EBURY PRESS
PLATFORM TICKET

Sangeetha Vallat, a seeker of stories, is passionate about books, travel, friends and conversations. Relinquishing a memorable career spanning fourteen years in the Indian Railways, she now lives in Dubai with her husband. Her short stories are featured in several anthologies and online journals. *Platform Ticket,* a memoir of her ticketing days in the railways, is her first book.

Platform Ticket

THE UNTOLD STORIES OF PEOPLE WHO MAKE TRAIN TRAVEL POSSIBLE

SANGEETHA VALLAT

EBURY
PRESS

An imprint of Penguin Random House

EBURY PRESS

Ebury Press is an imprint of the Penguin Random House group of companies
whose addresses can be found at global.penguinrandomhouse.com

Published by Penguin Random House India Pvt. Ltd
4th Floor, Capital Tower 1, MG Road,
Gurugram 122 002, Haryana, India

Penguin
Random House
India

First published in Ebury Press by Penguin Random House India 2025

Copyright © Sangeetha Vallat 2025

Illustrations by Reshma Manoj of reshdsign

All rights reserved

10 9 8 7 6 5 4 3 2 1

ISBN 9780143469223

Typeset in Adobe Caslon Pro by MAP Systems, Bengaluru, India
Printed at Gopsons Papers Pvt. Ltd., Noida

www.penguin.co.in

100%
Paper from well-
managed forests
FSC® C191020

To the ocean of hands that jostle at the ticket windows and the tireless railway community that serves with dedication

Contents

Prologue: Engine

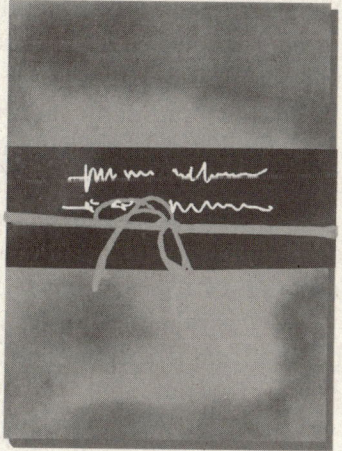

The grey file with red flaps lay ominously on the table. Bold, black letters glared at me. *Case no. 6/201Z. V. Sangeetha—102729312306.*

I chewed my nails and pulled a cuticle. Crimson beads trickled on to my blue kurta. Whenever I visited the railway office, I wore blue—my lucky colour. The first time, I had met a top official regarding a transfer to the Madras Division, which ended favourably. This time, I awaited the proceedings of a Discipline and Appeal Rules Case (DAR) registered against me.

We were in the Chennai Divisional Office. The Chief Commercial Inspector in charge of the case, CCI Jawahar, squeezed into a chair across me in the crowded office room. Earlier he had ordered a clerk to surrender his table for the inquiry session, and the clerk happily obliged, giving up his table and chair and his colleague's chair as well. The two then disappeared for a prolonged tea session in the railway canteen.

Jawahar cleared his throat and, with his nicotine-stained fingers, flipped the file open. A lanky, bespectacled man with three impeccable rows of holy ash and a vermilion dot on his forehead occupied the chair next to the inspector. He had a pen poised on a sheaf of paper.

'We begin the inquiry proceedings in the case against Mrs V. Sangeetha. Myself, CCI Jawahar and the Divisional Office Clerk Mr Saicharan; dated 26.02.201Z.'

My heart plummeted as Jawahar's voice rose above the din of the office intersection, and I curbed the urge to correct his grammar and crossed my arms.

'Preliminary hearing of Case no. 6/201Z; Defendant Mrs V. Sangeetha, Staff no. 102729312306.'

CCI Jawahar looked at me, his swarthy features dispassionate and neutral. 'Mrs V. Sangeetha, shall we begin the proceedings?'

'Yes, sir.'

'Are you aware of the charges against you? Do you want defence help, or do you wish to plead your case on your own?'

'Yes, I am aware of the charges,' I paused. Somehow, the air in the room felt bereft of oxygen, and my lungs seemed to be working overtime to keep me breathing. 'And I choose to plead my case.'

Saicharan's pen furiously moved on the paper as he transcribed every word we uttered.

'You are charged under the violation of Railway Services (Conduct) Rules 1966, Mrs Sangeetha. What do you have to say in your defence?'

I swallowed before responding.

PLATFORM NO. 1

THE ONLY TIME MY GRANDFATHER ever smiled and addressed me with a few kind words was when I told him about my appointment in the Indian Railways and sought his blessings. It was a few months after I reported for duty at my first station. And I could have gone on without telling him, but for my amma, who forced me to do it.

Ours was a big family with twenty grandchildren, and every summer holiday, we gathered at our grandparents' home and annoyed them with our non-stop banter and games. While my ever genial and exuberant *muthasi* welcomed the constant noise, *muthasan* showed his

1

displeasure by thundering at us to 'shut up' or 'play outside' or 'do your homework' or 'switch off the ceiling fans' when we slept until noon.

On these occasions, muthasi ambled up the squeaky stairs on her creaky knees, switched the fans on, and pulled her towering husband out of the room as he devised new ways to torture his progeny. He soon realized his genetic pool was of stubbornness and indiscipline and walked away, ignoring our existence.

I stood before muthasan as my amma nudged me to inform him about my job. She stood a little away, giving me the thumbs up. Not particularly encouraged, I reluctantly inched towards my grandpa. His pockmarked face frightened me. He saw me from the corner of his eyes but remained engrossed in his *Malayala Manorama*.

For how many hours did he read this newspaper? I wondered if he hid behind it to avoid talking to any of us.

I was uneasy standing close to him, so I shifted my leg and fabricated a cough announcing my presence. His nostrils flared as he snorted and peered at me through his thick glasses. Then, in his booming voice, he asked.

'*Endha*? (What?)' His favourite word.

'No-n . . . nothing.' I quivered, and he went back to his newspaper.

'Muthasa, I have something to say to you,' I tried again.

He lowered his newspaper, irked, and stared at my frail frame. 'Won't you say what it is, girl?'

'I got a job in the railways.' In my haste, it came out as a long string of gibberish. Igotajobintherailways.

'What?'

'I . . .' I sucked in a breath and forced myself to say it calmly this time. 'I got a job in the railways and am posted at a station in Karnataka.'

His thick, smoke-darkened lips designed a smile. 'Are you old enough to get a job?'

'Yes. I am twenty years old.'

He gestured for me to come closer and inspected me. His smile broadened, and he asked me to elaborate on my job. As I explained, he listened intently, and I saw his grey-glazed eyes brim with pride and happiness.

'Did you know I worked as an Assistant Stationmaster in the railways?'

'Yes, *Achan* told me.'

He bobbed his head, lost in some railway station. 'Good, go do your job well.'

And with that, the audience with His Highness was over. He returned to his world of stabbings and elections. I waited a few minutes, expecting more conversation from him now that we were related via the same paymaster, but his newspaper interested him more. Our parallel-track existence had only paused for a brief encounter.

I walked away from him, head held high, feeling all important as my cousins surrounded me, asking about my 'conversation' with muthasan. I told them it was between two railway employees and there was nothing to share with the commoners.

* * *

Two weeks after I celebrated my twentieth birthday, a clerk from the Madras Divisional Office, Southern Railway (SR) showed up at our home in Tambaram, Chennai. He delivered a brown envelope with the Government of India seal. Madras had just been renamed Chennai; for me, Madras is an emotion, Chennai is home.

As I tore open the envelope, the words swirled. It was a call letter from the Railways to report to the Mysore

Division of Southern Railways the next day! I squealed with happiness. But I had expected a posting at a station near home, not in another state.

Mysore?

Happiness intermingled with anxiety, and both emotions reigned supreme that day in the Vallat household. My mother kept the letter in the puja room, and I sprinted to the PCO booth to check whether my friend Sunil Warrier had also received the call letter. We had been waiting for this call letter since the day we completed our job-oriented higher secondary schooling.

In 1991, the Indian Railways introduced a brand-new Vocational Course in Railway Commercial (VCRC). This course comprised English, Business Studies, Accountancy, Computer Science, a General Foundation course, and a new subject—Railway Commercial Working: Theory and Practical—which dealt with all the commercial activities of the railways. This project was the initiative of the then Central government, which believed that an influx of fresh, vibrant young minds would add a much-needed impetus to rejuvenate the administration. The aim of the VCRC was to equip these young minds with the workings of ticketing, parcels and goods booking.

It was a breakthrough move, and the newspapers declared the course launch with full-page advertisements:

The Central Board of Secondary Education in collaboration with the Ministry of Railways and National Council of Educational Research and Training has launched a job-linked vocational course on Railway Commercial at the plus-two stage in schools. The course is being launched as a pilot project in five selected centres in the academic year 1991–92. Students will be short-listed via a three-stage process of elimination—a written exam, an interview, and a medical examination. Following this, selected students will undergo a two-year special training course along with their plus-two. Students who clear their 12th grade or senior secondary school examinations with a 55% pass percentage will be eligible for recruitment as Railway Employees—Commercial Clerks and Ticket Collectors on a pay scale of Rs 975–1540/Rs 950–1500.

* * *

A constant refrain everyone faces as we grow up is—what do you want to be when you grow up? Doctor or engineer? The list of choices has expanded to include other, sometimes more noble and fascinating, pursuits since I was a child. But even in the late 1980s and early 1990s, limited as my career options were, my answer was always: I want to read books.

Born into a middle-class family—my achan worked at the office, and my amma worked at maintaining the house—it wasn't lost on me that reading books would never be sufficient to harness all my dreams. So, when the newspaper advertisement boasted a government job in your hands when you turned eighteen, everyone eligible in my neighbourhood and school applied for it—even those who wanted to pursue medicine and engineering.

I was the only one, with my tangentially distinct world view and nose buried in a book, who almost missed the application deadline. If it had not been for the prompt reminder by a friend, I would not be writing this book today.

The written Railway Recruitment Board (RRB) examination was scheduled on the second Sunday of February before my class 10th board examinations. In the year when the big wigs met to end the Cold War formally, instead of feverishly prepping for the finals, I remember spending hours glued to the book, *10000 GK Questions* to crack the RRB test. I believe we significantly raised its sales that year.

My efforts triumphed. I was the only one from our school who cleared the RRB examination. Having been selected from the thousands who appeared from our city and lakhs from three states—Tamil Nadu, Kerala and Karnataka—where the exam was conducted, I was propelled into an instant celebrity status. I enjoyed all the attention until I received the interview letter mentioning the date in May, just before the board results.

I was sixteen and terrified. What should I wear? How must I address the panel? Should I show them my sports certificates or wait to be asked? A million questions swarmed in my head, and my fear scaled higher each day.

On the interview day, my parents and I reached the venue three hours before time. A mother and son walked towards the closed gate of the RRB office in Poes Garden, near the superstar Rajinikanth's house. My parents approached them, exchanged pleasantries, and we waited for the watchman to open the gate. Others trickled in, boys and girls, alone or accompanied by their parents or guardians. No one else had both parents with them, except me. Attribute it to the boon or bane of being a single child, I guess.

We were called in alphabetical order. I looked at the various hues surrounding me. I was the only one dressed in muted brown and mustard amongst the girls, who practically shone in their whites, pinks and blues. Some looked scared, while some exuded confidence. The boys befriended each other without preamble as if they had been waiting to meet each other, laughing and cracking jokes within minutes. The girls took time to warm up to each other. My new friend, Sunil Warrier, dressed in a white-and-pink striped full-sleeved shirt, black pants and black shoes looked quite professional, and he was one hell of a talker. Until then, I hadn't met someone who gabbed more than me. We sat between our parents and spoke about school life and hobbies.

The candidates waiting outside grilled those who came out of the interview room. We wanted to know the questions the panellists asked. A few halted and explained in detail. Others just walked away, locking their experience within themselves. I can say now that most of those who helped others and discussed the interview questions were the ones who joined me at school for the course.

My turn came post-noon. They called me in before my new friend.

Three members from the railway board and the principal of the school that offered the VCRC course, comprised the interview panel. When I answered that English was my favourite subject, the principal was visibly excited. He started the questions.

'What is a sonnet?'

This was easy. '16, no, 18, no . . . no, sorry, 14 lines.'

His eyes twinkled. 'Relax. Now, what is a diphthong?'

I felt the blood drain from my face and I wanted to rush towards the door in search of my parents. Liberate me. I wanted to scream. The word was Greek and Latin to me. Should I cook up an answer?

'I don't know, sir.' Honesty was the best policy.

The teacher in him spurted out the details. 'Diphthong is a Greek word. (Aha, gotcha!) A word that has two sounds. A sound which combines two vowels . . .' He continued with examples and asked me to cite examples to assess if I understood, but the RRB chairman cleared his throat and grunted in impatience.

They sent me out after a few general questions about where my dad was employed and whether my mother was a working woman. And why I wanted to join the railways.

By the end of the interview, I was practically skipping on my way out, thankful that the ordeal was over. A pack of curious candidates surrounded me, and, with a flourish, I explained everything that had transpired inside. Sunil Warrier and I bid each other goodbye, exchanging our addresses to discuss the results. A week later, I received a letter from him thanking me for my help.

Because, when it was Sunil's turn, the interview panel asked him the same questions. He answered them so comprehensively that the principal fell off the chair.

I cleared the interview and the medicals to everyone's delight and my bewilderment. Later, I and the others, a group of forty students, enrolled in a posh school where we studied the VCRC along with the regular stream of higher secondary education. As the Indian Railways was slated to employ us right after school, we knew we had no college life. Therefore, we had unadulterated fun for two years. After all, only a pass percentage of 55 was expected from us, and we were the school toppers of our earlier schools.

Our intellect, however, did not spare us from witnessing the reality of life and the class divide. The elite of this new school took time to accept those of us from middle-class families. While many students arrived by car and bike, we walked or travelled by bus, train or autorickshaw.

Our band of middle-class brainiacs didn't let the jeering and taunting stop us. Slow and steady, we let our presence known in the school clubs, sports, dramatics, arts and science, and our talents spoke for our standing.

One of the many episodes that strengthened our bond was the creation of our class magazine in grades 11 and 12, containing poetry, stories, art, etc. We fumbled a little in grade 11, as the concept was new. Even so, we were in the top three. And in grade 12, we were the undisputed winners. The title of our class magazine was 'MEMOIRS'. Perhaps, one of us was destined to write a memoir.

Even after all these years, the bond that connects those were inducted in the VCRC from every zone of the Indian Railways is formidable. Every VCRCian has a family in every other VCRCian; the enveloping comfort of love and camaraderie is in every part of the country.

* * *

There's many a slip 'twixt the cup and the lip, as the idiom goes; a hiccup developed in bagging the promised job right after we passed class 12. As it turned out, 400 graduate candidates selected by the SR-RRB registered a case in the Railway tribunal on us, the forty VCRC of the Southern Railways, stating that they should be given priority for posting. The case dragged on, and the railways opted to assign these 400 candidates their postings in and around Chennai, delaying our job prospects. And we were all thrown into different divisions in Southern Railways.

In the meantime, we could not join a college because the official orders could come any time. Hence, we all settled for distance education and picked up odd jobs in schools and offices. Two years passed in waiting, and I turned twenty.

The arrival of the brown envelope was a long-awaited blessing. I shook with nerves and excitement, the telephone glued to my sweaty cheek at the PCO; Sunil informed me that most of the forty batchmates had already received their call letters. The authorities had split our team and ordered us to report to various divisions of the Southern Railways (SR)—Mysore, Bangalore, Salem, Ernakulam and Trivandrum.

Only four of the forty, me included, hadn't received the original order issued by SR on time because of the nationwide postal strike that surfaced just as the orders were dispatched. So, Sunil and I, residents of Chennai, and two others living in Madurai—Priya and Balaguru—received hand-delivered letters. The other thirty-six recruits had already reported to their respective divisions and reached the Zonal Training School (ZTS) at Tiruchirappalli for a two-week training.

An unfortunate circumstance because those batchmates were nine days senior to us in service before we even joined. In government services, each day counts. When lists for promotions come up, the disparity in seniority always plays a role.

Then our parents scurried to book the tickets and get a uniform ready (blue sari and white blouse for the girls, and white shirt and brown pants for the boys), and this, that and everything. It was like planning for childbirth all nine months and suddenly when the contractions occur one is unprepared. The four of us reported to Mysore Division along with our fathers, and by the end of the working hours of the Divisional Office, we had signed our service register and read the oath.

'I, Sangeetha Vallat, do swear/solemnly affirm that I will maintain devotion to duty, never act in a manner unbecoming of railway personnel, and will uphold the dignity of Indian Railways ...'

We then collected our first free railway pass—a thin paper in shocking pink. (A pink slip on joining!) It had my name and an employee number. I must have zoned out as I stared at that number. My number amongst the millions of railway employees. 'Overwhelmed' was an understatement for me at that moment.

But before the euphoria could seep in, the clerk announced that the train to our destination would leave in the next ten minutes. And if we did not report to ZTS Tiruchirappalli by the next day, there would be dire consequences. This was enough to get us dashing through the platforms, lugging our bags and boxes, with our fathers at our heels.

PLATFORM NO. 1A

MY FIRST TRAIN JOURNEY AS a newly minted railway employee began in an unreserved compartment bulging at the seams. The four of us settled in the passage near the washroom with our concerned fathers. As they worried about what us after the training, my friends and I chatted without concern. We had made it. And we would meet the rest of our friends the next day.

At Bangalore station, we changed trains and settled in a congested compartment. As the train left the station, we realized the goof-up when we asked a passenger the time the train would reach Tiruchirappalli.

We had boarded the wrong train. Rather, the wrong compartment. This train split at a junction where a few compartments advanced to Madurai (MDU) and the rest to Tiruchirappalli (TPJ). And we had hopped into the MDU segment of the train. Passengers advised us to alight at Erode Junction (ED), where the train stopped for thirty minutes to fill water, clean the toilets, etc.

None of us slept that night (sitting or standing) as we dared not miss our stop. The train was late. We were supposed to be at ED at night, but it was daybreak when the train finally rolled into the station.

At the Zonal Training School (ZTS), we arrived after the classes for the day had already begun. We met the principal and handed our orders. He rattled off a long sentence in Kannada as our orders were from Mysore. He then noticed our puzzled, sleep-deprived faces and switched to English.

'Your batchmates have completed half of the training, and you're just arriving? You have two options now. You can join the next batch that would begin after two weeks or join them now.'

'We will join our batchmates,' we replied in unison.

'In that case, instead of A to Z, you will learn P to Z with them, and later A to P. Is that acceptable?'

Everything was acceptable. Nothing else interested us more than being back in a classroom with friends.

The two weeks of training at the ZTS, back in a classroom after two years was joyous. After our friends completed their training and left to join their stations, a separate class and a tutor were assigned exclusively to the four of us—Sunil, Priya, Balaguru and I. Deepavali holidays intervened, and the principal pitied us young souls, allowing us to travel home for festivities. But he couldn't be partial toward us, so, for the first time in all its existence, the ZTS closed for Deepavali.

This is how we students of the VCRC set a precedent wherever we went.

Completing a written examination at the end of the training period, we travelled with our parents to the Mysore Divisional Office, where our official orders awaited us.

* * *

With unsteady hands, I read the station's name written on the paper. I did not know where it was, nor did the clerk who handed me the orders. I scanned around and saw equally baffled faces. My friends were flung far and wide. The 'lucrative railway job' did not seem lucrative or prestigious anymore.

I scampered to the large railway map of India hanging on a wall inside the divisional office, procured a wobbly plastic stool and stood atop. A search of the map of Karnataka showed a tiny fleck at the end of a line. Indeed, was it that? Surely, that blink-and-you-miss-it station could not be mine. That line seemed like the end of the world. There was no railway track beyond my station. It was the final terminal on a broad-gauge line. 424 km from MYS.

Most of the luckier ones, who had completed their training and reported to MYS earlier, had received their postings in and around the city. But we were tossed to different corners of the division. Balaguru's station was 500 km from MYS. His was the farthest posting. Tears threatened to flow from his eyes. Sunil's was the closest: 100 km from Mysore.

My batchmate Priya, a short bunny-toothed girl with glorious silky long hair, and I were posted to adjacent stations, that were 30 km apart. Resigned to our fates, my parents and I, along with Priya and her father, boarded the train to our destination.

This was becoming a habit. Travelling in unreserved compartments swarming with women wrapped in unwashed, musty blankets (Amma and I had a bout of sneezing), wailing, snot-dribbling children and swaying drunk men. The passenger train lumbered at a snail's pace. In the subsequent stops, many more bodies crammed into the overflowing carriage. My parents squeezed me between them. All of us, stiff like cadavers, perched on a seat meant for three. After five gruelling hours, the night passenger train crawled to reach Bangalore, a distance of 150 km. We grabbed some bread and water at the bustling city station and caught the train to my destination.

It was the district headquarters, so there was a direct train (small mercies).

Priya and I, Railway 'Commercial Clerks' (our designation), huddled and discussed options with our parents. We would find a working women's hostel in between our stations and stay together, shuttling for work. Living alone wasn't something we could even consider at that time.

En route, the scenic countryside eased my mind off the reality of heading to an end-of-the-line station. As the monsoons had just ceased, the train wended over many brooks and cut through lush farmlands. I stuck my face to the grille, and the chilled morning air numbed my nose and lips. Vast swathes of countryside, fields, trees and villages dotted with huts whisked past. Many houses had green moss and plants growing on the tiled roofs. The verdant scenery appeared cosy with steam rising from the chimneys.

At Priya's station, we witnessed smoke-belching vehicles and factories—a big town. I had great hopes for my station; it was a district headquarters, after all. Priya and her father sallied forth, and my parents and I cruised on.

Then my station loomed ahead—carpets of grassy farmland as far as the eye could see. The train halted, and the platform blazed with life; perhaps the station was secluded from the main town, I surmised

Apprehensive and excited, we descended on the throbbing platform which, like steam after a hot shower, metamorphosed in precisely eight minutes. A desolate ghost town greeted us as our train was shunted to a distant track.

The scene I witnessed was straight out of an art-house movie by Adoor Gopalakrishnan or Satyajit Ray—empty parallel tracks flanked by vacant platforms. A crow on a cracked stone bench heralded my arrival and pierced the haunting stillness. The semaphore on the side of the track stood with its red hand at 90 degrees, indicating a stop signal. My old life stopped here, and a new life was to begin. Was I home?

I gazed at the blue skies, the long winding tracks, the white-and-red semaphore, and a colossal peepul tree where the platform tapered and ended. This was my station.

A face peeked out from an opening near the shuttered stall. The board in faded lettering read Shetty's Vegetarian Light Refreshment (VLR), inducing hunger instantly. VLR stalls and I have a history. Every summer vacation as long as I can remember, the moment the train halted at Palghat Jn, at an unearthly 04.00 hrs, I demanded pazhampori (sweet banana fritters) from the VLR—Amma's excuses about it being stale evaded my ears. The pleasure of sinking my teeth into the oil-dripping snack is incomparable.

Achan clanged the shutter of this VLR until the face rolled it up.

'*Aenu beku?*' (What do you want?) A Pinocchio nose darted out.

I went near Achan, leaving Amma to guard the baggage even though no one was around. This was an extremely significant risk. We belong to the generation who secured their luggage with a chain and lock. While travelling, one of us would sacrifice sleep inside the train to sit guard over the luggage.

Beku in Tamil means a fool, a stupid person. For a second, I wondered if that man called us fools. He understood our confusion and gestured 'What?'

'Sir, food?' I mimed the universal sign of food.

'*Chitranna solpa idhe. Banni.*' (There's some chitranna left. Come.)

I had no clue what he said, but we followed him inside, as he raised the shutter a little. His daughter, in school uniform, smiled at us. She played the interpreter. We were introduced to chitranna (almost a staple food in the region), a tasteless plate of yellow rice with coconut chutney to accompany it. Another prominent dish in this area is chow chow bhath: one serving of uppittu (upma) and one serving of kesari bhath (sheera).

Mr Shetty, in charge of the VLR, informed us that the station saw six trains per day, and he opened his shop only during the train timings. He served us the leftovers after a busy sale. When I told him I was the new railway clerk, his stunned surprise matched our shock.

'You are the first lady employee in our station!'

Amma bawled her eyes out.

* * *

This station had two platforms, and finding the station manager's office wasn't tricky. Amma dabbed her eyes and shuffled along. At one end of the main platform was the

VLR stall, followed by a squarish opening with a collapsible metal door (which was never closed). Three steps down to the left was the Booking Office (BO).

I gaped at my workplace. A sort of Palladian window, the half-moons, semi-circular arches, offered a peek into a world that would be my habitat soon. A blackboard hung across the straw-coloured, pockmarked wall. It was crammed with writing and appeared to be some illegible guide to step across timelines. I stared, nonplussed, at the grilled opening in the wall. As soon as my name entered the station staff register, I would be sucked into this wormhole—another dimension of cards, tickets, exact change, shift schedules and heaps of currency denominations. Unaware then that this and many such windows would serve as 'windows to a new world', I moved away to explore the station premises.

Across the BO was a small, shuttered shop with a board proclaiming, 'Abu's stall'. A short, frail man wearing a skullcap and a tall young girl locked the shutters and walked out, smiling at us. Beside Abu's Stall was the Stationmaster's room, where a man in a white uniform pored over a book scribbling vigorously. Adjacent to it was the Station Manager's (SMR) room. Farther down was the Parcel Office, dwarfed by a colossal peepul tree standing proudly marking the end of the platform. A few yards off the platform was the Railway Police Force (RPF) office and the Running Staff Restroom. Another blackboard painted on the wall near the station manager's cabin displayed the train name and time. Below it, three red sand buckets were slung on a stand, for use in case of fire.

The board outside the SMR's room read: Mr Shetty. I wondered if everyone shared the same last name in this part of the world and if I would find Suniel Shetty lurking somewhere. A slight, delicate and pale-as-chalk gentleman who mirrored my nervousness greeted me. He had just shut the room and was on his way out.

I introduced myself, and he blinked thrice. His shock subsided a trifle only after he added my name to the station roster, and I officially became a 'commercial clerk'. After every sentence, he chuckled like a baby. A tooth on his lower jaw rattled, and I couldn't stop staring at it. As he walked me to the booking office, the stationmaster came out of his room to inspect the entourage. A handsome guy with Ray-Ban sunglasses and a tight tucked-in half-sleeved shirt. He welcomed me in Kannada and later switched to an accented English.

As I learned later, the sunglasses were his style statement. In all my years working at this station, I never saw him without them, and I wondered if he wore them even while sleeping. He introduced me to his family in time; his wife ran a saree business from home. I bought my first and only Mysore silk saree, a pink-magenta standout, from her. Recently, I came across his photo on Facebook without Ray-Bans, he has perfect eyes.

Inside the BO, a man in his thirties wearing a pista-green shirt and brown pants (the railway clerk's uniform) exhibited uninhibited happiness at my arrival. Narendra Hegde had protruding ears complementing his bald pate. Huge wooden cupboards with racks and rows of tickets lay open on either side of the counter opening.

In a nasal twang, he said. 'Welcome, welcome, *banni banni.*' He seemed so happy and enthusiastic that I actually felt welcome for a minute. He told me the person I was replacing had fled from the clutches of this desolate fleck on the aforementioned map. That wiped the smile right off my face. Mr Hegde was the first one to train me on the job. I picked up nuances of the functioning of the commercial department of the railways from all my colleagues—neat and legible filling of the booking registers, meticulous issuing of tickets, collecting cash and immediately arranging the denominations in their appropriate slots before collecting money from the next person in line, a lightning quickness in using the calculator, asking for change from every single person, and the weird way of counting cash with the left hand, even though I was a righty.

As I conversed with Hegde, the Chief Booking Supervisor (CBS), Amarendra Pillai, walked in wearing the same green-brown uniform. Pillai had a small, scrunched-up face as if God created him and then cupped His hands on his face and squished it. He worked in the parcel office. Like all railway stations in India, this station, too, had a shortage of staff.

An exuberant personality, Mr Pillai took me under his wing, and from then onwards, I had the protection of the king of the tickets. He quite vociferously proclaimed himself as the king.

'When King is here, what's to fear!' He bellowed in the station.

Soon, he became my Mary, and I was the meek lamb. Everywhere he went, I was sure to go. His job comprised counting bundling the cash, writing the challan and remitting the station's daily earnings to the bank. He counted the currency peculiarly with his left hand. I soon mimicked it.

The railways paid us a daily conveyance allowance of Rs 14 for bank remittance in those days. Sometimes, we took an autorickshaw (the one-way charge for which was Rs 10); at other times, we walked the 5-km trip to and fro, and had an ice cream or pani puri while returning. I even accompanied Mr Pillai and his family to the weddings of politicians' children. Pillai's wife, a charming beauty, made hot potato bhajjis and tea whenever I dropped by, and treated me like their daughter.

Sometimes, I pulled Pillai's leg, claiming that I learned ticketing from Hegde. He would get all indignant and bristly.

'I am your first teacher at this station,' he insisted.

And he was my teacher in many ways. In Harry Potter terminology, Mr Pillai was my Dumbledore.

PLATFORM NO. 2

MEANWHILE, MY FRIEND BALAGURU TRAVELLED 500 km and reached his station. He found the unfamiliar dish, ragi mudde, served in VLR inedible and survived on water and fruits. His only solace was that our classmate Jotheeswaran was posted at a nearby station.

Balaguru slept in the waiting room for two days and shifted to a shared accommodation with an older man from the postal department. He was afraid to ask for leave or duty adjustments from his seniors and reconciled to

sending notes or letters to Jotheeswaran, Jo, at the next
station through the guards and TTEs.

Oh, the guards and the TTEs were our courier guys
in those days. I sent letters, notes and sometimes food to
my friend Priya through the train guards. My batchmates
Meenakshi, Bharathi and a few others posted in major city
stations used these guard-couriers to send home sweets,
among other things. During the festival season, these girls
working in the inquiry counters received loads of sweet
boxes as gifts from the local shopkeepers and vendors on the
station premises. Even after eating and sharing with their
hostel mates, the sweet boxes were numerous, so they sent the
remaining sweets home through the TTEs of the Shatabdi
trains that reached Chennai within a few hours. Their fathers
collected the sweets and returned home-made snacks and
dresses to them through these friendly messengers.

Balaguru, used to homely meals, suffered in his new
station. The cuisine here was different from what his
mother cooked. I was the only fortunate person in my class
of forty to have a parent cooking and taking care of me.
The sambar at Balaguru's town was sweet and watery, but
the vadas were good. For days, he consumed only vadas for
sustenance. Working in an environment where the language
was a big hurdle coupled with loneliness and unusual diet,
he wept silently and even harboured thoughts of running
back home. An STD booth near the station connected him
with his parents every other day. Soon, the cash he carried
from home depleted, and he waited until the end of the
month for his salary to call home.

* * *

At work, Balaguru was instructed to issue tickets for a train
only after it departed from a station two stations before his.

When the train left that station, the *khalasi* gonged a long bell. The passengers rushed to the ticket window, and he issued the tickets. The khalasi sounded a short gong when the train reached the adjacent station. And the passengers would yell to crank up the speed.

Once, a lady approached his counter before the long bell and asked for a ticket. My friend scratched his head, trying to remember the words in Kannada . . . He meant to say, '*Ghanta odisu mele ticket niduttene.*' (once the bell is rung, I will issue a ticket) but what he said enraged the woman and she screeched obscenities. Balaguru watched, oblivious to what she yelled. He had said, '*Ganda odisu mele ticket niduttene.*' (Once the husband beats you, I will issue a ticket.) Ganta–Ganda is a letter and a world of difference.

* * *

Later, assigned to the parcel office, Balaguru dealt with commodities with minimal human interaction. Women folk brought fresh vegetables to book them as luggage. These were treated as perishables, to be booked and loaded immediately into the luggage brake van of the train on which the passenger travelled. At 10.30 hrs, a group of women with baskets of vegetables showed up at the parcel and luggage office. The train to their destination was at 11.30 hrs, and the subsequent train was only at 16.30 hrs. Caught up with heavy workload, Balaguru forgot to order the *hamal*/khalasi to load the baskets of vegetables on the 11.30 train.

The ladies descried the clerk's error when one went to check her basket in the brake van, as the train came to a stop at an intermediate station. She created an uproar and gathered all the ladies, and they detrained. The collective cries of the women asking for their missing vegetable baskets thrust the train and the station into turmoil. The angry women assembled on the tracks; the stationmaster intervened and instructed the incoming goods rake to stop. The women boarded the goods train, and alighted at Balaguru's station, demanding their vegetables. Their livelihood depended on the sale of these perishables. The next train was in the evening. Again, the SM detained a goods train passing in the opposite direction. The ladies loaded their vegetable baskets and again hiked up their sarees to clamber into the open wagons. Seated amidst blocks of coal, they journeyed to their destination. Fortunately, Balaguru did not face an official enquiry because of his supervisor's intervention.

When Balaguru visited Jotheeswaran at the next station after a week, he realized his life was much better. Jo was a solitary clerk in his station. The station did not have a lavatory. For someone city-bred to attend nature's call in the fields like animals was unthinkable. Reality slapped him in the face. While his cousins gloated of flashy colleges and swanky offices, he was in a village lacking basic facilities.

The main aim of all of us, the new railway clerks, was to accumulate CLs (casual leave) and CRs (compulsory rest granted if one forgoes the weekly rest and works continuously for seven days) and go home to our parents and native city—to get back to a life of comfort and home-cooked food. The more significant aim was to work out a transfer to the Chennai Division; we kept sending application after application until some of us made peace with our destiny. Some, within a few years, married and settled in Karnataka.

When posted in smaller stations there was abundant free time between trains, and many of my batchmates utilized it to prepare and clear the civil services. My mobile contact list boasts of bureaucrats and diplomats. Amma wished for me to try the civil services. I bought competitive books and elected to do my post-graduation in a subject conducive to the UPSC electives, but I enjoyed reading fiction rather than these. My buddy, now a Chief Secretary, told my amma, 'Aunty, Sangeetha is enjoying all the perks and benefits associated with the high positions without the work tension. She has friends everywhere to provide her with the best possible experience.'

True, indeed. Recently, I visited my friend, the Chief Secretary's home state and what a rousing welcome I received. My stay and sightseeing trips were splendid, with an armed guard accompanying us.

* * *

Balaguru fondly recalls an exhilarating charged-up working day at a station. The Mahashivaratri Mahotsava of Ukkadagatri Temple on the banks of Tungabhadra River is celebrated for a week with joy and pomp, for the miracle man Ajjaya. Hordes of people from the village and from the far reaches of Karnataka and other states flock to the station. Grand food and lodging arrangements for the devotees are made. Lakhs of devotees are accommodated inside the temple premises. A big fair is held every new moon and thousands throng to the shrine. Devotees believe that people suffering from mental illnesses and those possessed by ghosts/devils are cured if they pray to the deity after a dip in the river. This tradition has existed for over 400 years since Sri Karibasaveshwara Swamy lived and performed miracles.

At a small window opening where only one hand could push the money/ticket, the booking clerk Balaguru, worked in tandem with the TC, TTE, issuing tickets, filling up Blank Paper Tickets (BPT, a pink handwritten ticket prepared for destinations for which a printed ticket is unavailable) and the Excess Fare Ticket (EFT, a white receipt book usually used by the TTE to penalize ticketless travellers or collect the difference of fare in a change of class, etc.). Heaps of currency notes and coins surrounded these men, who punched tickets synchronously within the tiny space between the ticket tubes facing the pigeonhole.

The passengers' appreciation and applause for the quick service boosted our morale. But satisfying the public is never easy; there will always be someone who censures the incompetence of railway employees. A standard dialogue from my seniors whenever I worked quickly, efficiently and cleared lengthy queues was: 'Whatever you do, these passengers are unhappy. Why raise our BP and work fast? You and I get the same pay; no one will acknowledge your efficiency here.'

But I can vouch on behalf of all the VCRC employees spread in all the zones of the Indian Railways that we never bothered about recognition from the railway authorities or aimed to please every customer who crossed our way. We work efficiently because we do not know otherwise.

* * *

Our friend Jotheeswaran's experience as soon as he disembarked the train trumped the experience of all the other batchmates. He collected his orders and boarded a train with two other friends. From a junction, they diverged to their respective stations. Curious about their posting stations, the boys asked the locals on the train about their stations. No one spoke English or Tamil, the only languages my friends spoke.

When Boy 1 asked the man reading an English newspaper, he twirled the tips of his moustache with his index finger and thumb and nodded, 'It is a good station. Big place.'

Then, Boy 2 wanted to know about his station. The man tugged his ear, 'Beautiful place. Kind people. My wife is from there.'

But when Jo asked, the man folded his newspaper and asked the other locals. They were all perplexed. 'We haven't heard of this place before. Do you know for sure it is in Karnataka?'

An anxious Jo requested the TTE to detrain him at his station.

The train halted in the middle of nowhere—no platform or a building. Jo searched for the station on both sides of the track. After walking for about ten minutes, he found a cowherd.

'Where is the station?'

'!!'

'Ahh, Kannada!'

'?'

'Station . . . t-r-a-i-n.' He imitated a locomotive, shouted 'choo choo' with his hand on his mouth, and chugged a little until the cowherd's eyes glinted in glee. He clutched Jo's shoulders and tooted 'choo choo.'

When the duo tired of playing train, the new clerk pleaded with the boy to show where tickets were issued, employing vigorous hand gestures.

A yellow board displayed the station's name from his posting order. A lone building stood sentry over the tracks. The dun, decrepit, single-storey structure looked like something out of a horror movie. On one side was a grimy, jolly-panelled wall where devotees had tied tiny red and black threads. Then, a wooden door or a gate opened to the fields (this was the entrance to the village.) With an imagined flair of the superstar Rajnikant, who in his first onscreen appearance opened an iron gate and announced his arrival on to the big screen and into the hearts of millions, the new commercial clerk announced his arrival to . . . well, there was no one other than stray dogs and rustling fields of sorghum.

Then Jotheeswaran saw a room with a lock. An unkempt, stinking, snoring man blocked the entry to the door. When prodded with a stick, he squinted, yawned and engulfed the railwayman in fumes of onions and toddy.

After showcasing more of his acting skills, my friend understood that the stationmaster had gone on leave, and the drunkard was the local watchman of the premises.

He showed Jo where the keys were kept—above the sunshade (duh).

The office room did not have much, but it was the beginning for him. The launch of a career that would span many years in similar-looking offices and, at times, better, but mostly the same or worse. Like first love, our first stations are unforgettable. Jotheeswaran still recalls the view from his station at night. 'The glow of the moonlight lent my village an ethereal look. The sea of dense green longish grain heads swayed in the breeze in the mornings, displaying vibrant shades of golden, red and brown, depending on the ripeness of the plant. At night-time, the distant echoes of the rumbling trains and the rustling jola fields broke the unsettling stillness . . . at that time, it was scary, but now, many years later in hindsight, the memories are nostalgic.'

The stationmaster returned after a few days; by then Jo had taken control. The on-the-job training we had during our school days served him well, but grasping the station names and their direction was a tough call. Moreover, the stationmaster everyone referred to, was the hamal or a porter, a lower-rung employee who managed the station in the absence of a booking clerk. The hamal commissioned himself as the stationmaster.

After a few months, Jotheeswaran availed a few days' vacation to write his graduation examinations. My friends and I had signed up for distance education courses and pursued our graduation. So, along with ticketing and adjusting to a new life, we were always seen with a book—perused in moments of peace between issuing tickets. A few of my juniors who had done the VCRC course even joined regular college because their postings, too, were delayed, and sadly, their batches received their posting orders in fragments. Five first, then ten, sometimes two, but somehow all received their posting orders.

So, our Jo's mother, proud of her son's employment, wrote to him, 'Dear, can you bring home something unique to your area? We need to give it to our neighbours and relatives. Everyone would expect something, now that you are a government employee.'

The package he carried home couldn't be given to anyone because of the belief that gifting spicy things ensured a break in relationships—he had carried kilos of Byadagi (Bedgi) chillies. It was the unique cash crop in his area. (Thankfully, my amma didn't ask me to buy betel nuts from my place of posting to distribute among the relatives.)

When Jo returned from writing his exams, something happened that taught him much about people. The kind we live with.

As soon as Jotheeswaran detrained, the hamal who administered the station in his absence boarded the same train. He had relied on the hamal to manage the station in his absence because the officer in the Divisional Office rejected his leave letter.

The hamal said, 'There is a shortage of Rs 5 in the earnings.'

Jo said, 'Oh, ok, Rs 5 I can handle.'

'Not Rs 5. Rs 5000.'

My friend blanched. The monthly salary was less than Rs 1200, and Rs 5000 was huge. (The first salary I received from the railway job was Rs 1045.) Usually, the station earnings wouldn't be more than Rs 2000 to 3000, but a local temple festival had hiked up the earnings.

To add to his his woes, the auditor picked that very day to visit his station. The auditor queried about the vast difference in accounts and cash on hand and said, 'I thought you, the young breed of railwaymen, were better than the older ones. But I can see I was wrong. What have you done with the cash? Did you spend on drinks? Lost it on cards?'

Jo bristled, 'Sir, don't let out words you cannot take back. I am an honest, God-fearing person. I will remit the correct amount tomorrow morning.'

He called his friend, Balaguru. There was only a Magneto phone in his office and no STD booths nearby. Jo dialled the next station on the Magneto phone, waited for his friend to reach from his one-room accommodation, and requested him to arrange for whatever cash he could. Then Jo decided to go to the village and ask his acquaintances, the house owner, and everyone who came by the station.

The locals didn't accept many of us when we joined the railways. They looked at us like museum exhibits or aliens. Many of their children in our age group had failed their studies and were wasting their days, and they viewed our success in gaining employment with envy. Our coworkers treated us as competitors as if we had usurped the jobs meant for their children. The passengers never respected us and even taunted, '*Ei hudugi* (girl), call your father to issue tickets.' They couldn't believe we were railway employees.

However, gradually, they accepted us. As they say, Rome was not built in a day, nor was our relationship with the people in our station, village and town.

In the absence of electricity, Jo hunted for a candle and matchbox in his tiny office while the jackals and foxes howled in the darkness. His troubles were further compounded when he looked for drinking water. The lone bore pump near the station building was rendered unusable by the villagers, who pumped out the last drop of water and splintered it while he was away. The repairers had to come from the nearest junction, and the pump would take at least a week to resurrect. Jo dispatched an empty, clean pot through the guard of the passing train, and the pot filled with drinking water arrived in the guard's brake van of the last passing train. Wary of snakes and scorpions in the fields, he rummaged through the shelves and found a flashlight. In the pale illumination, he locked the office and waded through the black marshy mud. When it rained, the black soil turned mucky. He balanced the flashlight in one hand and held his slippers and an umbrella in the other as he squelched through the soggy ground.

When Jo pleaded with the locals to help him with money, they all mobilized the amount. A 100 here, a 500 there, bit by bit it totalled Rs 5000. An old man contributed the funds set aside for his eye surgery.

Jo reached his station building, his feet caked with mud (he laughed saying it was as if he was wearing high heels), counted the cash, and tallied it with the accounts. As promised to the auditor, he remitted the money without discrepancy.

Three days later, the hamal returned with Rs 5000. He had lost the station earnings while playing cards and had travelled to the next town to make up his losses.

* * *

My friend Venkatapathy recollected an incident where learning the local language saved him and his friend's life. In interior Karnataka, people only spoke the regional language, and with the Cauvery water dispute going on, they disliked people from Tamil Nadu.

The situation worsened at the state borders whenever the courts convened to discuss the Cauvery water dispute. The anger towards everyone and everything from Tamil Nadu was at its zenith at the time, and those of us from Tamil Nadu lay low. I even changed my introduction from 'I am from Madras' to 'I am a Malayalee'.

The border stations were denuded of passengers or trains and carried only the railway staff and RPF with dogs. People burnt effigies of the Tamil Nadu CM, and chaos reigned.

One day, when the courts adjourned without any resolution, our batchmate Venkatapathy, posted in a station in the heart belt of such disputes, received a call from his uncle in Chennai.

'Venkat, you remember my friend's brother Idrees? He is trapped on a bus near your station. He speaks only Tamil. If fanatics catch him, that's it. You go and check. Keep him with you until things subside.'

'Ok. I will call you soon.'

He immediately ventured out in search of Idrees and found him near the bus shelter surrounded by a mob of men, wielding sticks and flags. Fortuitously, Venkatapathy could speak the language like a local. He had also learned to read, so he could understand the boards on the buses and movie posters. Idrees quivered and crumpled on to Venkat when he saw him. He caught his hand, tears streaming in a steady trickle. Venkat whispered, 'Stay quiet.'

In the local dialect, Venkat bellowed, 'What happened? Why are you harassing my deaf–mute friend here?'

A tall man from the group stared at Venkatapathy who held his stare, blistering, although inwardly he quaked. The predators moved to their next prey. Venkat prayed that Idrees wouldn't open his mouth to utter thanks. They both helplessly watched others on the bus being beaten.

After a few days, when Idrees recovered from his fear of a near-death situation and the agitation subsided, he went home.

* * *

We all went through different initiation processes into railways; some look back fondly, and some do not want to remember those days. My colleagues at different stations always treated me well. There were a few bitter incidents, but the good ones eclipsed them. Perhaps, that's why I am writing this memoir.

PLATFORM NO. 3

MY PARENTS WERE PLEASED WITH my counterparts and the station premises. Mr Shetty, Nagendra Hegde and Amarendra Pillai radiated warmth and promised to care for me. But when Achan asked for the address of a working women's hostel, the SMR went on a blinking fit. Immediately, we were royally marched to the railway quarters, as this slice of Karnataka hadn't heard of a working women's hostel. What a shocker. All our plans went kaput.

A hamal carried our luggage. He introduced himself with a hearty smile, 'Myself, Hanumantha. Two months, I join Railways. My house there.' He showed me a house in the farthest corner of the street. So, he had joined two months prior, a newbie like me, and stayed in his quarters. (Twenty-eight years have passed, and he still works in the same station. He never vacated the quarters despite shuffling to other stations in the section.)

My batchmate Rajan, with whom I must have spoken twice or thrice at school (a rare occurrence that I don't talk or grab others to speak to me), was also posted in my station. He had joined nine days earlier and was staying in one of the quarters in my block; he got his allotted quarters the day after his arrival. We worked together over the next few months and failed to become pals. My new colleagues became my chums sooner than this guy.

Hanumantha stopped in front of a blue door. 95D. It had a minuscule lock on it (my achan used a bigger lock to secure our luggage to the train seat). The hamal broke the lock with a stone and said, 'Welcome your new home.' This, too, had belonged to an absconding soul. We wondered what forced that person to desert his post. A one-room kitchen with a backyard and a small washroom. Just bare walls with scaly, tawny paint, no shelves or nails. My new home. (I swung by this station and quarters after twenty years; my name was still on the outer wall of Block 95: 95D - Sangeetha. CC and the station code.)

* * *

I was one of the lucky ones from our batch to get official accommodation within an hour of joining the station. Some of the girls posted in major stations found hostels. They recall the horrid times with a mix of aversion for the hostel premises and warm memories of the sisterhood. Three girls shared a room meant for two. Grimy rooms, a cranky warden, strict rules and watery food. They made such compromises as they had to save money to send home a chunk of their salary, and frequented restaurants only when friends from other stations came to stay.

The weather was cold; there was no hot water in the hostels, and the girls bathed with chattering teeth. Scared of the other older women, who gawked at them sinisterly, they resorted to bathing two at a time. Once, when they returned after a vacation, the room smelled rotten. A thorough investigation revealed a dead rat. It took two days for the warden to arrange a person to clean up. In such difficult times, having each other's companionship helped them sail through.

Although we all studied together for two years and forged strong bonds, the bond formed while being posted together or at adjacent stations was much stronger.

My friend, Sidharth who is now a diplomat, recounted his days sharing a room with our quirky batchmate. When Sidhu's parents visited him, the roommate complained, 'Aunty, your son is using my bucket in the bathroom. I bought it.'

'Why dear, I will get you a bucket don't use his, ok?' Aunty advised her son but couldn't control her laughter when the boy said, 'Aunty, he is using my mirror to comb his hair.'

Sidhu, to spite him, resisted buying a separate bucket and mirror, and sometimes ate the bread purchased by his roomie.

Some of the boys posted in a radius of 15 km rented a house together in Mysore. It was this house that became our party pad. We celebrated birthdays and other important occasions together. Our group of friends posted at various stations in different divisions of Southern Railways booked tickets to Mysore, and we stayed together for a day or two, cooking, singing songs, touring and watching movies. We had a friendship anthem too. At night, we slept on the terrace looking at the stars, sharing jokes and stories about our work life—the memories are vivid.

Nowadays, we plan our reunions in resorts at regular intervals. And playing train is something we do whenever we meet. Unmindful of the staring guests all over the resort, we do the winding railway engine, bogies, guards, etc., screaming 'Kooooo chug chug chug choo choo . . .

* * *

There were instances where my batchmates struggled to locate the station mentioned in their posting orders. It was arduous as no one knew where the railway siding was located. A siding was an offshoot of tracks from the main line or the station into a customer's premises. A friend, Harshkant, posted in a siding, scoured the area for a long time. The station was positioned in a low-lying area from the road, and reaching the siding was like following a secret trail. Surrounded by tall eucalyptus trees, in the centre of the woody area were the sidings of a Karnataka state industry, a TATA steel plant and a SAIL plant. His work included recording when the wagons were received, when the unloading started and when they were released. The two senior clerks posted there acted like visiting professors, and the whole burden of work fell on Harshkant.

His father left him after requesting the SM to give him a spare room till he found accommodation. Harshkant didn't speak Kannada, and nobody guided him to find a house. Finally, the guy who provided milk to the station gave his home for a hefty rent. It was a hut, with space for bathing and sleeping. One could hardly live there. All day he spent at the siding and, if possible, a few nights and holidays too.

During the weekly rest days, to wash clothes, Harshkant visited a friend's aunt's house in the city. He washed his clothes and slept on the terrace while the clothes dried. Then, he spent time with the family and returned to his dingy accommodation. I didn't know such difficulties because Amma washed and ironed my clothes. I had a royal life.

Another batchmate, Ilayaraja, often stayed overnight at his station because, by the time he reached home, it was time to head back and issue tickets for the morning train. On one such night, he hummed a song resting his back after a tiring day of sitting and staring at the tracks. It was a wayside station where few trains passed, and very few halted. He imagined the dark star-lit sky beyond the red tiles on the ceiling as he lay on a straw mat when he saw a movement on the tiles. The streetlight lit up the room and created shifting shadows. Then hearing a thud beside him, he jumped with his legs entangled in the bed sheets.

As the tube light flickered to life, he saw a snake wriggling over his makeshift pillows of 'Daily Trains Ticket Register and Coaching Tariff.' Like Bruce Lee, he took a snake pose, trying to scare the snake into relinquishing his pillows. The snake watched his antics with a bored expression and yawned. Then, it looked at the skinny chap as if to say, 'Don't bother, I am leaving.' It slithered into an opening in the wall near the door and disappeared. From then on, Ilayaraja slept with the lights on while the snakes practised traipsing on the ceiling.

Once, while sleeping at Priya's railway quarters, I woke up in the middle of the night as my fingers touched something soft and squishy. I shrieked, and when the tube light sparkled, my face con torted in horror, and Priya collapsed laughing. Three tiny pink mice were sleeping in my warmth. The mother mouse was nowhere to be seen. Either, the mouse gave birth beside me, or, as Priya deduced, they must have fallen from the wooden beam in the ceiling. Or I miraculously birthed three mice.

* * *

Leaving Amma to bemoan our fate, sitting on the floor of my new quarters, 95D, Achan and I explored the quaint little town to buy the bare essentials I needed to survive.

The main town was a good 2 km from the station. Yellow and red flags fluttered on bamboo posts everywhere creating an air of festivity. Loudspeakers blared songs in Kannada. Flex boards with intricate Kannada script hung from the trees.

1st November was Karnataka State Day, and the celebrations continued until the month's end. Every time I remember my initial days in a new place on a new job, I chuckle at what my achan told me that day we jaunted across the town.

'Looks like the town is celebrating your arrival.'

The quarters fringed the station. Between the station building and the quarters was the Health Unit, and the doctor's residence was next to it. Other than the roads all over the ground, lush, soft grass flourished. The doctor's primary purpose was to issue the sick certificate to employees who could not perform duties. And most of the employees were not 'sick'. Other times, the doctor—a huge pot-bellied man—remained cooped up in his house.

At the rear side of the station premises was a cluster of houses, a temple and meadows.

The goods shed neighboured the station building, a few yards from the end of the platform beyond the VLR stall.

A few roadside shops sold vegetables, fruits and groceries. Beside the station road, a tiny restaurant with just two tables and two benches advertised of chitranna on a blackboard. The roads were broad, bordered by mimosa trees, shedding pink fuzzy flowers with intermittent clumps of areca and coconut palm. In the heart of the town was the main road—Nehru Road, the artery, where all the businesses were concentrated. Several shops sold tyres and hardware, a few fancy stores, two theatres—Vinayaka and Laxmi—and a Venkateswara sweet stall, where you could get the best melt-in-the-mouth mysurpak in the world (they have no branches).

I noticed numerous shops had the name 'Green' prefixed on their name boards. Later, I learned that they were one of the prominent families of our town. The other prominent inhabitants were an affluent Iyengar family who organized music and dance shows at the Kuvempu Auditorium, and many famous national-level politicians.

* * *

Being the only female employee, men trailed me like ants on a sugar spill. The eligible bachelor from the Green family frequented the station and drifted in the premises too often after my arrival, alleged my colleagues. It was as if he had taken up the task of reserving tickets for all his friends and relatives. Two years later, he would gift me—a salwar kameez dress material, in GREEN.

There was this hulk of a cement vendor who frequented the goods shed; I was a fan of his sonorous voice and walrus moustache. He had zero interest in me, and we bonded over books and movies. He had a vast coffee plantation and resort in Coorg. I called the goods shed on the railway phone just to hear his 'Hello.' We did not have BSNL phones, only the railway phones on which we could speak within the station or the one in the SM's office that dialled the other stations in the section.

Another person who fluttered near the coop was a tall, fair, handsome man with wavy hair and a dimpled chin. He was the Iyengar scion and was estranged from his young wife. He displayed adorable shyness in talking with me and quietly stood in the queue, watching me issue tickets. If others were at work and I was counting tickets, he would come inside the office inquiring about ticket availability. His wife later returned to live with him, and he brought his cute little daughter to meet me.

My unmarried and young colleague Farhan who became my best buddy in the station, once casually asked if I wanted to marry him and continue issuing tickets as partners.

Ahh, the pleasures of being young and sought after!

* * *

Achan returned to Madras after a week, but Amma couldn't leave her twenty-year-old single child alone, so she stayed back. Amma called her brother in the police service posted in New Delhi, asking him to meet the railway minister or the Prime Minister and arrange for my transfer to Madras. Poor uncle was in a fix. We announced to everyone in the station that we would be leaving soon and put off buying the important things for the house . . . we slept on a straw mat, although the weather was chilly and had no stove or kerosene. Amma struck a deal with a neighbour to cook three meals for us on payment. The neighbour, a young girl about my age with three children, crushed in poverty thanks to her abusive alcoholic husband, pounced on our offer and cooked tasty fare for her family and us.

Amma soon realized that we were funding their rations, which chipped away at our savings. As weeks turned to a month, we bought a mattress and blankets. Then, a kerosene stove and vessels. She stood in long queues to buy kerosene because the kerosene shop only functioned whenever the in-charge was sober. News spread like fire as soon as it opened. She dropped whatever she was doing, picked up the white 5-l can (later it became two 5-l cans) and dashed to the shop. Getting a new gas connection was complicated, and we were confident we would be leaving soon.

* * *

My friend Priya started life alone in her railway quarters at her station. No train services would suit her shift timings if she stayed with me or vice versa. A colleague sublet his quarters to her. Priya was also a lone woman in her station. A neighbour offered her measly food at a monthly rate. For many days, she survived on papads and curd rice. Already a puny girl, she looked emaciated. We bought her some vessels, a stove and provisions. Her mother came over for a week and gave her a crash course on cooking before she went home to her younger daughter who was in school.

Amma soon made friends and conversed in broken Kannada. She taught the women to make vadams (rice papads). Come summer, all the women in our quarters followed Amma's recipe. We adjusted to simple living where we only needed a refrigerator during summer and relied on our neighbours. We avoided purchasing a refrigerator or TV because we already had one back in Madras. Oh, we were busy saving money. During winter, milk and curd were safe inside a cardboard box.

Amma cooked tasty dishes that took forever to make on the kerosene stove and sometimes smelled of paraffin. On weekends, we watched movies on our neighbours' televisions. We ordered a teakwood cot at the behest of a railway guard, which is still in excellent condition even after twenty-eight years.

Reluctantly, life fell into a routine. Achan, bored of staying alone in Madras, said he might try for a transfer to this town. My parents began a long-distance relationship through letters. On Sundays, we went to an STD booth and worked out an adjustment. We waited at the phone booth for Achan's phone call from an STD booth back home.

I learned the nuances of ticketing. The theoretical knowledge I gained over the two years of schooling helped, but we followed the railway maxim—'Turn the page, learn the work. If one asked a difficult question to a senior who was unaware of the answer, they quickly said, 'Turn the page, see how it's done, and then do it.'

* * *

I assisted the seniors for the first few weeks and observed their working style. Independent shifts came after a month. Lakhs of printed card tickets freighted from the ticket factory needed checking before relevant entries were recorded. The task of maintaining the registers fell on me. When everyone praised my handwriting, I happily wrote reservation charts of four coaches every day. Seventy-two multiplied by four times names, gender and age. I was too vain to understand that these men were fake praising my handwriting and making me write those charts. Computerized ticketing systems had not yet reached this part of the world, so charting was all manual.

There were huge registers, one for each train for which we had a reservation quota. In the narrow space within the ticket vault, crammed between the columns and tubes of the card tickets, I had to handle these registers, taking care not to tear the pages while turning them to find the page specific to the date and class mentioned in the reservation forms. If one person asked for a sleeper class, the next would render a form for first class. That's another register. I was quite frail in those days, and shuffling the registers exhausted me. After marking the entry on the register, I had to mention the train number, class, gender and age on the rear side of the tiny card ticket.

If there were any error in writing the gender or the date of travel, or a mismatch in class, it would be murderous on the day of travel. I combed the reservation forms and made the entries meticulously. Sometimes, it was difficult to decipher a colleague's handwriting on the register, and mistakes crept in, leading to episodes of trauma.

Once the chart was written in triplicate, we glued one copy on the train coach. With the overused carbon, one had to put pressure on the writing. Sometimes, we didn't have full-sized carbon sheets, and small bits were placed together. We made the indents for these periodically, but the supplies were delayed. Sometimes, the same berth number would be mentioned on two different card tickets, and a wrong entry was made in the register—a double booking. When two passengers claimed the same berth, they rushed to the ticket window, yelling and agitated. Apart from issuing unreserved tickets for the three general compartments, the night duty clerk also had to resolve the chart discrepancy. The clerk had to check the registers and peruse the reservation forms hurriedly to ascertain whether the error was on the part of the passenger or the clerk.

If it was a clerical error, we had to safeguard the teammate involved, and somehow plead with the TTE to give his sleeping berth to the passenger to avoid a complaint. There were cases when one or more celebrity passengers were promised the same cabin or a coupe in first class. We had quite a rich VIP traffic, and it was CBS Amarendra Pillai's prerogative to do the first-class cabin and coupe allotment. He bungled the allotment several times but being a smooth talker, he managed to sort things and massaged the egos of these personalities.

I watched agog as the king handled the inflated egos of these VIPs and, in turn, inflated his own ego. It was a thorough lesson on human relations and human behaviour.

PLATFORM NO. 3A

OUR STATION WAS THE TERMINAL railway station on the BG line, and many famous Hindu temples were reachable by road from there: Sringeri, Subramanya, Udupi and Mookambika. An incredible waterfall, one of the best in India was just around the corner. As the Mangalore line was closed for gauge conversion works, to reach these temple towns and tourist spots one had to go by road from our station. We had no dearth of visitors, especially VIPs. They detrained at our station, visited the temples and boarded the night express. Sometimes, these VIPs were ushered into the Station Manager's room for a quick session of tea and biscuits from the VLR.

I had the opportunity and privilege of meeting Dr Raja Ramanna, the physicist and architect of India's nuclear weapons programme. He and his wife visited the tourist spots and temples right after he retired from his post as the founder and director of National Institute of Advanced Studies. My amma and I met them in front of the first-class coupe. He was reticent, but his wife was friendly.

The dynamic and beautiful BJP MP, Sushma Swaraj, also visited. We met her inside the first-class coupe, on her return journey. Amma was mesmerized by her politeness and glowing skin.

Karnataka politicians, including MLAs and MPs, were a common sight at our station. And I remember, once a famous politician informed the station to hold up the train until he arrived. Luckily, he reached before the scheduled departure time so the passengers, mostly from his constituency, were spared the inconvenience. The SM waved the green flag with relief after the politician and his entourage boarded the train.

Coincidentally, whenever all these personalities boarded the night express, I happened to work a shift at the parcel office where there were few customers for luggage booking, which permitted me to loiter outside on the platform, taking in these sights. Even if I happened to be on my weekly holiday, I would be on the platform because I had inside information on the VIP movements.

Iconic Kannada star Dr Rajkumar and his family also travelled to our station. On rare occasions, I caught sight of these personalities when they detrained the express train that pulled in at our station in the morning. But that day, I had been on night shift, and as usual, I waited on the platform to see the morning train roll in and enjoyed the scenario where the locals welcomed their guests. I bounced in excitement and saw a trace of a smile on the matinee idol's face. (Perhaps I imagined it) I was on the parcel shift on the night of their return journey. I saw Shiva Rajkumar (or Shivanna), his son, a star himself, walk on to the railway platform wearing spotless white pyjamas and carrying a pillow while boarding the train was just like Aamir Khan's viral videos where he carried a pillow and boarded a flight that did the rounds on social media a few years ago.

Shivanna was a trendsetter, Aamir Khan caught on quite late. A shy Puneeth who hadn't yet debuted as a lead followed his father quietly. I never knew at that juncture that he would rise to great heights only to later leave millions of fans heartbroken. When I heard about his untimely death, the vague image of a young man came to my mind. He was only a year older than me.

At the Kuvempu Auditorium, dance dramas were regularly enacted, and legendary dancers performed. The Iyengar family were the organizers, and we, the station people, were seated in the front. Amma and I watched fantastic dance performances by Vani Ganapathy and Padma Subramaniam and conversed in Tamil with them. The dancer couple, the Kirans, who garnered attention later, performed in our town in their earlier days. When they boarded the train in sleeper class, I met them near their coach and congratulated them on their stunning performance. Carnatic vocalist T.M. Krishna, then a spanking new musician, had one of his earliest solo performances in our town.

My colleagues joked that I could soon join politics because I even had publicity to capture the vote bank. I was pretty famous with the locals and the visitors as The Lady at the railway station. That was when my CBS, Amarendra Pillai, took me to attend the wedding of our district MP's daughter. The who's who of the state and central politics attended the spectacular wedding, and I also posed for a photograph with the couple. If they now open their marriage album, they will wonder who this skinny, bespectacled character was!

* * *

After counting thousands of card tickets, I learnt ticketing in my spare time. Yes, we counted the individual ticket bundles, checked if every bundle had 250 tickets and ruled out errors, because a missing ticket meant a loss of money. I memorized the names of the stations in the section, and a bit of Kannada needed to issue tickets—*ellige, eshtu* and change *kodree*—and took up independent duty. Even now, when people ask me, 'Do you speak Kannada?' I answer, 'Mostly only the ticket-selling language.'

Another thing we all observed during our tenure in Karnataka was the type of currency bills that were in circulation. Back in Madras, people leapt to the sky and created a fuss about the quality of the notes—refusing to accept even a tiny tear or sticky tape on a currency. But when we joined our stations in various parts of Karnataka, we were shocked to see these currency notes. Almost all the small denominations were soiled, grimy and sticky. You accepted them and issued a ticket, and the passengers took it back without a fuss when you gave such notes as balance. There was this banknote that circulated a lot—one half was a Rs 10 note, and the other half was a mix of Rs 5 and Rs 2. This note was accepted as a Rs 10 note, the latter being the highest denomination it carried. I had my brush with counterfeit currencies, too. Railway stations are the easiest targets for floating fake money. The booking clerk would end up coughing up the replacement currency or cunningly float the fake notes back into circulation.

* * *

Rajan, who had joined before me, completed his training in ticketing and later worked shifts in the goods shed under the Chief Goods Supervisor (CGS). The CBS and CGS were at loggerheads over trivial issues, and we became their ammunition. Over time, these two supervisors became possessive of us and treated us like their toys. The station manager introduced a rule to rotate staff between the booking and goods sheds. All the seniors dodged, while we the new entrants were shunted.

During my shifts in the goods shed, the CGS would send me to the booking office (BO) on trivial errands to spite the CBS. I longed to reclaim the bustling ticket windows from the solitude of the GS. Soon, Rajan went home on leave from the BO and then switched jobs to a private company. As a solo pawn, I shouldered the ego clash of the supervisors. Once, the CGS invited me home for the Ugadi festival, and the same day, I had to join the booking staff at the CBS's home, too. I was neither here nor there, and both here and there. I consumed two festival lunches of almost the same *saaru, palya, majjige* and *holige*.

* * *

Work in the booking office galloped compared to the sluggish pace in the goods shed, where wagons rumbled in only once or twice a week, but when they did, the work crippled me. I would walk the length of the goods train, sometimes more than 2 or 3 km, noting down the wagon number and originating railway, the tare weight, and check the waybill on hand to rule out discrepancies. These details had to be surveyed even when an empty wagon arrived for loading. Our incoming freight included cement, rice and oil tankers. The outgoing freight was mostly areca nuts.

During my goods shed duty, I noted the details of the wagons walking over the brambles near the tracks, gnawed by insects and having my clothes snagged by thorns. The dangers when suddenly the rake moved while I squeezed between the wheel gaps and crossed under the wagons to the other side were life-threatening.

I lost weight. I was almost size zero (even before Kareena Kapoor) and flaunted my fitted kurtas. (There was an excellent tailor near the quarters who stitched fantastic kurtas—with such a perfect fit and comfort. I haven't found a tailor like him ever again.)

It was a sneeze fest inside the goods shed, especially when bags of cement were due for delivery. While working, I wore a bandana like a balaclava on my face and head. Rats and bandicoots scurried across the damp bags of rice or wheat to be taken to the Food Corporation of India warehouse. Sometimes alone in the cavernous room, any faint thump unnerved me. When we had wagons to unload, the customers brought their workforce to unload the commodities. These men, dusted in cement from head to toe, sat circling me, sipping tea and regaling stories of ghosts seen on the tracks. Although I laughed at these tales and acted brave, it terrified me at night.

My uncle in the police department, who was entrusted with the task of my transfer to Chennai, loved to narrate anecdotes—some true, some made up. When he commanded a police unit in a small town in Tamil Nadu, his juniors reported about the ghostly activities ruining their sleep.

'*Ayya*, every night at 1 a.m., we hear the sound of anklets. It repeats at regular intervals for thirty minutes. We think it's the ghost of a woman who died on the railway tracks. Because of this, we are uncomfortable during night shifts. Can we arrange for a priest to exorcise the ghost?'

'Don't be foolish. You are all brave policemen. What's this nonsense? Go back to your posts.'

'Ok, Ayya.' The men clipped their heels, saluted and left.

After a few days, the women from the police quarters also complained about these strange sounds; my uncle posted two men to patrol near the railway station and tracks.

The policemen caught a man dressed in khakis wearing an orange overcoat marching on the tracks with a giant hammer and hitting the sides, emitting a clang.

'Hello, hello, are you crazy? Why are you hitting the tracks? You will damage the tracks,' shouted one of them.

The man calmly answered, 'Sir, I am the railway gangman. I must check the nuts and bolts in the tracks, tighten them and check the points in the line to ensure the safety of the tracks. I can only do this after the last train has left the station.'

The policemen sheepishly reported this to my uncle the next day, thus solving the case of the anklet-wearing ghost.

I relayed this to my friend Ilayaraja when he reported an incident from his station.

He told me that there was an enormous banyan tree across from the ticket office on the other side of the tracks where he worked. He enjoyed watching the leathery, glossy green leaves and counting the number of prop roots. During the first two years of working in that station, it was just a banyan tree under whose shade he smoked during breaks.

One day, a local villager asked him, 'Why are you standing near the banyan tree?'

'It is a tree I like, that's all.'

'Sir, a few years ago, a group of railway contract labourers put up a tent near this tree. One day, an unmarried man in his sleep couldn't extricate his legs; he imagined the roots had entwined his legs. It frightened him, and he fell ill. Within a few days, his fever spiked, he vomited blood and died. In his delirium, he blabbered that a *yaksha* or a *mohini* called him to follow her, conjugate with her and leave the earth.'

Ever since my friend heard the story, he shuddered upon seeing the tree. On a lonely night when the full moon glowed over the tree, a dark-as-night person stood outside the office and, in a husky voice, asked: *Gaadi yaavaaga baruthe*? (when will the train come?) Ilayaraja sprung from his seat, sweat pouring from his brows. He took a few seconds to calm down and figure out that it was not a ghost but a flesh-and-blood human. For many months, my young, unmarried friend worried that all his untold desires would fructify only with a mohini.

I told Ilayaraja to ask his parents to find him a bride instead of waiting for a mohini.

A lot of hearsay does the rounds in railway stations and end up becoming folklore. Next time you see a massive, gnarled tree near the platform, don't look for marks of a yaksha. Folklore is fun to listen to. Just listen, enjoy and move on.

* * *

The booking office work comprised issuing unreserved tickets for the passenger and express trains and reservation tickets for the night express train to Bangalore as well as the other wayside quotas allotted to our station.

The reservation process was unhurried and never served a lengthy queue but had a steady trickle of customers. It required great concentration in handling the enormous reservation registers, noting the details as per the reservation form, calculating and collecting the right fare.

There were several engineering and medical colleges around our town, and the students crowded our office whenever the holiday season came up. Most of them were boys from far corners of India: Chhapra (CPR), Darbhanga (DBG), Ara (ARA), Muzaffarpur (MFP), Dehri on Sone (DOS), Misrauli (MFL), and my favourite New Jalpaiguri (NJP), to mention some places. Recently, I checked the details of this station and inferred there is Jalpaiguri Road (JPF.), Jalpaiguri (JPG) and even Raninagar Jalpaiguri junction (RQJ), as if they ran out of names and the funny thing is that these stations have some five to ten stations between them.

We had a limited wayside quota for trains to these destinations, and when these were filled, we had to send a telegram to the central junction in our section, from where the train originated. These telegrams were written in coded railway language and sent through the train guards. A typical coded message would read: EMBOAT M 20 T No 1234 From station To station Date. EMBOAT was for second class, and first class was SFESI or FESCI. In these times of computerization, such codes have ceased to exist.

The names of all these stations were new to me, and without the resources we have now, I relied on the heavy-bound books, one for each zone comprising the details of all the stations within that zone. In those days, Indian railways were divided into nine zones, and calculating the distance from our station to the destination station was a laborious task; by the time I issued one ticket, the queue would stretch beyond the station entrance. And students thronged my nook whenever I had the evening shift.

Blame it on my conversation skills; these young ones, mostly my age, found a listening ear in me. I asked about their family back home and inquired about their studies while handling those heavy books. Sometimes, I calculated wrongly and received a debit notice during auditing.

These boys requested that we send the telegram by postal services for onward journey reservations instead of relying on train guards and TTEs, as was the norm. They offered to pay for this, but we knew that postal telegrams would not work. Still, we promised to send telegrams but never did. Instead of the money which they offered, we asked them to buy carbon sheets for our station or obtain Xerox copies of the reservation forms. Sometimes, there was a shortage of reservation forms.

When these boys returned after their vacation and thanked me for getting them confirmed tickets, I cringed in guilt, aware that these coded telegrams seldom reached the intended junction.

Also, there was a railway circular to collect Farakka Bridge tax while issuing tickets to a few stations in West Bengal. Passengers travelling to New Jalpaiguri had to be levied this tax along with the ticket fare. Sometimes, we forgot to add this to the ticket fare, and the auditors raised debit advice, sometimes even in paise! To be saved from debits, I collected the Farakka Bridge tax even though the train never traversed West Bengal. When the students who knew better geography pointed it out, I stared them down, 'Who is in charge of tickets here? Do you want a confirmed berth or not?' I bullied them into paying this tax.

* * *

The issuing of unreserved tickets was an adrenaline rush. We would issue hundreds of tickets in twenty minutes.

The rule was to open the window for unreserved tickets only twenty minutes before departure because the train could get cancelled in case of untoward circumstances. Scores of hands pushed through the tiny window opening, screaming the destination and number of tickets required. I rarely had time to see the faces, just a fleeting glance. As a ticketing staff, I have seen a gazillion hands—stubby, manicured, burnt, albino, with chipped nails or an extra finger, dark, fair, gnarled, wrinkled, calloused, deformed . . . So, after working for so many years, the physiognomy often looks familiar when I meet a new person. Somewhere, some features connect the neurons in my head to a face I have seen on some platform through the porthole.

My hand would whizz in lightning speed, asking the passenger: Ellige (Where)? Eshtu (How many)? And change kodree. (Give me change) Full ticket, *ardha* (half) ticket, *mathe enu beku* (What else do you want)? Then, I would calculate the fare, my fingers furiously playing with the calculator, collecting cash, returning the change, and pulling the tickets out from the ticket tube. I had palpitations if I didn't have a calculator in sight. The tickets were inserted in tubular columns on a wooden cupboard and I had to stretch to reach the top rungs. Then I stamped the date and time and issued it as I simultaneously asked the next person: Ellige? Speed was of essence. Working in automatic mode, I issued tickets. No other thoughts . . . the only time my head was blank, and I focused on the task at hand.

Many passengers and my colleagues called me 'Express Lady', and I enjoyed being the only woman amongst the 70-odd railway staff in the station. It was when Dr J. Jayalalitha was the most powerful woman in Tamil Nadu, and I was compared to her.

Our station was the originating station for the night train, and four reserved coaches formed the station quota.

The other coaches were filled up by the two subsequent stations—one in which my friend Priya worked and the other, the station that followed hers. Some days, she and I did night duties on the same night. She at her station, and I at mine. We discussed the number of unreserved tickets we issued for the three general coaches. I almost filled up the three coaches, and the passengers she issued tickets for scrabbled up in the remaining space. On weekends, the train would swell to bursting capacity. Passengers purchased a ticket even after I warned them that the train was packed. They demanded a ticket, and later pleaded for cancellation and refund. As per the rules, we deducted Rs 10 per ticket as cancellation charge. But sometimes, I pitied the poor passengers and whispered that he could sell it to the next person in the queue, who would return for cancellation—it was an unending loop.

* * *

My friend Priya visited me on her 'weekly off'; we watched all the movies that were newly released. Language and star cast were no bar for us. Tamil, Kannada, Hindi and English; if the movie changed on a Friday, we would see it before the following Friday. Aamir Khan's *Raja Hindustani* is one film we watched more than five times! The movie ran for a long time, and we took relatives and friends to watch it. Only a few films were simultaneously released in our theatres and India-wide. We were small-town folks who waited. My friend and I watched Aamir Khan romance Karishma Kapoor, and when the next week had no other new release, we watched it again. Then, a cousin came to my town, and I watched the movie again. Because it ran for so long, the guard's wife, my friend, wanted to see it, so I accompanied her. The following week, Sunil Warrier stopped by, and we had only five hours to spare before he caught his train back to Mysore; yet again, I watched *Raja Hindustani* with him. I had the dialogues and songs memorized by the time the movie changed at our theatre. When I went to Chennai, the beggars on the electric trains screamed '*Paarrrdesi paarrrdesi jaana nahi*' and I almost chorused with them.

When the movie *Border* was released, we were worried that a fire might erupt in our town's theatre as it did in Uphaar cinema in the capital. Priya and I prayed before we entered the cinema.

We found restaurants serving anything besides chitranna and explored the region's cuisine. There was a restaurant, Hotel Malnad, which still, in my opinion, serves the best chicken manchurian. It was the first chicken manchurian I had tasted.

Growing up in Madras, with only Achan as the breadwinner, we rarely went to restaurants. And now we were earning, although our salary was a pittance compared to others working in the private sector. Sitting in the restaurant, as we perused the menu card, Priya and I calculated the total price of the dishes we selected before ordering. A sense of accomplishment coloured our faces when we paid the bill and added a small tip for the waiter.

When girls and boys our age were enjoying college life, we were financially independent. Of course, our purse strings were still in our amma's fist, and we were responsible for contributing to the family savings. We used the little pocket money Amma permitted and splurged it on movies and restaurants.

Priya and I were not too close during school days. But we established a great connection over the two years we worked in adjacent stations, away from our other friends. The love and companionship, the secrets we shared, the giggles and the tears are truly treasured memories. During the period we worked there, she had to rush home on receiving news of her father's sickness. Through the railway phone, she conveyed a message to me. When I called her station, she had already left, and her CBS told me that they hadn't informed her of her father's demise. I fumed and threw words at her CBS, unmindful of the consequences. 'How can you send her alone? You could have informed me, and I would have travelled with her. Poor girl, she will be devastated when she reaches home.' The CBS was apologetic.

Priya was a brave girl. I admired her tenacity when she returned, the head of her family, the provider.

Our batchmate, Inbaraj, who worked four stations away, regularly dropped in. We planned our weekly holiday or night off and met at my home. Amma cooked lunch and fussed over him. He troubled her to cook his favourite food, and Amma even waited on him as he drank his glass of milk, slurping with a spoon. We watched movies and later had dinner at street shops. The egg dosas were delicious in the roadside eateries where one held the plate in one hand and ate standing. Once, when Amma was in Chennai, the three of us stayed in Priya's quarters. We cooked food together, which turned out inedible, and then went for a late-night show. After watching *Independence Day*, we walked home because there were no autorickshaws late at night. This was because it was an English movie, there were few moviegoers, and the road was deserted. As a dog howled, Inbaraj started running. He was so scared, and we girls erupted in laughter. We pulled his leg often, 'What a daredevil you are, abandoning your friends and running away.'

To get back at us, every time he boarded the train back after spending a day with us, he shouted from inside the train, 'My darlings! Take care of our children; don't loiter without feeding them. I will be back soon. Don't miss me.' The two of us turned red as everyone on the platform watched us.

* * *

As my first year in the town ended, Amma and I grasped the futility of hoping for a transfer. Amma checked the price of a refrigerator and television, and set aside money in her monthly budget.

A guard's wife who was between Amma and me in age, provided us great company. She accompanied Amma to the shops, and Amma taught her many recipes. We sometimes borrowed her vessels, chairs and teacups as the need arose. Amma revealed that she instilled in her the habit of carrying enough money whenever stepping out of the house. There could be an emergency, or we might have a sudden craving to shop. Aunty escorted me to the movies and we gossiped about the new stationmaster.

Her husband, the guard, was a specimen. We called him antique. When someone asked him a question, he gazed into their eyes, nodded his head, crunched his teeth, looked beyond the horizon and then answered. By then the person would forget the question. I wondered how this guard would react if there was an emergency on his daily run on the rails. He was often sent to the Zonal Training School to attend training sessions. Whenever he returned, his wife found packets of yellow thread in his luggage. Confused, she showed the thread to Amma. It was the thread the Tamils used in solemnizing a marriage—it was tied on the bride's neck. When Amma asked the guard why he had bought so many, after his ritual of gazing, nodding and crunching he said, 'My colleagues bought it, so I also bought it. I don't know what they are.' Even now, whenever Amma and I see these yellow '*thaali saradu*' we remember him.

When we weekended at my old station recently, it was pretty spruced up and all modern; this guard's wife drove us all over in her new car and showed us the new spots that had cropped up in our town. This town even has an airport now!

I liked my station and my new companions. The pastoral beauty and the pollution-free air of the town was pleasing. Life was slow in our little town, but people were kind and loving. Unbeknownst to us, it had become OUR town.

PLATFORM NO. 4

I PULLED THE WOOLLEN CAP down to my ears and briskly swung my arms like a discus thrower. A tiny flash of warmth spread through my shivering body. My eyes strained and watered as the chilly wind lapped my eyelashes. I trudged in the spooky silence until I collided with a white, immobile apparition. As my heart lurched, I cautiously clenched my palms. A simpering bray erased my doubt. Since my posting at this corner of the country—the farthest broad gauge railway station—I have encountered donkeys daily on the road and at the workplace.

Why was I so fascinated with donkeys? Hear me out.

In Chennai, hordes of cows and stray dogs loitered on the roads, sometimes buffaloes too. But never had I seen donkeys. Here, donkeys dotted the grassy paths, rooted to the spot as if stunned. An occasional whisk of the tail to swat a fly (the fly must have had immense perseverance to irritate the donkey to stir) confirmed to anyone watching that it was not a statue. But my initial surprise at seeing these many donkeys morphed into an embarrassed shock when my eyes clocked the long, elongated, oversized and dangling . . . aah, you know what!

You had to see it to believe it.

I was an unmarried twenty-something who hadn't been initiated into the distinctions or dispositions of male anatomy. Imagine my state when I couldn't peel my eyes off *it*, although I knew the small town would judge me for staring.

One incident that my cousins and I still reminisce and laugh about took place when they came to my humble corner. Two cousins, one unmarried and one with her daughter, travelled by train to my station for a holiday. While the married cousin helped my mother at home, I showed my other cousin (six months younger than me) and our niece, a sprightly girl of five, the station premises.

As always, the donkeys lined up in random places. On spotting one, my niece squealed, clapping her hands, 'This donkey has five legs!'

Oh, boy! My cousin and I turned scarlet and pulled our niece away, clamping her mouth shut. The niece is now in her thirties, and naughty aunts that we are, we still embarrass her by talking about the 'penta-pedal animal', asking, 'How many legs does a donkey have?'

Five-legged donkeys aside, others in my batch had remarkable experiences with the local fauna. One of my friends, Bharathi, posted in the city, told me about a dog, who became her protector.

She had to walk a few kilometres to work whenever she had the morning shift. The trains for the day did not begin that early, and there were no autorickshaws at that ungodly hour. En route to her station, she traversed a dense copse of trees where the weak moonlight struggled to sieve through. Muttering *slokas*, she sprinted through, her heart thudding. Once, she sensed a movement behind. Immediately she picked up a stick and turned around, 'Hello. Who is there?' She saw a dog. She tried to shoo away the dog, but it gazed at her, never growling. She trotted, and the dog stalked at a distance. As soon as she reached her station, the dog watched her climb the steps to her office, then scrammed. This became a regular practice for the two. Every time she had the morning shift, the dog waited near the trees and accompanied her to the station—an angelic companion.

* * *

Bidding farewell to my donkey friend, I bolted across the narrow path towards the station, festooned by dewy grass sparkling in the moonlight, as if a drawstring had snapped from a pouch scattering diamonds. The dew threatened to dampen my ankles and I mumbled the choicest of cuss words. The recipient of my favour? A colleague who had dumped his night shift on me. Enamoured by his 'spirits', this colleague ditched the ones he ought to relieve at work. As a result, the junior-most employee in the station, yours truly, had to take up his rostered shift.

The night before, I had secured the workplace after midnight, tallying the whole day's earnings and the 'proof book'. On the 11th, 21st and 30th/31st of every month the night-duty staff had extra work—tallying the ten days' earnings. These 'SN2' registers were long, like Draupadi's never-ending saree, and handling them was a laborious task. Invariably some of these nights would be earmarked for me. After tallying all the books, I sprinted home to the railway quarters for a quick nap.

Mostly, Amma escorted me to the night shift. It was eerily silent after the last train departed, and while everyone else snored in their beds, my work extended for an hour after the train's departure. Then we trudged to our quarters, beaming a torch.

But Amma wasn't there the previous night. She was in Chennai. The CBS had assured her I wouldn't be rostered for night duties during her absence. And that was why the gentleman who morphed into a villain when inebriated and dumped his night shift on me deserved all the cussing.

And so there I was, on my way, alone, to open shop at 04.00 hrs. Amma never accompanied me in the morning but waited at the end of the block, watching me walk to the station. The express train from Bangalore was due to reach my blip-in-the-map station in some time, but before that was a meter gauge train for which I needed to issue tickets.

The last few yards, I jogged to reach the station building, rubbing my palms and blowing on them for warmth. I had been born and raised in Chennai, where only one season persisted—the summer. So, it was this posting at the gateway of the Western Ghats that introduced me to winter. I absolutely enjoyed the nip in the air.

Upon reaching the station, I walked to the ticket office. Then I opened the colossal lock and tugged the rusty latch. My glasses fogged, as I pushed and prodded until the long key snugly fit into the grove. Using my full strength—I was wafer-thin in those days—I shoved with my shoulders, and the door finally creaked open. Groping the wall to find the light switch, I prayed that a resident lizard wouldn't lick my fingers.

The tube light flickered then, letting out a buzzing sound, breathed its last.

CRAP!

I nudged my way to the table, waving my arms.

OUCH!

The blasted heavy rosewood table nicked my knees.

Mouthing a volley of curses, I flicked the switch for a 25-watt bulb dangling from the chipped ceiling on a long wire. It brightened a portion of the room like a stage spotlight. I jumped as two cockroaches scuttled across. By the dim light, I rummaged for a stub of a candle kept in the office for such outages and emergencies. The candle lit, I stretched, standing on tiptoes, opened the ticketing window—an arch-shape in wood, a tiny grilled wall with a narrow opening wide enough for a palm—and pulled a towering chair whose seat was level with my waist. I held on to the heavy wooden ticket racks and hoisted my petite frame aloft.

The meter gauge train was a two-compartment box car painted in powder blue, resembling a toy train. On a typical day, I sold three tickets for this train. A few passengers crossed over the tracks, unconcerned about walking to the booking window for tickets. The train's guard would levy those passengers the ticket fare and share the money with the driver. Some principled ones wrote up a receipt and handed the collection to the ticketing staff at the end of the line. This train shuttled chock-full during summer vacations or monsoon time.

At the end of the line, you find one of the highest plunge waterfalls in India. The torrential rains this region enjoys enhances the sublime beauty of the cascade amidst scenic, lush greenery. When the fog cleared, one could see the splendour of a rainbow reflecting in the misty vapours. Ah! What a sight! Since I joined this station, I have feasted my eyes on the falls several times. With cousins, aunts, uncles and friends, whoever visited me. I would take them on the blue train to glimpse the cascade.

This day was neither a holiday nor a monsoon. March marked the beginning of summer, yet for a *Madrasi*, it was still winter. I stifled a yawn and peered into the gloomy darkness.

The loco pilot (the train driver) and the guard trotted together, laughing merrily. The duo waved and hollered in unison, 'Good Morning. Nice to see you in the morning.'

When I travelled in trains during summer vacations, I often wondered about the black boxes with the names suffixed with Guard or Driver in brackets and other details. So, when I became a railway employee and saw these black boxes on my platform, I couldn't hold my curiosity and enquired about it. The guard who just waved an exuberant good morning explained in detail. In case any of you have noticed these black tin boxes and wondered about them, here it is.

The running staff, the drivers and the guards each had a black metal box with their name, designation, etc., that travelled with them on the train. The black box is called the 'line box'. It contained the safety equipment required by these railwaymen in times of need during their duty on the train. The various safety equipment they carried were the detonators, LV board, tail lamp, tri-colour torch, first-aid kit, carriage key, tailboard, and books and forms required for ensuring a safe run. It was in the news recently that these boxes were to be replaced by trolley bags. However, the railway men are against it. They say when the guard steps out of his brake van in an emergency someone could push the trolley and take them. These metal boxes are heavy and difficult to move. But it's a failing battle, the loco pilot's line box has been replaced by a tool box which has to be handed over after duty.

I grinned and shrilled a 'good morning' to the driver/ guard. I envied their fellowship while I wilted in loneliness. If my favourite stationmaster (more on that later) were on duty, he would come for a chat. But otherwise, it was a solitary morning for me.

So, I wasn't bashful while I idled in the crack of dawn, watching the waving duo. Youthful, spirited and moderately good-looking, I was the princess of my kingdom. Each one of my colleagues'—old, young, married, single—faces lit up on seeing me. It enthralled me, no less.

Although this was a small station with two platforms, and three trains onward and three inwards, not including the blue train, plentiful were employed. The Indian Railways was, and continues to be, among the largest employers. But the strangest thing was, barring me, every other employee here was male. I yearned for girly talk and the company of women. I sighed and at that moment, however, I was unaware I was to have my wish granted. And how!

After a year of enjoying my queendom, my station welcomed a new porter, a lady porter. Ecstatic, I ran to meet her. Zahira Begum was a small, thin older woman, all grey and wrinkled. She flashed a smile, crinkling the crow's feet near her eyes. My relief mirrored and surged through her upon meeting a fellow species at this distant station.

She had taken up her spouse's job after his demise, and this was her first post. The parcel-office shifts we shared were such fun. Her voice was remarkably similar to that of the extraordinary singer *Salma Agha,* and I spent many hours listening to her sing ghazals on demand. Whenever I hear *'Dil ke armaan aasoowon mein beh gaye',* I remember my dainty companion, who entranced me with her songs.

* * *

I checked my watch. The blue train must have left, and the express train would arrive soon. A few men nodded at me as they paraded to the platform to receive their guests. Technically, they were supposed to buy platform tickets from me, but everyone knew the ticket collector post was still vacant in our station. A few months later, a young chap joined us but soon left for a bigger station.

I craved tea, but VLR wasn't open yet. Mr Shetty would open his shutters only when he heard the approaching train. On some days, his daughter Shalini, a class 10 student, helped him. She was the closest substitute to a female friend I had (until Zahira Begum reported), other than the ever-busy Fathima, who ran the shop on the platform along with her *abbu*. I missed my achan a lot when I saw these girls with their fathers. Shalini and I often chatted and giggled over inane subjects. But these were not railway staff, and I couldn't carry on any work-talk with them.

The night express rolled in, I fastened the room and strolled to the platform. The train jingled satisfactorily at its safe arrival.

I loved watching the platform come alive. Hordes of people lugging heavy boxes lunged out. Mothers tugged sleepy children to walk faster. Fathers haggled with the only two licensed porters of the station. The men who waited to welcome the travellers hugged their daughters and grandchildren, reserving a stiff handshake for the sons-in-law.

A pair of ticket examiners detrained after the first rush of passengers, uttering something. During my earlier vigils of arrivals on the platform, I had observed several TTEs praying and sometimes touching the train's steps before boarding it. That's how I knew the ticket examiners were thanking the gods for their secure passage. Since then, every time I board a train or a flight, I pray for a safe journey and of course never forget to thank the gods at the destination.

I paced towards my office door and opened it just before they reached my door. The TTEs remitted their earnings collected over the night journey, a WL (wait-list) passenger paid the reservation charges, a second-class passenger opted for an upgrade to first class if available, or the penalty for ticketless travel.

'Are you on duty today?' One of them, a rotund man in the standard black jacket with the Indian Railways logo embroidered on the breast pocket, raised his eyebrows.

'Yeah, I was watching the travellers.'

'I can understand. This is the major entertainment for you.' The other, a dark bearded fellow, quipped as he pulled a chair and sat.

'Not exactly. We have movies and drama theatres, too. Even the other day, we watched danseuse Padma Subramaniam's performance at Kuvempu Auditorium.' I reserved the right to complain about the ordinariness of my station.

'Oh, don't get offended, Sangeetha. Are you still looking for a transfer or are you settling well here?' He pulled out his collection book, counted the cash, and waited.

'I will get a transfer soon.' I had been repeating this mantra for several months and was on the verge of becoming a perennial joke among the staff.

I set the carbon in triplicate and wrote the receipt after counting the cash. I then repeated the procedure with the bearded TTE.

'Where are the others?' I asked, moving my pen.

'Only one more. We manage four coaches each nowadays. The new guy has a camera and is clicking pictures of the platform and the sunrise,' scoffed the portly one.

'We do have the most beautiful sunrises.'

After a quick chat, they dispensed their work and retreated to their retiring rooms. 'See you later, Sangeetha. Keep trying for that transfer, yes?' the bearded one waved goodbye.

I liked these avuncular men. Sometimes, they shared funny anecdotes about their journeys and the passengers they met. And it felt good to be included in their conversations, almost as if I was bantering along with my uncles at home, laughing at their jokes.

I arranged the cash (always the heads together, the denominations in descending order) and was impatiently tapping my foot when there was a knock at the open door.

'May I come in?'

'Yes, please.'

A tall, honey-coloured, smartly dressed man (the night stubble grazing his square jaw) in a tailored black coat (not the uniform handout) and sparkly shoes sauntered in.

'Er, excuse me. Are you the clerk?' he asked.

'Is it too hard to believe?'

'Oh, no. I wasn't expecting a kid. I thought maybe you were with your father . . .'

I stared at him. 'I am not a kid. Don't waste my time; quickly remit your collection.'

He bit his protruding tongue, counted the soiled notes and watched me write the receipt. Then, ruffling his bag, he pulled a bunch of purple flowers with the long stalks bunched together.

'Happy Women's Day!' He extended the bouquet, flashing a smile.

'What?!'

'Er, I picked these at the edge of the platform. Thought of putting them in a glass of water. Aren't they beautiful?'

'*Tch*, they are. What did you wish me?'

'Happy Women's Day. I want to call my wife. Is there a phone booth? I must get her a gift tomorrow. Is there any decent shop here?'

'What is *Women's Day*? And the phone booth is on the road outside the station, beyond the quarters. Yes, there are a few fancy shops on Nehru Road.'

He pulled up a chair and explained the new fad of celebrating Women's Day. However, he added, women ought to be celebrated every day. He showed me a picture of his wife and a year-old daughter from his wallet.

'Come and join me for a cup of tea. Let's celebrate Women's Day.'

I was thrilled to be acknowledged as a 'woman'. Ever since I came here, I have been the 'young girl' or 'kid' to everyone in the town. Failing to control the blush that spread on to my cheeks, I mumbled thanks.

I shut the office again after stuffing the meticulously arranged cash (whatever the emergency, the cash had to be arranged; I was too finicky about organizing back then) in the drawers and walked to VLR stall at the end of the platform. He ordered tea and biscuits. We enjoyed our little celebration as the sun lent a golden tinge to the barren platform; dewdrops glistened on the brown train and the meadows beyond the tracks.

I have had many Women's Day celebrations since that day. WhatsApp and Facebook stacked up with forwarded messages and umpteen wishes, espousing the power of womanhood. But every 8th March, I fondly remember 'Charles', the TTE, with whom I celebrated my first Women's Day.

PLATFORM NO. 5

WHEN THE HAMAL TOLD ME that the station manager had summoned me, the twine in my hand snapped. The card tickets flew like confetti all over the floor. Sounds of *tch–tch*, *sheesh*, and not again wormed into my ears.

'Don't worry, I will be back in a jiffy and bundle the tickets,' I chirped, faking cheeriness as I inwardly groaned at the prospect of searching for the errant tickets, arranging them in serial order and bundling them within the twine. The twine would often snap again after I had arranged the tickets; I had to crawl, bend and scruff my knees, searching under the shelves and moving the rusted almirah.

The first task entrusted to a recruit joining my station was counting the tickets. Touch, feel and hold them before you issue them. Nay, there's nothing romantic about that. Hundreds and hundreds of card tickets lined up the shelves, as adult tickets, half tickets and concession tickets to all the stations in our section and a few major junctions. These tickets had a serial number that helped calculate the number of tickets sold daily. Multiplying this number by the fare for the respective stations helped us derive the earnings on a particular shift.

Sometimes, a number was skipped: the dubious case of missing tickets. This could be attributed to negligence in the printing factory, or a fraudulent clerk in the station who might have helped his financial shortage by selling a ticket and pocketing the cash. Later, when some other staff inserted that bundle of tickets into the ticket tube, they would have to compensate the fare of the missing ticket (there are a few knaves in any system). Hence, to rule out discrepancies, the ticket clerk counted all the lakhs of tickets arriving from the ticket printing factory and marked them 'correct.' As the inventory in-charge, I maintained an account of the tickets on hand and informed CBS if the stocks dwindled. So, he could order and replenish them.

Although Indian Railways was the largest employer, there were no extra personnel to count the tickets. Usually, a novice joining the payroll was burdened with this tedious task. I had been doing this for the last six months (along with my independent shifts), and I moved my thumb and index finger, whispering numbers even in sleep. If currency notes and stock prices appeared in Harshad Mehta's dreams, in mine, I saw tickets. If you surveyed the person who snapped a significant number of twines and let the tickets fly, I would be the front runner. Blame it on my clumsiness and stubby fingers. I requested a colleague with sharp, long nails (which I envied as I looked at my chewed-up nails) to help me bundle the tickets. Being the only lady employee of the station had its perks.

My batchmates posted in major stations answered the phones, no ticket counting for them. Thousands called the railway inquiry line, inquiring about the availability of trains, berths, seats, lower berths, tourist spots of a region, bus numbers and, sometimes, whether a movie was running in a theatre.

My friends wrote the probable questions and answers in Kannada and read them out. Some of the words in their non-Kannada accent sounded hilarious, and their seniors cracked up. Some callers even professed their love on the phone to the faceless voices.

Each of us had novel experiences at work. My batchmate Sidharth recalled his first morning in the station near the Kolar Gold Fields in Karnataka. Early morning as he walked on the platform to the ticket window, he was shocked to see a veritable number of people on haunches scrutinizing the ground near the tracks. On enquiry, the crouchers said they were looking for gold dust. Every day men, women and children fastidiously sifted sand and carried home shards of gold.

* * *

On my way to the new station manager's cabin—the old manager had retired a few weeks ago—I wondered if I was to receive good news. I missed the old SMR, a frail, pale, short man who missed a tooth or two and wobbled if he stood on the platform when the train blared. He had a daughter my age, so he treated me kindly and nannied me. His replacement, a much younger person opposite in looks and behaviour, had no interest in this station as he was awaiting a transfer to his wife's hometown.

So, I sprinted to meet the SMR, hoping and praying that my transfer orders had arrived. Amma and I hoped my Delhi uncle would work a miracle. We underestimated the challenge of working out a transfer from the Mysore division to the Chennai division. (A few years later, Mysore, previously under the umbrella of Southern Railways, forked into a new zone—South Western Railways.) My poor uncle pushed my transfer application whenever and wherever he could meet ministers or their powerful PAs. While most of my applications ended up crumpled in wastepaper baskets, one did reach the Minister of State for Railways, although considerable time had elapsed since my mother's first phone call.

The SMR had a smirk on his face, and I curbed the words tumbling out of my mouth regarding my transfer.

'This year is the 50th year of Independence. There's an order to play special announcements for every incoming and outgoing train in Kannada, English and Hindi. It's better if people hear a lady's voice. So, I have put you in charge of it.'

'But . . . I don't know Kannada. Why me . . . ?' The words escaped my lips before I bit my tongue.

'As if we have another choice. You are Miss Sunshine, the only lady employee. I cannot have a class IV announce in Urdu over the public address system; otherwise, the next choice was Zahira Begum, your best friend.'

Mumbling under my breath at his sarcasm, I reached the parcel office, where the Chief Booking Supervisor, my Dumbledore Amarendra Pillai, delivered the rubber rolls. CBS was my father figure. He was the Don Corleone of our town and proudly announced to everyone that I was his heir. People who came to him to book 'special' tickets, the sort who couldn't stand in the queue or wanted specific coupes in first class and such other specifications, were asked to meet me in case of his unavailability.

Oh, I felt supreme as I held a conference with the who's who of the town. It all melted away to powerlessness when I had to plead with the booking clerk on duty to book the reservation form I gave instead of the one proffered by the ones standing and peering at us from the queue. The colleague with a bulbous nose who initially trained Rajan in the BO felt betrayed at his absconding and took it out on me. He made me squirm with guilt as he operated in an excruciatingly slow manner when I took a form for an inside booking. The customers glared at me for the disruption.

* * *

So here I was, asking CBS for a well-written train announcement in Kannada. The SMR gave me the English version, and the versions for other two languages had to be translated. I knew my Hindi was better than the folks here who conversed in a dialect of Hindi. In Chennai, most of us opted for Tamil as our second language in school and chose to study Hindi through the Dakshin Bharat Hindi Prachar Sabha. I cleared my prathmic, madhyama, and rashtrabasha examinations. My cousins even now ribbed me about one of the fill-in-the-blanks questions in my prathmic exam. The final question was *'Dawaat mein* _____ (dash) *nahin hai.'* The answer I wrote was, *'Dawaat mein dawa nahin hai.'* Dawaat was not a medicine bottle like I thought it was, but dawaat meant inkpot. *Siyahi* (ink) was beyond my vocabulary.

Armed with the script, microphone and music player to play patriotic songs, I began rehearsals. No wonder the large important stations had recorded voices over the speakers. I felt prouder than Sarla Chaudhary; the voice we all hear from the speakers in the railway stations across India. I switched on the microphone, and my colleague Farhan, my best friend in the station, exploded in laughter as I squeaked in Kannada. Fortunately, there were no trains for the next few hours, and we provided entertainment to the stray animals and a sprinkle of people on the platforms.

Within a few days, my voice became the voice of the town. I felt like Ameen Sayani, the radio announcer of 'Binaca Geetmala' (a countdown of popular Hindi film songs and a craze among radio listeners for decades) announcing *Behno aur Bhaiyo* . . . Sometimes, I prank announced the names of the staff who went out for tea breaks, and they came running when they heard their names booming from the loudspeakers.

* * *

The station buildings received a coat of fresh paint on the walls after scrubbing clean the flaky walls. The new colours chosen were powder blue for the walls, and navy blue for the doors and windows. Large potted plants were carried by trains from the headquarters, along with huge, gilt-framed pictures of Mahatma Gandhi, Pandit Nehru and Netaji Subhash Chandra Bose. The entire station gleamed, and a celebratory mood wafted all over. (By the month's end, the potted plants, pictures, everything vanished. I'm not sure if they ended up back in the headquarters or someone's home.)

The flag post stood at the end of Platform 1. We decorated the flag post with streamers and I supervised all the activities. Paper ribbons twirled in the wind. My station looked fabulous and my work mates endorsed my enthusiasm. CBS spared me from regular shift duties.

The SM asked if I could draw rangolis or flowers on the platform as an added attraction. When I exhibited my non-existent drawing skills, he arranged for a lineman, an artist, to showcase his talents on the platform. He bought coloured chalk and covered the platform floor with intricate scenery.

My colleague with thick soda-bottle glasses that enlarged his eyes like billiards balls, who enjoyed drinking right before and after duty, who dumped his shifts on poor unsuspecting colleagues like me, raised his displeasure at the celebration activities.

He called me aside, swaying his finger while seated at a table where the photo frames of the freedom fighters were displayed.

'I don't accept this discrimination. Why are you not garlanding the photograph of Dr B.R. Ambedkar?'

He went on a tirade about the great statesman, and I apologized for my blunder. I quickly decorated the photo of Dr B.R. Ambedkar. Over the years in railways, I observed the disparity amongst castes, which loomed large when promotion lists emerged.

Pleased to see the garlanded photo, my colleague vanished to celebrate and didn't turn up for his shift.

The railways was known for its woes with habitual drunkards in its ranks, especially the lower rung. One to two in each station were drunk on duty, shunning work or on extended sick leave. It was a skill to manage the station when you had like 10 per cent troublemakers on your staff and get the best out of the remaining 90 per cent.

Just a week before, we had lost a colleague in another station to liver failure. The saddest thing was his wife had killed herself a few months ago as she couldn't tolerate his drunken abuse. It broke every heart to see the two orphaned children.

Meanwhile, a clerk slugged a quarter bottle in another station after closing the ticket window at night when the last train departed. He passed out. The clerk was horrified when he awoke in the morning disturbed by the passenger for the day's first train. A rat—an office inmate—had nibbled off the tip of his nose. Like Surpanakha with a chopped-off nose, he yelped in agony as the night's intoxication faded.

* * *

When a new officer took charge in the Divisional Office, he surveyed his division's important, minor and obscure stations. He interacted with the lower- and middle-level commercial staff, operations wing people, and the public whom he seldom met in the cosy office rooms at the headquarters. He received first-hand knowledge of problems and issues affecting the division's performance.

One pervasive issue pertained to the long gaps in the musters left unsigned. Red crosses, on account of the long-drawn disciplinary proceedings against the porters and other class III and IV employees, landed them in trouble with the personnel department. The officer sought an accurate picture and reckoned that most of them were irreparable drunkards, but when sober, were a dedicated and efficient lot. The situation worsened by payday, and when bonus was dispersed. The new Divisional Officer called those employees individually from each station to the headquarters. They were instructed to be present in full uniform all day and specifically to greet him when he entered or exited his cabin. The troublemakers had to be punctual and sit on a stool in the corridor all day. There were innumerable friendly inquiries from passersby. Also, they couldn't afford to sip their favourite drink sitting just outside their boss' cabin. More importantly, this allowed these men, for the first time, to be angry at their boss, then to brood over their situation, and think of their children and families who lived in poverty even as they drowned their conscience.

After a week, a few accepted they had gone too far and repented. After a session or two of counselling by the officer, they were back at their stations; some were transferred to a new station, giving them a fresh lease on life. Payments were paid to joint accounts with their spouses, and sometimes family members were counselled. Some needed more than a week in the corridor, but eventually, everybody relented. The moment they could see their fears taken care of and were assured of love and respect, they strode to their everyday lives, giving back much more to the organization.

* * *

The SMR instructed me to reach the station early on the 15th of August to do the trilingual announcements during the train's arrival and wish everyone Happy Independence Day.

On 14th evening, after a hectic day of arrangements, I picked up my bag when my colleague's son came to the office. His father had enjoyed a few extra pegs and was unwilling to wake up for the night shift. So, the onus fell on me, the 'extra' or the 'rest giver' (RG), to pick up the burden of the night shift. I hustled home, apprised Amma and wolfed down a quick dinner.

Amma chaperoned me to the night shift, where she helped me count cash, bundle it up, wrap the day's reservation forms, etc. By midnight, we galloped home and slept fitfully. She was an unpaid part-time booking clerk.

On the wee hours of 15th August, I jaunted to my work spot. When the stationmaster informed me that the express train from the city was trundling in, I threw my exuberant voice into the mike wishing the sleepy passengers: *Dayavittu gamanisi . . . (Your kind attention, please.)*

We had the photos of the national leaders placed on a table strewn with flowers. Around the same time the Prime Minister hoisted the national flag at the Red Fort, the SMR hoisted the national flag in our town. Instead of enjoying the 'night off' and sleeping, I loitered in the station premises. Throughout the day, we distributed sweets to everyone who stepped into our railway station.

PLATFORM NO. 6

'I DON'T WANT TO MARRY her!' said my dear colleague Farhan the day after his engagement.

I froze, clutching an adult ticket and a half ticket. My jaws declined to cooperate in uttering the few words from my Kannada vocabulary.

'Madam, *bega kodree* (give it soon),' pleaded the passenger.

'*Neevu correct change kodree* (You get me the exact change).' I assaulted him with my standard dialogue.

There are times when we are pally with the passengers, enquire about the children and aged parents, and allot lower berths. In the days before computerized reservation, the ticket staff held power over whether you slept on the lower berth or winched up the upper or the side upper berths. Nowadays, the powers are vested in the circuits of the computer. And there are times when bogged down by a personal issue, the staff lets it reflect in their demeanour. After all, we are humans too.

This reminds me of an incident. One builds a relationship with the customers at work. Sunil Warrier was posted in a tourist spot where there were no trains or tracks, just a tiny building with a single counter that operated between 10.00 and 17.00 hrs every day. It is called a satellite reservation office. Living in a tourist place has its benefits as well as disadvantages. Firstly, everything is priced high, rents are higher, coupled with minuscule house rent allowance (HRA) and there's no travel allowance (TA)—perks my friend had enjoyed earlier and without which life was financially burdensome. However, customers showered their love and respect by supplying him fresh milk, bananas and coffee from the plantation. The locals were compassionate. Quite soon after the episode I am writing about, he left the railways for a job abroad.

Before this, when Sunil was posted in an iron ore siding, he had difficulty finding a house on rent with basic facilities. Newly married, he was apprehensive about bringing his young bride to such an area. He spent many days hunting for a house with an attached bath. Somehow, he convinced his house owner to build a makeshift washroom inside the house before he brought his city-bred wife. The bride settled down in her new home and at the behest of her cousin's advice woke up early to cook and pack lunch for Sunil. For a few days when he returned from work, bathed in iron dust— hair, dress and shoes all a shining red—his wife kept mum.

At the end of a week, she cleared her throat and asked, 'Are you really a clerk in the railways?' Sunil was taken aback and asked her why she had asked. Pressing her tongue against her cheek she said, 'The way you come home covered in iron dust almost like a bronze statue I wondered if you were a porter and cheated me into marrying you.'

So, in a way, he was relieved for a change of scenery. Moreover, his wife was pregnant when he moved to this holiday destination. Unfortunately, she miscarried. Not once but thrice. So, when she became pregnant again, the neighbours, the hospital staff and everyone cherished her. This baby was beloved, a gift from God. On the day of the delivery, she was in the hospital; both their parents sat with her, but Sunil couldn't find a reliever. He tottered to open the office. Usually a person of sunny disposition, he acted surly and curt with the customers. Working in small towns, everybody knew you and vice versa. An affluent plantation owner came by and realized that something wasn't right.

'What is it? You seem tense,' she said.

'Sorry if I let my issues reflect in my behaviour.'

'I have never seen you like this. Tell me what's worrying you.'

'You know, my wife is at the hospital delivering our baby, and I couldn't find anyone to take over my shift, so I am here while my mind is with her.'

'Hmm. Do one thing: issue tickets for the people in the queue and then close the office. You need to be with your wife. Call me on this number if someone lodges a complaint about the closed counter. My brother is a big politician. We will take care of it.'

His mind did not think of the consequences. Like a drowning person reaching out for a hand, Sunil quickly disposed of the queue, half pulled the shutter and locked the room. He informed the shopkeeper next door and rushed to the hospital. The baby was waiting for the father. They wheeled in his wife just then because an emergency delivery superseded hers.

As he climbed the stairs, a doctor caught him.

'God is great. Your wife will deliver a healthy baby soon. But I have to tell you, I am surprised that you never asked me during the miscarriages or the recent scans about the gender of the baby. Although illegal, usually people bug me. Now, I want to reveal the gender.'

'Doc, my wife and I prayed for a healthy baby. We have already decided two names: for a boy and a girl. It's God's gift. Nothing else matters. In some time, I will know the gender. I can wait.'

'But I cannot. It's a boy!' With a quick hug, the doctor left.

When the baby was nineteen days old, Sunil decided to join his uncle abroad. He resigned his job and relocated to the Middle East. Many years later, he tracked the doctor who delivered his boy and sent an email to the hospital with a picture of his son. He wasn't sure it would reach the doctor, but he received a reply after a month.

Dealing with customers is an important skill that we, the frontline staff, the face of the railways, require. Any customer who enters the railway premises, sees us and converses with us through the ticket window forms a good or bad opinion about the railways by how the person issuing the tickets or the ticket collector on the platform behaves. A caring word and a smile go a long way.

* * *

Sunil recounted an incident with a divisional office (DO) billing clerk. His travel allowance bills were never correct. The accounts were consistently bungled. There was no way to contact the clerk in the DO, and no one addressed his issues. So, he relied on the TTE to pass on his grievances to the staff of the personnel branch at the DO. He sent a list of duty hours and stations he worked at to enable the bill clerk to verify with her list. A rectified bill and balance payment were paid after three months. By then, the next two months' accounts would be wrong, and this continued for the subsequent five billing cycles. One day, he wrote a personal note with the TA documents to the bill clerk.

'Madam, just reminding you about the previous arrears, and I know you're busy. But thank you for the time you took to rectify and pay the arrears. Keep in mind my TA bill, please.'

Just a three-line note.

Surprisingly, the bill clerk paid the accurate amount for the next two to three months. What he tallied and filled in the form would always be paid. After three months of sending a note, Sunil headed to the DO and met the bill clerk.

'Madam, thank you. I received all the arrears.'

She smiled and said, 'Till this time, no one has thanked me; I was surprised to see the thank-you note. I do my work, but no one acknowledges, and I am frustrated.'

Her way of venting was to pay the wrong amount and make people run behind her.

She added that every time she got his paper, it was the first bill she handled. And nowadays she also tried to pay the correct bill amount to the others.

Such is the power of kindness and gratitude. Whenever I requested leave at the stations where I worked, and the supervisors granted it, I thanked them profusely, and when I wasn't granted leave, I rarely picked up a fight but modified my plans. I empathized with the pressures of drawing up a roster in a short-staffed situation.

* * *

Now let us address Farhan's great reluctance to go ahead with his wedding.

He squeezed beside me in the narrow space between the two ticket racks. Working in harmonious alignment we cleared the morning rush for the express train to the big city. I closed the shutter when the guard sounded the whistle and the train slowly trundled out of the platform.

Arms akimbo, I stared at him. 'Are you crazy?'

'Yes. I am crazy in love!' He flopped on to the table and cracked his knuckles. I swatted his hand (soft, hairless, more feminine than mine). When I hauled the rickety high chair, my kurta snagged on a nail and I struggled to free it. He pulled the chair closer to the table and gently tugged my kurta. I quivered at his breath, warm on my neck. The cabin door opened, and the stationmaster walked in. My cheeks turned hot.

'Oh, you have company.' A mix of mischief and disappointment, evident in his eyes.

'I came to give these sweets to Sangeetha. Why, sir, you expected her to be alone?' Farhan quipped.

'Yeah, I came to ask her for tea at VLR.'

'Ok, Sangeetha. I will see you tomorrow. You enjoy your tea with sir.'

'Wait . . .' I grabbed his hand, and the stationmaster raised his eyebrows. 'You can't leave without telling me the whole story.' I turned towards the stationmaster.

'Can you please give me five minutes? Why don't you go ahead and order? I will be there soon. I have not even tallied my accounts.' I flashed a beseeching smile at the SM on whom I had a titanic crush.

Everyone in the station was privy to this news, from my colleagues to the hamals to the other stationmasters—even my amma. Oh yeah, the concerned party was aware . . . Why am I talking about us? This chapter is dedicated to Farhan.

I know what you are thinking: as if it stopped me earlier from digressing.

The SM pursed his lips and left us alone.

'Now, tell me what happened?' I demanded.

'I know I told you I like this girl whom my uncle chose for me. She's chubby and cute, but her sister is smart and bubbly like you. Yes, she reminds me of you. I think she will suit me better than this girl I am supposed to marry.'

'Nonsense! Didn't you see this sister that day? Suddenly, you can't decide she is more suitable than the other. You are batshit crazy.'

'I am going to their house now. To talk to the sister.'

'What!!?'

'Yes, you heard it right. Now go. Your SM is waiting.'

He left me fuming. I quickly closed the office and sprinted to the VLR stall.

A tiring shift made certain that I didn't have time to think about Farhan or his dilemma. The evening shift colleague bailed out on me, and I continued after a quick lunch break. The saving grace was that the SM, too, had an adjusted shift (done earlier—not to match mine. Don't get ideas). We took a couple more tea breaks together (wink, wink).

When I cleared the reservation queue, I also counted the cash and tallied the accounts. I had the habit of tallying accounts whenever there was a lag in the queue.

After an exhausting double shift, I went home and crashed. Farhan and his romance, forgotten.

After two days, I met my crazy partner. He was unshaven and hollow-eyed.

'The sister rejected me. Now I am stuck with the other one for life.'

'Don't feel depressed. Allah knows what is right for you. Everything happens for a reason.'

'But I am very unlucky. Nothing good happens to me. First you, now this girl.'

Farhan had once asked me if I wanted to stay here and continue to issue tickets together instead of trying for a transfer to Chennai. My heart was in Chennai.

'*Arre yaar!* We are best friends. Let's not complicate things. You relax. This girl is the right one for you. Quiet and pretty. The younger one sounds too feisty. Trust me, you will be fine and happily married.'

'I don't know. But how will I look at my sister-in-law, and will I always regret losing her?'

'Huh. She was never yours to lose. Don't begin your new life with such thoughts. You wouldn't be doing right by your wife.'

He sulked the rest of the day, and as the wedding date neared, he yielded to kismet.

* * *

His was the first *nikah* that I attended. We assembled in the modest house Farhan built with his railway salary; he was the eldest son and had two younger brothers and a pampered sister (who married her sweetheart against Farhan's wish).

As soon as Amma and I reached, we were ushered to the women's enclosure. There were two shamiana enclosures in the compound. After a while, I felt jittery and escaped the confines to search for the groom. Fortunately, his youngest brother took us to watch the proceedings. The paternal aunt bossed the mother of the groom, a wispy, silver-haired, toothless woman.

A lady held a bowl of black powder, and—as per tradition—the aunt brushed the groom's teeth with her finger. Then, after he rinsed his mouth with water, each of us dropped a pinch of sugar into his mouth. Farhan was dressed in a pure white kurta pyjama. His kohl-rimmed eyes exuded mirth. Someone placed a *sehra* of jasmine over his white embroidered *kufi*.

Then, the *baraat* filled the line of cars and vans. The groom sat in a fancy car arranged by the bride's family, and the congregation reached the bride's house. Sprinkled with *ittar*-scented rose water, we entered. A young man, the bride's brother, welcomed the groom and offered him a sherbet. I tagged along with the women of the family to meet the bride. She was in a dark room, lying down. As we entered, someone switched on the light. The bride, dressed in a red Banarasi silk sari with white flowers encircling her braid and wrists, promptly recovered from the recumbent position and sat up. I found her fair, flawless skin and chubby appearance endearing. She had her eyes closed. Her bud-like lips, without a dash of lipstick, looked naturally pink. I was ecstatic for my friend marrying such a beautiful girl.

'Why are her eyes closed?' I asked.

'It's a custom. Since morning, she hasn't eaten or opened her eyes. She must first see her husband's face and eat something sweet fed by him.'

'Oh, nice.' Now I understood why she was lying down. I wondered how she dressed up with closed eyes.

My gaze wandered for her sister, who had captured Farhan's heart. A tall, skinny girl dressed in a bright salwar bounced into the room.

'*Asalam alekkum*,' she gave us a collective greeting. Her eyes rested on mine, a tad longer than the others.

The qazi and his man filed in, and we all moved aside.

The two men squatted and whispered, asking for the bride's approval of the match and willingness to be united in matrimony.

The bride mumbled, '*Qabool*'. Thrice.

With closed eyes, she signed her name at the specified spot. Then, a tray of sugar was kept on the bride's lap; she spread her palms on the tray.

By then, the qazi left to get the approval and willingness of the groom. A commotion burbled from outside, and my nerves rattled. I prayed that Farhan would not diverge. My heart hammered until someone informed us that the groom's uncle, an older man, had fainted. He was revived and nourished with a chicken fry grabbed from the cook's tent. The groom signed the register; the nikah was solemnized. Then, the qazi read the *fatiha*, the first chapter of the Holy Quran. He blessed the young couple and discussed marriage vows that must be upheld.

Farhan's oldest aunt tied a black beaded chain on the bride. As per tradition, this chain had adorned the neck of the aunt since the nikah ceremony began. It is a belief that in transferring the chain the new bride would live a fulfilling life, just like the aunt. Dried fruits and dates bundled in a red silk cloth were placed on the bride's head. Then, the bundle was loosened to let a few raisins and dates tumble on the bride. The rest was distributed to the women.

The groom accompanied his *ammi* and offered his bride a gold chain, the dowry the groom pays to marry the bride. This was an assurance of her financial security. Then, the new couple sat side by side, and the groom held a mirror through which the couple saw each other's reflection. She blinked her eyes open. She blushed, he blushed, and all chorused '*Alhamdullilah*'.

We all relished the mutton biryani, raita, *mirchi ka salan* and the chicken fry. Long tables were arranged with chairs on both sides and large plates of biryani were served, which were shared by four people. Amma (she was first horrified but placated by the aromatic biryani) and I shared our meal with a young couple—a cousin of the groom.

Amma and I clasped each other as tears filled every woman's eye to see the bride bid farewell to her family. We reached the groom's house for the *walima* (reception). As soon as the bride entered her new home, her mother-in-law placed the Holy Quran on her head to symbolize her duties as a wife.

A group sang ghazals, lights lit up, laughter and fun continued. After a sumptuous dinner, we returned home.

Farhan shifted with his bride to the railway quarters—94D. His mother and his brothers stayed in the house he built. The bride was shy and didn't speak much. Her sister came by often, much to my dismay and my friend's fluttering heart.

I received my transfer orders to Chennai within three months of his wedding. We kept in touch off and on. I prayed for his well-being on his birthday, every year. He never remembered mine. With the advent of Facebook, WhatsApp and mobiles, staying connected is easier.

Just the other day, we chatted for a long time. His wife (according to him) has transformed into a loud, foul-mouthed, bulky, grey-haired woman rearing four children. My friend still has regrets. And I wonder . . . Perhaps if I had supported him, would he have taken a brazen step? Would his life have been better? Or is his wife who cooks, cleans and maintains his home and family a suitable companion? After all, the grass looks greener on the other side.

A never-ending conundrum of ifs and could and would.

PLATFORM NO. 7

IN RAILWAY STATIONS, THE juniors were sent as rest givers (RG) to the adjacent stations in the section. Booking clerks, TCs, stationmasters, and the like are sent as rest givers and leave reserve (LR) to other stations. A 'section' defined loosely in this context is usually a series of stations in a line towards a major station. When a booking staff wanted to avail a weekly rest, if an acute staff shortage persisted, or someone wanted emergency leave, the RG/LR undertook their shift. Sometimes, the junior would have just completed the stipulated eight hours and was asked to continue because the relieving staff absented from work.

It was sometimes confusing for the RG staff to get accustomed to the new BO set-up; the rows and columns of tickets and their positions differed in each BO. We had to be extra careful *not* to issue wrong tickets or calculate fares from the station we regularly worked on rather than the fare from the current station we were working on that day.

I was at Priya's station. She had not yet returned after her father's demise, and perhaps the CBS, who harboured anger towards me for my outburst earlier at his decision to send my friend alone, planned to torture me. He might have granted leave to many of his staff and created a crisis. Or maybe I was reading too much into it.

I continued duty for more than twenty hours—thanks to some foxy colleagues who knew how to exploit the deputed relief. A few months in railways was too short to learn the language or the names of the stations, let alone raise a complaint.

My wait for the train homewards seemed like an eternity. Forty minutes late was uncommon in our section. Even if I had walked, I would have reached home. It was already 19.40 hrs. *Hit the bed* was the war cry in my head. And it would take another thirty minutes to my destination. Thankfully, home was just a jump away from the platform.

Sitting on the cement bench outside the office was heaven compared to the relentless banter of the reliever. I talk a lot, too, but I despise cribbing or self-pity. He went on and on about his wailing children, nagging wife and barking dog. I was so tired, and my brain was ready to shut down.

A sudden drizzle of rain jangled on the platform shelter, and I watched as the passengers scrambled. A habitual traveller smiled and walked past me. His routine was to chat briefly when I was on duty. He frequented my station too.

He could never grasp how a Keralite settled in Chennai could get a job in Karnataka and travel 400 km to work. As if I did.

A colleague who never bothered to converse with any customer and never smiled at work had a different kind of experience.

Once, a customer complained against this person for not returning the balance change due to him. In the complaint letter, he added that the clerk abused him when he asked for the balance and typed all the bad words allegedly used by my colleague.

After the investigation by the Complaint Inspector dealing with such complaints against the commercial staff, the clerk was punished with a 'pass' cut (a booking clerk receives three privilege passes in a year) and a warning not to repeat the offence. My colleague traced the complainant's address and visited his home.

'Anyway, I got the punishment, so let me call you all the abusive words you mentioned in the complaint. You and I both know I did not utter any abuses that day.'

That customer never returned to our station and travelled to the next station to get his tickets done. We, the new entrants, the young and vibrant breed, treated our customers better and nurtured a relationship with almost everyone we interacted with.

It helped me immensely—my conversations with strangers.

I dozed sitting on the platform bench when a garbled announcement startled me. A few minutes later, a train rolled in; I jumped on to it and settled in a window seat. Only a few passengers occupied the train; I only wanted a few inches. There was no option but to pull down the shutters as the rain intensified. I knew I had another twenty-five minutes to hibernate. The driver decided to accelerate as I lolled to sleep—just pure bliss.

As a young child whenever I travelled by train, I occupied the window seat. With no siblings to fight for this seat, I enjoyed the sights. But when I felt drowsy, although my parents assured me they would take care of my belongings, I remained awake, anxious that I would lose my slippers. So now, sitting alone without my parents to care for my belongings, I huddled with my bag and firmly rested my feet on the floor.

For how long I slept, I don't know. When I opened my eyes, the rain had stopped. I couldn't decide between opening the window to check for familiar landmarks and checking the time on my watch. As the train zipped, making out anything in the darkness was nearly impossible. And nothing familiar appeared. My watch conveyed it was about time I docked. There was no sign of the train reducing speed. Now, I panicked. Had I overslept? Was the train on its return journey? Gosh, where was I?

Helpless. Clueless. Ticketless. Life can bring together a lovely combination at times.

I tapped the sleeping man opposite me and asked if he knew why the train was taking longer to reach my station.

He blinked, then sneered, 'You took the wrong train, madam; this is going away from your station.'

'But I took the train from Platform 1.'

'So? The incoming train was late, so the outgoing train stopped at Platform 1. Didn't you hear the announcement?'

Yes, in my brain-fogged, sleep-deprived condition, I had taken a train in the opposite direction. Well, it was becoming a pattern.

Dread dripped out of my every nerve. I had never been to this junction before. None of my friends were posted here. I didn't know a ticket collector or a squad staff in this section, and it would be a mess if I was caught without a ticket. That was the first issue I had to handle.

Taking a bed in the station dormitory needed a ticket, so that was ruled out, and, in any case, I wanted to get out of the railway premises as soon as possible. Thank God, Amma was in Chennai and wasn't waiting for me at home. At least she wouldn't be worried to death. Otherwise, she would pester the SMR to send a search party.

* * *

Perhaps I should have followed what Jotheeswaran did when he went to another station on duty as a rest giver. After the evening shift, he had to continue the next day's morning and night shift. So, instead of travelling home, he spent the night in the waiting room. The night duty clerk was responsible for issuing tickets to the 07.00 hrs train the following day. But the train was running late, and the night clerk left without issuing tickets. My friend took up his post, and when the gong signalled that the train had left the earlier station, he issued tickets.

By then, the passengers in the queue were angry at the late arrival of the train but could show their angst only at the person inside. The grumbling swelled when they saw that the person sleeping with them in the waiting room was issuing tickets. 'Look at this irresponsible guy. Sleeping in the waiting room instead of performing his duty. These clerks are all drunkards.'

Well, when people readily form opinions, we cannot do anything. Jo stoically issued tickets without letting the grumbles affect him.

* * *

My head formulated plans like a good planner. Plans A, B and C came easily. Plan A seemed most feasible. Get out and find a hotel to stay in for the night. Being alone in a hotel was intimidating, but was there any other way? I tried to relax.

But life had other plans.

It was close to 22.00 hrs as the train sounded the horn and entered the platform. Mission accomplished, it announced. Even before the train came to a complete stop, I leapt and looked for the exit. Follow the exodus, my mind dictated. I thought I saw a known face at quite a distance. It was him. He was the regular passenger who smiled and conversed with me every time. Boy, was I delighted. He could help me find a hotel.

This was not a part of any of my plans.

I couldn't keep track of him though, and he suddenly disappeared. He had a scooter, I remembered, out of nowhere. Dashing to the exit, I asked for the vehicle stand. I sprinted before I got a full reply. Every second mattered. It was as if I was on a timer trying to perform several tasks at once. When I reached and stood panting at its entrance, my only prayer was that I would recognize him with the helmet on. And, more worrisome, will he recognize me outside of my usual territory? I heard the tiny squeak of a horn amidst the commotion of everyone trying the 'survival of the fittest' battle.

He lifted the helmet's glass; the words came out, 'What happened? You sleep train?'

'Yes,' I admitted. 'I sleep wrong train. I want go hotel for stay. Go tomorrow night duty.' I matched my English to suit his.

'Ok. Sit my scooter,' he replied.

22.20 hrs. I wondered how he could reach home so late and start off the next day so early to catch the Intercity Express at 06.00 hrs. Earning a living was not easy—he was travelling almost four hours a day to and fro between home and work. As he rode the scooter,

I looked around, trying to locate a decent place to stay. Fortunately, I had 300 bucks with me.

But whenever I pointed out one, he said, 'Another good one, I take you.' The city lights soon became fewer in number, and I felt jittery. What is this man up to? It was time to speak up. 'Where are you going?' I asked, ensuring the tone didn't reveal my perturbation. He laughed and said, 'My house, my family good. Hotel not good.' He seemed to take some pleasure in having fooled me. I was stunned. Sweaty, smelly and tired. How could I be comfortable in a new place? And could I trust him? What if he was a serial killer? The relationship I had with him was selling him a ticket.

After a good twenty minutes, we reached his place. I was happy to see that it was on a crowded street— someone would turn up if I screamed for help. He parked and led the way upstairs through a rickety staircase. Sure, this must be rented and not his own, I thought, judgementally. I was confused about how to greet the family and what I would say. I hoped he had a family. What would his family think when he entered his home with a young girl in tow? Kannada was still a strange language to me. I wouldn't be able to manage as much Kannada as he managed English.

The apprehension on my face was unmistakable as the lady opened the door. The hall was dimly lit, and her brows and lips communicated a big question mark.

The man introduced me, 'She is the stationmaster madam,' and added that I had fallen asleep on the train.

'Come in, please,' she greeted in regional Kannada. Her wide smile helped diminish my embarrassment.

I scanned the room as I padded in. 'Shocked' would not even come close to the feelings I experienced. Three children were sleeping on thin mattresses on the floor—a sparsely decorated room. I followed the man into the kitchen, and the lady asked questions as if a rapid fire was in progress. Perhaps the discussion was where I would sleep. For sure, I was a burden to the family of five. I could not make out where the couple slept. Just then, an elderly lady—his mother—exited the washroom. Another member—so now six. I nearly fainted. Where did he expect me to sleep? Why did he bring me here? And what was the woman ranting about? Perhaps scolding him?

I saw the lady kneading some dough, and she looked at me and indicated she was making chapattis for me. I told the man that I had had dinner. 23.15—I stole a glance at the watch. My body was crumbling. He said she wanted me to eat with him, since I was there for the first time. Briskly she served hot rotis. The plates and low-height stools were laid on the floor. I felt ashamed about what I had imagined about their conversations.

The mother stood by me wearing a broad smile. After dinner, the wife handed me a clean nightie. Words failed me. They motioned me to the space next to the kids and switched off the light. I said my prayer and thanked them, too. They nodded when I asked them to wake me early so I could go with the man and take the Intercity Express.

Suddenly, the place and the people did not seem new or strange to me. Incredible warmth filled my heart. I heard the mother murmuring something, possibly a sloka or prayer, and I glanced at where she had settled down. My eyes moistened. She lay on a bed sheet in the small passage between the hall and the kitchen. The man and the lady put some mats in the kitchen and folded a few clothes for their pillow.

Love? Kindness? Friendship? What would I call it? I was in danger of losing sleep as I was busy pondering. But their cosy one-room–kitchen–shared bath house got the better of me. I slept.

* * *

I yawned and stretched as I woke up, and it hit me that I was not in my home. The kids were not there—neither was the man. My watch displayed 10.00. They hadn't woken me, and it was intentional. I excused myself to go to the bathroom and borrowed herbal powder to brush my teeth. Breakfast was ready, and the wife constantly talked to make me feel comfortable. I hoped my smile would be a good response. She handed me a torn portion from a newspaper with the train timings.

It was close to 11.30 hrs when I trooped out lest she cooked lunch. She accompanied me to the nearest autorickshaw stand and waved goodbye. I felt tears rolling down my cheek. What made them show so much tenderness towards me? Their compassion was overwhelming. Every aspect of their hospitality lingered in my heart. My journey back home was filled with the old lady's smile. A rush of loneliness engulfed me as I opened the door to my home and trotted in. A new thought filled me, quickly dispelling the loneliness. I made a decision. Where I have an opportunity, I would show kindness sans barriers.

The smiles the man and I exchanged on that night's duty had a new and different meaning.

PLATFORM NO. 8

A FEW MONTHS AGO, MY husband and I went on a pilgrimage to temples of Karnataka in the Mangalore belt. After days of satisfactory *darshan*, we reached the railway station to board the train to Bangalore. Done with the spiritual trip, it was the time for spirited conversations with my cousin's gang in Bangalore before our journey to Chennai.

As we reached the station, I remembered that the yellow Bajaj scooter-owning stationmaster had worked there before joining my station. I took pictures of the platform and walked the length and breadth of it, peered through the ticket window (I often do this in any railway station

I happen to be in and sometimes strike up conversations), and glanced inside the SM's cabin.

I sat with my husband on a cement bench. A fan above clanged dangerously, and a wing got cut off and slashed the air. Luckily, it fell on a spot where no one was sitting. I sprinted to the SM's cabin (I so wanted to get into the cabin) and informed the duty SM about the mishap. He switched off the fan and removed the blade. I resumed my seat and called him, my SM. I had gleaned his mobile number through a friend but never dialled. His wife picked up the call; I explained who I was and waited for her to hand over the phone to him.

'Hello. Sangeetha?'

My heart somersaulted.

'Yes, it is me. How are you?'

He had undergone surgery and was recuperating. There was a layer of tiredness in his voice. He had retired from the station I was sitting in, just a year ago. With a promise to call him after a few weeks, I let my mind wander. The husband, as usual, was glued to his mobile.

* * *

It had been four months since I joined the railways and my station. I had completed my shift and was dashing out of the station with Priya, who had showed up on her weekly off—we were late for the afternoon show of *Judaai*. He parked his yellow Bajaj scooter and strode into the station. For a second, our eyes met.

Priya talked non-stop about the new stationmaster in her station, whom she fancied, but I couldn't concentrate on what she was saying as the beautiful face I had just seen floored me. He was gorgeous, handsome, attractive . . . well, you get the drift. I caressed the scooter on my way out.

The next day on duty, I met him again. The Adonis was the new stationmaster. His name figured in a famous Bollywood number, and I couldn't stop humming it.

He was much older than me—fourteen years separated us. His wife and kid lived in another city where his wife worked, and he had moved here because the section he worked had closed for gauge conversion.

Quite aware nothing could come out of my fascination for him, we developed a friendship. I spent my spare time between shifts at the parcel office sitting in the SM's cabin listening to his lilting Kannada as he conversed with others. The linemen, passengers, porters, guards and everyone else hobbled inside to enquire about this and that. The blabbermouth that I was, and still am, I talked a lot—asking questions about signals, the railway equipment in the office and the details he scribbled on the register. He patiently explained, and we spoke about movies, actors and the books I read because I always carried a paperback to work.

I did not have a fixed roster. They shuffled me to wherever a shortage of staff arose. So, when I had to pick up a shift that matched his roster, it delighted me. The BO roster link begins with the afternoon shift, followed by the next day's morning and night shifts. After the night shift, we had the day off.

The afternoon shift was the longest. It involved issuing unreserved tickets for two passenger trains, handling passenger reservations for four hours and the responsibility of writing the chart of four coaches. My colleague usually dumped this shift on me. I generally whined but was energized on days when this SM was on duty.

Once the 14.20 hrs train left, there was a break till 15.30 hrs for the reservations to begin. The SM and I walked to the tea shop near the goods shed, a thatched shop where the sun dappled through the Gulmohar trees that spread a carpet of red and yellow flowers. We sat on rugged tree trunks sipping our 'By 2' chai. I had never drunk tea until I joined railways; my doting parents nurtured me on Horlicks.

On some days, CBS or other colleagues also accompanied us. This chai was served in an ounce glass, a fresh, fragrant tea that we sipped leisurely. The tea vendor offered a piece of newspaper to sit on, so the SM's white uniform didn't stain. He was in spotless white, sometimes with short sleeves, other times, the long sleeves folded neatly, his wristwatch with a brown leather strap on his wrist, trapping the curly hair.

He called me Chutki. In the movie DDLJ, Kajol's sister was called Chutki, and he said I resembled her and bopped my upturned nose.

* * *

Whenever we girls discussed our dream guy, I vehemently declared that my guy should have a lush moustache. The South Indian in me preferred men with thick facial hair above the lip. A beard was an added attraction for the Mallu blood in me. But this guy was clean-shaven, with a clear skin and a perfect square jawline.

He used to keep a moustache and donned a beret cap before his mandatory service in the Territorial Army. Years ago, assisting the army personnel, he served in flood-hit regions. To please me, he kept the moustache a little longer even after his TA stint.

In a Malayalam movie released close to this time, the hero played a stationmaster. The SM and the heroine sang a duet on an engine. I wanted to hop on an engine and do the *Titanic* pose. Once, when the SM supervised the shunting of the engine, I pleaded to be allowed into the engine. It wasn't advisable for safety reasons, and when he opposed, I sulked for a day. The next day, he asked me to get on a stationary engine, and the loco pilot explained the various buttons and levers inside.

Ever since I'd joined this station, another aspect that intrigued me was the token exchange. The block signal instrument would release a token that had to be handed over to the loco pilot for him to proceed, and on his return, he would hand over the token received from the previous station. The token was tied on to a wooden loopy thing, and I sometimes volunteered to do the handing and taking over. If the train was moving fast, the SM stopped me from obtaining the token because I might get pulled by the force.

I was curious about all aspects of railway work and tried my hand at everything.

* * *

When we returned after tea, I opened my kiosk, and he went to his cabin. Later, if the queue for reservations was lengthy, he ordered tea from VLR to the BO, chatted while I issued tickets and sipped tea. Maybe this is why I can efficiently multitask; if I concentrate on one task, I bungle it up. He never issued tickets but watched me work. I said it unnerved me to be watched, he chortled and came closer. My skin prickled. Then, in a confiding whisper he said, 'Do I object when you sit in my cabin and watch me work?'

So, the days I did the afternoon shift without him, knackered me.

* * *

Meanwhile, Priya was busy scripting her romance. I even went to check out that Assistant Station Master (ASM). He was young, shy, chubby and towered over my friend like a hulk. He was unmarried, and their story could have developed into something else, but the stars intervened.

My friend bubbled in excitement when she invited me to 'see' him. The ASM and an SM who joined her station from the gauge conversion section had planned to cook for us. The SM was a sweet, bald, older chap and a great talker. They were fun company and struggled to throw a feast. The trio were vegetarians, and I was the only meat-eating person. They had boiled two eggs which I ate with pepper and salt. The food was terrific; we promised to invite them for lunch soon. Which never happened.

Neither of them gave words to their feelings. Their silent gazes and blushes never transformed into holding hands or whispering sweet nothings. Bogged down by family pressures, he married and moved to another station. Priya worried about her younger sister's marriage prospects if she gave wings to her heart. Shackled by values and ideals, she allowed herself to be heartbroken but giggled away her grief.

Later on, when Achan came over, Priya, my parents and I toured nearby temples: Sringeri, Udupi, Mookambika, Murudeshwara and Gokarna. The journey through the Western Ghats with their rain-soaked trees and the sunlight filtering in enchanted us. Priya and I huddled to glimpse the mesmerizing sunset at Agumbe. Nature soothed her lovelorn heart. We travelled by buses and omni vans that functioned as 'share autos', packing lemon rice in plantain leaves and packets of potato chips for the way. Once we polished off the food we carried, we struggled to consume the ragi muddes served at the wayside hotels. Gokarna was the last stop and we reached there at night to see the whole town immersed in darkness: there was a power outage, and the hotel we booked had no generator. Achan searched for a shop, bought candles and bread and jam, and we had a candlelight dinner in our cosy hotel room. We spent a sleepless night swarmed by mosquitoes. The next day, after a beautiful darshan and a dip in the sea, we travelled back to our stations. It is one of the most cherished memories of Priya that I hold close to my heart.

We envision a future filled with shared laughter, yet sometimes a fleeting moment experienced could mark the last episode of togetherness.

Years later, she died of complications during her second pregnancy, and a few of us, her closest friends, attended her last rites. She continues to live in our memories. Whenever I hear a song that she hummed in those years when we met every week, my eyes moisten. Her daughter is a grown woman—beautiful, and accomplished in her studies. I recently chatted with her about the mother she never knew. We laughed and cried together. The daughter thanked me for talking about her mother and said, 'It is as if I know her now, but I miss living with her.'

During this phase of our lives when we went through the rigours of love, we laughed, we cried and we loved. Together. We simmered hand in hand in the blush of attraction and love. These memories will stay fresh in my mind forever. I miss you, my friend. I miss your crazy giggles and goofy banter. I wish you were here.

* * *

When the SM and I completed a joint afternoon duty, coincidentally, both our relievers did a no-show, so we continued the night. Amma was in Chennai, and usually, she chaperoned me to the night shifts. Wrapped in a sweater and shawl, she would open a plastic cover and arrange the contents on a table: a water bottle, torch and mosquito coil. She would then stuff her scarf inside the cover. The plastic rustled a lot, and Farhan once said, 'Aunty, the sound is grating on my ears.' From then on, Amma has always checked whenever she carries a plastic cover to see if it is the rustling kind or the soft type.

By the time the last train tooted, I was exhausted. Without Amma to assist me, I took longer to complete my work. The hamal, Hanumantha, was itching to go home after escorting me to my home. SM sent him home saying he would drop me.

That's when we saw the woman. Clad in an orange sari and sporting a bob, she stood near the entrance to the platform. Hanumantha said he had seen her earlier before the evening passenger train. The SM approached her, asking, 'Ma'am, did you miss the train?'

She screamed and cowered, turning to the wall near Abu's stall. Abu and Fathima, the father and daughter duo, were pulling down the shutter.

I walked outside to speak with the lady, but she became violent. Screeching, she almost clawed my face. The SM immediately pulled me to safety.

We convened in the BO—the SM, Hanumantha, Abu, Fathima and I. The cash tallying was neglected. I bundled the cash and shoved it into the cash chest, a hole in the wall with an iron door and a long key. Everyone tossed different ideas.

Abu offered to talk to her. He said he had seven daughters and could handle her. He moved closer; the lady stayed quiet.

'*Beti*, where are you from? Did you miss the train?'

'I am hungry.' She opened her handbag and said, 'No money.' Then she took a picture of a little girl and kissed it.

Abu and Fathima pulled up the shutter and offered biscuits. She grabbed them and stuffed her mouth. Fathima offered to make tea for all of us. She made sulaimani chai, which we sipped while Abu tried to chat. We all hovered around but didn't approach the lady because it agitated her.

I quietly extricated her handbag when Abu distracted her. There was no ID, nothing else other than the photo of the small girl. He gathered that she had arrived by the evening passenger train and was a resident of Bangalore.

The SM immediately alerted the SM of that station. Who in turn checked with the local police.

After an all-nighter, we all went home, handing over the duty, cash and the lady. When I returned to the station after sleeping for a few hours to check on the lady, the duty SM said that her husband had picked her up a while ago.

'Was she ok to meet him?'

'No, she was screaming. But he had someone with him who gave her an injection, and she passed out. They drove back in a car.'

'But didn't you ask why or what happened to her?'

'Why would I? Husband–wife issue. Maybe she was deranged.'

I was sad for the lady, miffed at the duty SM and said, 'Maybe he was making her crazy. She might be a rich woman. He wants to grab her wealth. Perhaps we will see her photo in the obit column . . .'

'Hello! Hold your horses. You need to sleep. Don't overwork your brain. Better go and write a novel.'

* * *

The SM's family travelled to our town for a few days and did the touristy sightseeing. His son was cute and chubby, a toddler. He was too heavy to carry, so I sat him on my lap and sang nursery rhymes. Amma and I invited the SM and his family home for tea and bhajjis. Amma sat on the floor working on her kerosene stove while I served them. Someone had a camera, and we clicked photos, but I lost those.

* * *

When unseasonable rains ripped the skies in our region, the tracks were flooded and trains ran late. Raging winds had uprooted the electric posts, and darkness engulfed the railway station. Even if there were no trains or no one at the railway station to make reservations, we had to keep the cubicle open. VLR and Abu's stalls were closed, and there was no way to check if we could get tea in the roadside shop. In all probability, the vendor wouldn't risk opening his tea shop in this weather.

Instead of sitting alone in the BO, I waded through pools of water gushing from the platform and reached the SM's office. Sitting across his chair, I watched him writing reports. When he caught my eye, I crimsoned.

The SM's cabin had many control panels and signalling equipment. When trains left a station in the same block to which our station belonged, a bell clinked, and a small green bulb lit up as long as the train was moving, and a red one as it halted. On other days, I asked many questions, sometimes dialled the Magneto phone, and gave relevant information to the SM in another station. Priya and I would sometimes speak on the block phone connected to the stations to our left and right, and plan our movie dates. The SM never allowed me to operate the block instruments without him as it was an offence to let civilians operate them. It was as if I was under training to become an ASM. My grandfather's genes were at work.

But that day, there were no trains in our block, so no lights, and the candlelights danced in the breeze.

With the rest of the trains cancelled, the station was placid except for the rain and the deafening thunder. A few stranded people huddled on the platform singing folk songs. The showers and the melodies made for a heady concoction as the candlelight cast shapes. Our shadows melded on the wall as I gazed at the mischief undulating in his eyes.

Unspoken words encircled us like vapour.

Tea shops being closed, we mimed the tea-making process and sipped scalding liquid from imaginary cups amidst the feeble radiance.

I shivered as the cold wind moaned through the open fields when we watched the rain. He crept closer to drape his coat on me. I stiffened like a scarecrow as his fingers grazed my shoulders. I pulled the coat and inhaled the faint hint of his cologne. Even when I returned to my BO to hand over the accounts to my reliever, I didn't remove the coat. I was no longer cold, and a warmth spread through my being.

Several shifts we were rostered together. For some time, he sat watching me tally the day's earnings. We talked. We gazed. We laughed. Then I went to his office room and watched him finish his pending work. We talked. We gazed. We laughed.

* * *

I worried about his impending promotion as he would then be transferred to a station where the SMR post was vacant. Luckily, our station SMR went on an extended leave, instructing my SM to take charge. Sometimes, if the CBS was unwell or on a training course, the SM remitted the station earnings to the bank. So, a few lady admirers at the bank demanded a lunch treat for his promotion. The SM invited me as well, and we rode to a restaurant where the two ladies from the bank joined us. I knew what I would wear if such an opportunity presented itself. I picked up a yellow polka-dot kurta. It was my desire all along to ride pillion with him dressed in a colour that matched the scooter. An electric burst coursed through my body. Sometimes I wondered whether it was the scooter or the SM I had a crush on.

After lunch at the most famous restaurant in our town, the bankers left. The movie *Ghulam* had just been released in our theatres, and the song *'Aati kya Khandala?'* was the latest rage. So, when the SM asked me if I wished to watch the movie, I worried about the many what-if scenarios for a split second.

At the movie hall, the seats were unnumbered; we slipped into a row where a few seats were vacant. I was thankful for the noise from the screen that hushed up my thudding heart and the darkness that veiled my consternation. Our arms rested next to each other, with the fabric of our sleeves rustling.

I froze when he shifted slightly in his seat and stretched his arm over my seat. Perhaps he was stretching his cramped hand. My chest was tight, and my heart walloped. He realized my discomfort and immediately took off his arm and never even rested it on the armrest. The fear and risk of being seen together in a theatre was foremost on my mind. With covert glances, we left the theatre when the end credits played on the screen.

We were the only people on the road towards the station, and I hummed the song, which Rani Mukherjee and Aamir Khan sang on a bike. With a disarming smile for the next few weeks, he sang, *'Aati kya Khandala'* whenever we met. And I glowed like a red-faced spider monkey.

All good things come to an end. Or new beginnings were brewing. I received my transfer orders, but the station decided that if I could work an impossible transfer so soon (two years was too soon in railway terminology), they realized I could arrange a replacement or a reliever in my place. So, I wouldn't be relieved until a person was posted in my place. The nitty-gritty is unclear, but my uncle and the lord above worked miracles, and another lady, a compassionate posting, took up my place in my station.

I was ecstatic when I received the news that I could leave the station and go home to my achan. I would miss my friends here, but then I knew I couldn't settle in this town. The SM was not on duty. Hanumantha said that he was unwell and resting in his railway quarter. I knew his door number but had never been to his home. I pounded on the slightly ajar door of his quarters.

'Come in,' said a shaky voice. He rested on a bed, but his face brightened instantly. Unable to look into his eyes, I stared at the wall as he apologized for his sparsely furnished abode and asked me to sit on the bed. Sitting on the edge of the bed, I pushed my relieving order towards him. A shadow of anguish crossed his face.

'Congratulations,' he murmured.

'Hmmm,' I lifted my face, and his forlorn expression pained me.

'So, you are leaving. Never to return.'

My voice was calm, although my heart was tumultuous, 'Why wouldn't I? We will always be connected by trains and tracks. We can travel anytime.'

'True. A railway connection would definitely be there.'

'Railway tracks run parallel to eternity. Or until the next crossing. It depends on our perspective.' I spouted philosophy and added, 'I will miss you.'

'Hmmm. You will forget this station and all of us.'

'I don't think I can ever forget my first station and my people.'

For a few minutes, silence reigned as our eyes spoke volumes.

'Hmmm. You need to leave now.' His voice sounded hoarse. With a wistful smile, he said he would not be at the station on my last day to see me board the train.

Tears streamed as I closed the door behind me.

A veil of dust covered the yellow Bajaj. My first ride on it turned out to be the last.

I met him a few years later when I caught a train at Mysore Junction with my husband. He accompanied us to our compartment, and we held on to the yellow handle inches apart. The train moved and with an imperceptible grazing of fingers, he zoomed out into a white dot on the platform. Once he came to my station in Chennai during an official training session and we shared a filter coffee on the bustling platform. I wished him on his sixtieth birthday and he breathed, 'You remembered.' Then, we spoke again after my pilgrimage with my husband from that platform of the station where he retired.

When this book was taking shape, I told him there would be a chapter on him. He answered with his trademark hearty booming laughter.

PLATFORM NO. 8A

MY GRANDFATHER WAS AN ASM in a small railway station before Independence. Achan and his brothers regaled me with stories about those times. If only muthasan had talked about his railway life, I could have added pre-Independence stories as well. A man of few words, he preferred grunts and snorts. He worked in the Madras Presidency, in a C-category station where the railway ASM/SM was the VVIP. Dressed in white pants, a white shirt and a white coat, a pilot cap on his head, carrying green and red flags and a whistle, he strutted across the station with an air of authority. All in white with the steam engines puffing out black smoke. Pity the launderer whose palms would have frayed.

Treated like demigods, the ASM and his family enjoyed a royal life. Muthasan stayed in the railway quarters, and his wife and children remained in the ancestral home in Kerala. The stories I heard were from school vacations when my achan and his siblings spent time with their father. The villagers gave their best produce of fresh vegetables and rice, and my muthasi cooked a large, sumptuous meal, which my dad and his twelve siblings devoured. Railway pay was not enough to support the extra-large family, and he retired at the peak of his cadre with a pension of Rs 120, within which many children and the couple had to wade through. Some children were still in primary classes, and only two daughters were married, out of which one was back home, widowed with four children.

My youngest uncle has bitter memories of the days spent in poverty after their father's retirement. But he shared beautiful memories of the scenic beauty of Lovedale station and the time he spent amongst the sheep-breeding people. The train journey in first class from Mettupalayalam was dreamy: the verdant spread, the swarming mist . . . the train had its engine at the rear, and first class was the first coach that ambled on the tracks. Sheep getting killed was rare as the Nilgiri trains crawled. But when that happened, there was celebration all around. Elaborate meals where a whole community partook. My uncle loved succulent meat but felt guilty about eating it.

There were no lavatories in the railway quarters, and the sweepers employed in the railways carried excrement daily from the homes and replaced clean trays. And this part of the country had the most beautiful girls; my uncle, then a teenager, harboured dreams of saving a beauty from the clutches of such an impoverished life. One girl resembled Cinderella, a princess in torn clothes, fair with pink dimpled cheeks, while her father, a sweeper, was dark as coal. It was no secret, and these girls were ipso facto treated as British. The girl was the heroine in several stories imagined by my uncle, a romantic at heart.

I wonder if muthasan stole any young girl's heart in those days.

* * *

Commercial clerks worked together with the stationmasters, and many of my batchmates shared fond memories of the SMs they admired. Not all were romantically inclined like some of us.

There was a Malayali stationmaster in a godforsaken station that had only one passenger train stopping either way the entire day, and the SM had to give tickets and book parcels, too. He was an acquaintance of my friend Harshkant. He had retired from the armed forces from the radio/communication wing. The guy was lively and fond of my friend. They met for lunch or an evening of rum or watched a night show. Harshkant listened agape to all his commentaries. The SM had a bunch of English novels, the Forsyth/Sydney Sheldon types, which my friend borrowed, and later, they discussed the books.

The personnel branch guys were notoriously cutting back on the NDA (night duty allowance) claims of these wayside stations, keeping arrears of over six months, and these middle-aged men with family pressures were genuinely affected. One fine night, our Malayali SM decided to teach the authorities a lesson and stopped a prestigious train (a city mail/some board-level goods train). He didn't give a 'proceed, all clear' signal and neither did he pick up the phones from the traffic controller for a while. The train halted in the middle of the tracks as the loco pilot could not proceed without the all-clear signal; the higher officials had to be awakened. The driver/guard was furious as the station doors and windows were bolted from inside, and nobody dared to cross a 'live' signal.

After twenty-odd minutes, our SM picked up the phone and said to the higher official, 'Sorry sir, I slept off, as I didn't have a reliever after eight hours of duty, and I didn't get my NDA for the past six months, and my pointsman asked why should we be awake when we aren't compensated. A few minutes of my dozing resulted in the disruption of your slumber. I hope you get the meaning.'

He was not even summoned to the headquarters. The next day, all their dues were sanctioned. For the next month, a section inspector was stationed at the section.

* * *

Another flamboyant SM worked a few stations away from Harshkant. Stories about him, embellished by whoever retold them, reached other stations, distortions and all. He used to have five businesses, two wives and several unknown affairs. If he was your workmate, you should be prepared to continue duty and thank God if he turned up. He always punched in at the wrong time, adjusting his other commitments, and somehow worked at his convenience. Once he had to reach his village at night, he sat in a private rural bus and demanded a ticket.

'Sir, this bus is going in the opposite direction. You please take another bus.'

He got down, met a group of people travelling to his village and a few plying in that direction, and ensured they boarded that bus. After the bus left the stand, all the passengers asked for a ticket to their village and forced the driver and conductor to divert to their place. The few passengers headed towards the earlier route of the bus deboarded, displeased. Such was his persuasive power.

* * *

Sunil Warrier, during a stint in a major junction, witnessed an incident involving a haughty, raucous lady officer and an SM with adept cognitive agility.

This SM, a Goan, a state champion boxer, a lovely, witty gentleman, was on duty at a busy junction. Once, on an incoming train, a high-ranking lady officer of the AF selection board was caught with an irregular ticket by a TTE. The defence employees and other police personnel had warrants issued that were treated as vouchers by the ticket issuing clerk. There are many types of warrants; some are fully treated as vouchers; on others, a percentage must be paid in cash. This officer had her defence warrant exchanged for a particular train but boarded a different train towards the same destination. The TTE penalized the officer. She created a ruckus and abused the railway employee. The TTE approached the SM, the Goan boxer, and asked the lady to sort out the penalty issue with him.

The lady barked, 'I am an officer. You can't treat me like a petty, ticketless traveller. You are taking advantage of a lady.' She interspersed this with vulgar words, addressing the TTE.

The SM calmly said, 'Madam, being an official of such a high rank, you should maintain your decorum. And use decent, nice words. If I forget who I am and just think how will it look if I call you a . . .?' And he listed out one hell of a list in colourful language. 'See, if I call you all this, will it look nice?'

The SM brandished a smile all the while. Then he called one of his friends at the AF station, a wing commander at the selection board. When the phone rang, he turned to the lady officer, 'If he picks up the phone, I will complain about you. Which do you prefer?'

The lady officer paid the penalty, apologized to everyone and scooted. If any other SM were in that situation, perhaps the lady would have lodged a harassment case on the guileless TTE.

* * *

People are so different. Some put everything into their work, and some do not want to take any extra burden on their shoulders. You see a 'Why should I?' attitude prevalent everywhere. One SM is starkly different from the other. No two railwaymen functioned the same way in any given situation.

Likewise, loco pilots and guards are thrown in the middle of the long tracks, where the onus of the safety of hundreds of passengers is on them; the decision taken in a snap saves them all. Recently, there was news about two loco pilots walking out of two trains, leaving thousands of passengers in the lurch. Such a hue and cry and trolls emerged from the incident. But didn't the reason cited by the loco pilots prove that it was the best decision not to operate a train when they were overworked and sleep-deprived? What if the trains had met with accidents due to the negligence of the tired employees? Didn't these two loco pilots actually end up saving lives?

The following is one such incident where a timely decision was made by the railway staff that guaranteed a smooth journey for the passengers on a long-distance train. My colleague Anwar Hussain, a train superintendent

(TS), thwarted what might have been a major riot. He had changed his cadre from a booking staff to a TS, whose duties involved controlling the entire train. He managed the operations of the running train, TTE, pantry and a team of AC and electrical technicians. As a TS, he also oversaw and assured the availability of water in all the toilets, and the water needed for the pantry car. Once, in the height of summer, he was on his run as the TS of the New Delhi (NDLS) bound train. A few stations were marked as watering spots on the route like Vijayawada (BZA), Nagpur (NGP), Jhansi (JHS). But the train reached NDLS dry because the stations enroute had no water to dispense. On their return journey, there was no water at the NDLS yard, and they were instructed to fill up water on the way. The train began its run at 22.30 hrs with no water in any of the compartments or the pantry. At JHS, the next watering spot, the yard was dry. The pantry manager informed the TS, 'If there is no water and we cannot even give tea to the passengers, things will turn ugly. Already, some passengers are clamouring for attention. I cannot provide tea or food.'

Anwar Hussain said, 'We will find a way.'

He quickly called the train controller, informed him about the agitated passengers, and requested a halt at an unscheduled station on the route. Bina Junction is a military cantonment. The pantry manager mocked the TS, 'As if it could be done.'

The TS informed BINA that the seventh coach from the engine was the pantry. The train halted at BINA and positioned itself to fill up water from an old, spout on top watering post.

After filling water at BINA, the train resumed its journey, and the pantry manager folded his hands and said, 'Hats off to you, sir. No TS has dared to stop the train. You have calmed the rioting passengers.'

Anwar Hussain glowed. 'If we put our minds to it, we can do anything.'

* * *

My second Dumbledore, Cyril Thomas, the Chief Reservation Supervisor (CRS), who joined the railways the year I was born shared an incident. He always repeated a dialogue to whoever came to him for a ticket, EQ, or anything connected to railways. 'The train will not go without you. It is my promise.' There are instances where his assurance ended getting him in trouble. One pastor came to him saying he had lost his ticket and wallet and was to travel to Chandigarh. Thomas issued a duplicate ticket and gave him Rs 500 for his travel expenses. After reaching Chandigarh, the passenger who had promised to send him the money forgot all about it. The funny part was that the CRS gave a duplicate ticket even without getting a requisition because the train was about to depart. Then Thomas found out from which PRS the original ticket was issued, and from that reservation office, he got the reservation form with the particulars of the pastor and called him by phone. Only then did the pastor send the money through someone. It was not just about the money; no one would help if the trust was broken. Thomas told me if these people do not return the money as promised, how would someone feel like helping such people? This might cloud our minds even if a genuine person warrants our help. A similar incident happened with a doctor's son from Patna; the CRS paid for a duplicate ticket and travel expenditure. In this case, however, the doctor's son sent an MO and a letter.

It's like when you carry a pen to the bank, and someone borrows it to fill in a challan, then walks away with your pen. Next time, you hesitate to share your pen and view everyone with suspicion.

In another incident, Cyril Thomas promised a defence officer a first-class coupe. Thomas was in the charting section and knew that the allotment was an easy-peasy job. But on that day Thomas was unable to attend work owing to personal issues.

The officer called, 'Mr Thomas. Sorry to bother you but I just wanted to remind you about the coupe.'

Thomas was in a fix. He tried persuading the officer that he had informed his colleague and had placed a note too. The officer then informed him why he had requested a coupe.

'I lost my right leg, and I am unaccustomed to removing my prosthetic foot in front of fellow travellers.'

'Officer, it is a civilian's promise that you will travel in a coupe. Alone.'

Thomas called his assistant and issued an order: Defence Officer travelling with defence secrets, hence issue a coupe for safety reasons.

* * *

The officials were of many kinds. Some were straight forward and a pleasure to work with, whereas some were corrupt and a pain. Once, my friend Venkatapathy, on duty, accompanied a high-ranking railway official on his salon. A separate cook prepared special food in the salon for the officer and his entourage. The cook took the provisions from the pantry car. All noted and accounted for.

When the official and his crew returned to the station at the end of the inspection, the official's wife ordered the cook to transfer all the leftover provisions to their car to be taken home. The cook discarded a coriander bunch, and the officer's wife, who had taken stock of the inventory earlier, asked for the coriander leaves. When the cook said he had junked the wilted bunch, she said, 'I decide if it should be thrown or used.'

This officer enjoyed many promotions and many more salon travels but, in the end, was discharged from service unceremoniously. Literally discarded like the wilted leaves.

* * *

Men and their egos never tire.

Once, a ticket collector on his way to the station was stopped by a traffic police and issued a fine. The TC pleaded and said that the police department folks frequented his station for tickets, and he and his colleagues always helped them. So, the TC requested that he be allowed to pass without penalty. But the police officer issued a fine, the least amount for a person with no helmet. For almost a month or so, whenever the police officials entered the station premises to drink tea, the TC clan harassed them for platform tickets and issued EFTs (excess fare tickets, a challan). The vengeful behaviour ended only after the intervention of higher authorities from both sides.

PLATFORM NO. 9

I BID A TEARY FAREWELL to my first railway family after two years and boarded the afternoon express to Bangalore. The BO staff's farewell gift was a small rosewood mandir. Even now, twenty-odd years later, all the gods in my house reside there. The goods-shed staff presented me a date-sheet key hanger. Although the sheets have crumpled, my amma cut out the numbers from a calendar and glued them on a cardboard sheet. It still hangs on our living room wall. We hold on to sentimental things. From Bangalore, on to the Chennai Express to 'Namma Chennai'. In the morning, as

I breathed in the stench of the Chennai Central Platform 9, it was bliss.

Boy, I was home! The vibrant people of Chennai, the friendliest people on earth, were ever smiling. Perhaps gazing at the glaring sun, the lips pulled up. The red-uniformed porters haggled for carrying the luggage; everyone paused to look at my goofy grin—delightedly humming a mashup of MGR songs, *Puthiya vaanam puthiya bhoomi* (New skies, new land); second line I switched to *naan paarthathile intha stationai thaan romba azhagi* . . . (To my eyes this station was the most beauteous.)

Maybe I will be posted to this station, I secretly wished, and almost skipped and pranced like Puratchi Thalaivar MGR (well, now this station is named after him.) The variety of parcels, from rubber rolls to butter tins to household vessels, lying haphazardly on the platform formed the welcome brigade.

Achan wrapped me in his arms and kissed my forehead, saying *Ende molukutty* . . . (my dear daughter, he was pretty possessive. Ende always preceded molukutty.) We rushed home because I had to report to the Southern Railways headquarters at 10.00 hrs.

* * *

Dressed in my lucky colour, blue, I bounded the stairs, ready for the next part of my railway innings. I reported at the Divisional Personnel Office (DPO), even before the clerks had settled in.

The staff ordered me to take a walk while they prepared my orders. I walked to the Southern Railways Headquarters office, admiring the breathtaking Indo-Saracenic architecture. Decades ago, this place was Adams Park, commemorating a lesser-known British governor, William Patrick Adams. The Moore Market Complex, where passenger reservation systems functioned, and the area around was just a mound of earth in 1904 called Narimedu or Hoggs Hill. The mound was flattened, and the sand was used to fill a ditch that became the Broadway in Madras. My head has accumulated many such trivia, thanks to the historian V. Sriram. After a sightseeing tour, I returned to the place in front of the clerk, who was visibly infuriated at me for reasons only known to her. Over the years, whenever I frequented this office, I greeted this lady. She has drawn up thousands of posting orders and never remembered me. But I jogged her memory, every single time.

Hemming and hawing for five hours, she issued me a posting order. Like the clerk in my earlier headquarters, from where I received my first orders to the small town, this one also checked her watch and ordered me to report to the station as soon as possible and before 18.00 hrs, so I would not have a break in service. Otherwise, I would lose two days, the day I left my previous station, and the day I delayed joining my new station.

Only some of this information registered in my mind as I was bewildered upon seeing the letter in my hand. It was not what I had dreamed of, but a railway station in the mofussil. A junction, a mofussil junction. Hell! That was not in the suburbs. Did it even come under Chennai's jurisdiction? My dream of working at Central Station went pfft and disappeared in the Chennai pollution.

What's with the countryside and me! Another bucolic setting.

I stuttered, 'How do I reach this station?'

'Take a train from the station opposite to this one and change over at the terminus.'

'There is a fast passenger to Pondicherry that stops at your station,' said another clerk.

'Do you know the timings?' I asked.

'Do I look like a timetable? Go to the station and enquire.'

Mumbling thanks, I sprinted through the corridors, boarded the packed elevator, and then on to the subway with the jostling vendors, school children, aunties and uncles. At the opposite station, a passenger guided me to take the electric train (EMU) to another station, which was the starting point of the Pondicherry passenger train. Collecting my ticket, I looked at the looming staircase before me. Just then, an EMU wheeled into the platform, and I saw people clamber into it to cross over to the next platform. I followed them, caught the electric train and alighted at the specified point.

I barrelled through the stairs and hurtled into the moving train. People tsk-ed and glared at me.

'Why this haste? What if you had fallen . . .'

I didn't have the energy to explain. In the ladies' compartment, I pushed through the sweaty women and saw the seated ones had already started cutting vegetables or stringing flowers. Non-stop chatter filled my ears. I informed at least ten people to detrain me at my station without fail. Unaccustomed to packed, swaying trains, I trampled on feet and knocked on elbows. The ladies shuffled their ample behinds and gave me a spot to sit, and I squeezed in. Confined by shiny midriffs, and hearing juicy gossip about strangers, I saw houses and trees fuse into each other like a distorted canvas as the train sped.

* * *

My pupils dilated as a vast lake glittered like mercury droplets on the side of the tracks. The setting sun cast a hypnotic glow and I drank in the beauty. A nudge from the midriff to my right and she said that the approaching station was mine. My joy doubled as the train juddered to a halt, and I could view the lake from the platform. I already loved my new station.

Mesmerized by its beauty, I sauntered to the ticket office. My friend from school, Siluvai Sekar, was sitting there issuing tickets. He had joined this station a few weeks ago, on a transfer from one of the smaller stations in the Trivandrum Division. Luckily for him, he had spotted a booking clerk in the Madras Division, whose home was in Trivandrum, so they applied for mutual transfer and both wound up not too far from their respective homes.

Excitement, happiness and pleasantries exchanged, he accompanied me to the SMR's office, where I handed my posting orders and signed the attendance register. The booking supervisor had left on the same train I had arrived on, so my friend added my name to the duty roster with a flourish.

In this station, both unreserved tickets issuing commercial clerks (CC) and the computerised reservation clerks, the ECRC or the Enquiry cum Reservation clerks, shared space inside the Booking Office. In major stations, there were separate cabins for CCs and ECRCs. If I remember right, this co-living arrangement had been practised for many years in this station. Lately, these two cadres of the commercial department of the railways have been merged unofficially. Ticketing was becoming hectic, and some friends were preferring early retirement. Staying home and following their passions seemed attractive as they had completed the required years to procure a full pension.

My posting in this station happened when the hierarchy of cadres was explicit. Here, the parcel office was in the corner of Platform 1, the farthest from the SMR's office and the BO was in the centre with a lake view.

I met my new colleague, a lady (yeah, I was a drop in the ocean in Chennai) whose husband and one-year-old kid were waiting to take her home.

The lady had a fresh strand of fragrant jasmine dangling, far lengthier than her scanty ponytail. Her husband had lovingly strung these flowers with banana fibre. It's the Tamil way of romancing: no red roses here, but jasmine speaks the language of love. She dawdled, strewing flowers on the floor, which the crawling kid popped into his mouth. While the father grabbed the kid's mouth open, the mother held a ticket with one hand and used the other to rummage through the child's mouth . . . The germs ingested by the toddler from the floor and the currency-handling hands of his mother—it was too much for me to handle. Not to appear rude, I tried small talk with them while Siluvai cleared the queue.

'Hello, sir. Do you stay close?' I asked.

'Yeah, in the railway quarters,' replied the wife, my colleague.

'Where do you work?'

'I am a landlord,' the husband responded.

It stupefied me, and I couldn't stop asking, 'So?'

Siluvai saved me from committing further gaffes. 'Hey, there will be a train on Platform 3 to the station near your home; why don't you go, rest and come in the morning?' He handed me a ticket.

I gathered my bags, waved, pulled the baby's cheeks gently, and walked out in search of Platform 3, while the landless landlord lorded over his employed wife.

* * *

The guard was waving the green flag; I raced and boarded the train. It was empty. The onward journey had been packed. I sat at the window seat to gaze at the lake, but a minute passed, and there was no sight of it. Sweat lined my forehead. I searched for someone to enquire. Unlike the

EMU, this train was vestibuled, so I trudged along. I saw a lone man puffing clouds of smoke, and I didn't stop. Then I came across four young boys, laughing aloud at some private joke, so I moved on. A whole empty coach and I reached the last compartment where a man in a khaki uniform with the insignia RMS (Railway Mail Service) chatted with an older man with a long white beard, like the poet Tagore.

'Sir, where is this train going to?'

'Kanchipuram, Madam.'

I slumped down on to a seat.

The railwayman quickly asked, 'Where do you want to go?'

'I thought this was the Tambaram train.'

'Ah, that's after this train. That's an EMU. This is a passenger train. Don't worry. You can get down and catch a train back soon.'

'What is the next station? I will get down there.' After all the theory I studied in school and the practical knowledge I gained working for two years, I did not know an EMU from a passenger train. So dumb!

'The next station is Reddypalayam. You will not get another train now. Only passenger trains stop there; the last train on this route would have crossed before we reach it.'

'Oh, what do I do?' I blinked back tears, willing them not to spill.

'Will that express train stop in Palur?' asked the old man.

'No. Palur will not be suitable for a young lady. Just last week, a rowdy gang . . .' The RMS man trailed off.

Then, the men discussed the best station for me to catch a train while I fretted.

They concluded that the Walajabad crossing was the best bet.

'Crossing?' I asked, fear cleaving through me afresh.

'At Walajabad, this train stops for a minute. Every day, right at that time, the express train slows and waits for a signal, hence the term crossing. You can get down from this train and climb into the express train that will take you back to the station you boarded. Then you can go home.'

'What if this train misses that train?'

The two men looked at each other and spoke in unison, 'That has never happened till now.'

So, I had nothing to do other than wait. My loquaciousness helped me to overcome the distress. We talked about my joining duty and immediately getting on to the wrong train. I was ashamed of calling myself a railway employee. The men shared biscuits, which I politely refused as I was aware of the dictum of not eating anything offered by strangers. However, I trusted these men to help me reach home safely. I heard growling sounds from my stomach.

The old man took a biscuit, broke it into half, put one piece into his mouth, and gave me the other half. Shrugging my shoulders, with a silly grin, I grabbed it and gobbled.

Amidst sacks of mail, the blue inland letters and postcards, three of us shared life stories. The old man was a retired railway employee on his way to his daughter's house. His wife and son had died in a road accident, so he stayed alone and looked forward to the occasional visits to his daughter and grandson, but only if the son-in-law permitted the visit.

The younger man lived with his wife and children. A typical man in his thirties trying to make ends meet, burdened with school fees and inflation.

I explained the process of landing a Central government job right after school and that it wasn't as easy as it sounded. I detailed the time and effort I put into clearing the RRB examination, how I managed to confront a panel of interviewers at sixteen, and after that the two years of education in school, and how while in school, a few of us from Karnataka and Kerala shared accommodation with benevolent relatives, who agreed to feed us and let us sleep under their roof. The umbrella of sheer luck in landing a government job shadowed our hardships. And then a posting at a place where we didn't speak the local language. Our difficulties were written off because we earned a government salary at such a young age.

It was pitch dark when the train slowed and crawled to stop. The RMS guy jetted down on the train's other side (off-side)—not the platform side. I gingerly held on to the handles and turned to face the train while my feet searched for the distantly placed rungs. As I plodded, the express train tooted on the adjacent track. While the brambles pricked and clung to my clothes, I manoeuvred the ballast pebbles and hefted up.

The door of the express didn't budge.

My glasses clouded. The RMS angel called out to a person peering through the darkness from the window seat and pleaded with him to open the door. He relented soon, forgetting his earlier reluctance when his eyes fathomed me—a damsel, my distress unmistakable.

A la SRK style, he offered to pull me up while my guardian angel cleared his throat. I ascended cautiously, and the train jolted. For a teeny-weeny second, I swayed but held on to the railing and disappointed the youth. The darkness swallowed the railwayman before I could catch my breath and thank him. After thanking the youth, I searched for women folk to sit with.

When the train reached the Lake station, Siluvai Sekar was waiting for me on the platform. The worry lines on his face transformed into joy as he ran towards me.

'As soon as you left, I realized I should have specified that a passenger train would be there, and next was the

EMU. I prayed someone would guide you, and you would come in this train.'

'Yeah, two good souls helped me. I couldn't recognize a passenger train from an electric train. I should be awarded.'

'Hahaha. My work is over. Come on, I will accompany you.'

The two of us boarded the EMU from Platform 3, and we stood near the door as the chilly January breeze nuzzled us. I was delighted to see a pale moon glinting off the water. Siluvai took a KitKat, broke it in half and offered me a piece. A beggar sitting near my feet pulled my dupatta and opened her palm.

My friend retrieved a one-rupee coin and offered it to her. She shook her head and pointed at the KitKat in my hand. Siluvai, the beggar woman and I relished a KitKat as the rustic scenery swished past.

For the subsequent three months, I worked in the mofussil station, commuting from my home. (It was a short time, but one of the critical incidents of my railway career happened in that period.) Whenever I was on evening duty, the RMS angel peeped into the booking counter and said, 'Good evening, madam.'

My gratitude swelled, and I gave him the sincerest smile. We never exchanged names. He remains a nameless face in the cloud of cherished memories.

PLATFORM NO. 10

'THE STAR WITNESS IS HERE.' The railway union lawyer ushers me inside the room. Three men are seated on a long table facing the rest of us. As I enter, the one-eyed parcel porter expels air through his lips, and his shoulders sag.

I avoid meeting his eyes and sit beside the Union lawyer.

One of the men from the panel asks me, 'Do you know why you are here, Mrs Sangeetha?'

'Yes, sir.'

'You have an important role to play in this case against the parcel porter. Railways are strict regarding such cases. The image of the Railways gets tarnished. Bribery is a serious issue.'

I wipe my clammy palms on my kurta. I attempt to speak, but no word comes out. I feel like someone had spooned out my throat.

'Please give her some water.'

I glug water, and the sound amplifies in the silence.

'Now, can we begin the proceedings?'

It is sheer good luck and God's grace that I occupy the witness chair, not the defendant's.

* * *

Most of my colleagues in the commercial department have never entered the parcel office or the goods shed in their entire career. Because of my posting in a smaller station, I worked in parcels, goods and passenger ticketing.

While I was rostered in the BO during my tenure in the mofussil junction station in the Chennai Division, the parcel office clerk suddenly called in sick, and the station manager summoned me.

Here, the SMR handled the duty rosters as opposed to the regular practice of the booking supervisor controlling the roster of the booking staff. Old politics ran deep in this station.

The clerk in the SMR office furrowed his brows, 'Have you worked in the parcel office in your earlier station?'

'Oh yes, I have worked in both parcels and goods.' That was me giving out information that wasn't asked for.

'That's good to know. Can you man the parcel office for the next few days? The clerk is unwell and is on sick leave.'

'You mean now? Immediately?' I eyed his shirt wondering when the stretched fabric would pop out the buttons.

'Yes. Now.'

'But I have already opened my counter at the BO . . .'

'It's ok. I will instruct someone to close and tally. You go to the parcel office.' He dismissed me as if I was something stuck in his shoe.

Such a stark contrast compared to the station master and station managers in my earlier station. They were kinder men who treated everyone with tenderness. Here, they exuded angry vibes. We could blame the hot, sunny weather or the abundance of female staff.

I observed a visible chemistry between the two clerks in the SMR office. The young reedy girl smirked as her senior dealt with me. Actually, she once asked me if Siluvai and I were in a relationship. I seethed and shut her up telling her not to sully our friendship. In three months, I received my transfer orders, and when it culminated with Siluvai growing a beard due to other reasons, this girl advised me not to betray him. She disputed my claim that there was no connection between my leaving the station and Siluvai's beard.

Handbag in hand, I went to the parcel office and sagged into the rickety chair, looking disapprovingly at my surroundings. A film of dust blanketed the shelves, crammed with files and papers. I convulsed, glancing at the multi-coloured flakes of paint blistering from the cracked walls and the ceiling that rained chalk on me whenever a train headed off. Overgrown weeds snaked through the window, lavishly spreading tentacles, and aimed for the roof where a gargantuan menacing fan rotated sluggishly. The artistic cobwebs in the four corners of the dingy room were my companions.

A worming decrepitude lingered in most of the parcel offices.

In several railway stations in India, the parcel office was located on the farthest end of the platform and bustled with activity sixty minutes before the departure of trains and thirty minutes after their arrival. Only in large stations does a steady line of customers trickle in. After the flurry of activity, the rest of the day was entirely free, and the regular parcel clerk slept in his quarters until the next train needed him.

I wished I had a book with me.

The parcel porter, old and nearing retirement, entered scratching his ear, dressed in khaki shorts and a shirt.

'Are you on duty today, madam?'

'Yes. What is your name?'

'Kaatupoochi.'

'What?'

'It is our god's name.'

Kaatupoochi means forest insect. How could someone name their son an insect?!

'When was the last time somebody cleaned this place?' I turned my head because his stare with one good eye and a glass eye on the other creeped me out.

'Last Ayudha Puja. The next one is in a couple of months.'

'What is that disgusting stink?' I scrunched my nostrils at the fetid air.

'Oh, those are the butter tins. Uthukuli butter is very famous.' My ignorance elicited a snicker.

'Hmm, I am not sure how everything works here. I hope you will guide me. First, clean up this place; this dust will kill me.'

'But madam, Goddess Lakshmi resides here. We shouldn't disturb her.'

Exasperated, I zipped my lips. It wouldn't be possible to deliver swift changes in a system that had prevailed for years. Anyway, it was only a three-day assignment.

I opened the registers and studied the local traffic while he sat cross-legged near the door.

* * *

My thoughts hankered to my earlier parcel office. Once, when my CBS, Amarendra Pillai, went for a training course, he deputed me to work in the parcel office until his return. Zahira Begum, the new lady porter had just joined our station.

Except the senior-most staff members in all the stations I worked at, I addressed everyone by name. Although I was considerably young, people preferred I didn't suffix a sir/madam. When the porters were much older, I felt awkward, but later it became my style. Perhaps people presumed I was arrogant. I certainly give off those vibes.

Zahira Begum always grinned displaying multiple gaps and entertained me by singing ghazals. Masha Allah, she had an enchanting voice. It was a *mehfil* when we worked together.

We checked our weights standing together on the Avery weighing scale placed inside the parcel office to weigh consignments that came for booking and whooped. It thrilled me to read the manufacturer and year: Birmingham 1907. I unleashed my imagination on what was weighed on this in the British era and during the fight for Independence. Ah, I miss those weighing machines in the platforms that added in fortune telling along with the kilograms, wonder where they have disappeared.

Hanumantha, the senior hamal who first took me to my railway quarters, brought me up to speed on the intricacies of the parcel office operation.

'What? No! I don't take extra,' I gasped.

'Madam, it's not extra, a little encouragement to pack and load with care. That's the unwritten rule here. I will deal with everything. You should tell the customer, "Do as the porter says". Rest assured, you will do fine here.'

'But it's not right.'

'Madam, you cannot change the pattern. You are here for just a few months, and then you return to your tickets. Just go with the flow.'

I fell into the groove. Some items that excited and irritated me were the booking of hundreds of day-old chicks, the cheeping of which resonated in the room and gave me a headache. Sometimes, I felt like wringing the tender necks of the chicks. I had such a murderous rage at their incessant chirping.

The parcels that everyone looked forward to, however, were the rubber rolls. Neatly packed in gunny sacks, the rubber rolls—sent from rubber estates in Kerala to various industries throughout India—were considered gold mines in railway stations.

Whenever a train brought rubber rolls for delivery, the parcel office would see an influx of people who herded to catch the action. I was surprised when I emerged from my cabin to receive the train's cargo load and signed the forms the train's guard extended. The clerk and the porter on duty always attracted envious looks; it was no secret that we would go home with a bulky wallet at the end of the shift.

Hanumantha handed over my 'share' of the day's earnings, every day. I put my initial qualms to rest and hopped home merrily. I spent the money on movie tickets and dresses. As everyone else who sins, hides behind an explanation, I told myself: if I don't do it someone else will.

One day, a peasant approached me with a strange commodity. Pigs! Yes, he had ten squealing piglets on a leash. After he left the piglets under my custody, one among them turned rogue, scurried out of the parcel office, and began romping about on the platform. Fortunately, there were no trains then, and Begum and I pounced on the errant piglet and managed to capture it after a short, breathless chase. Nightmares haunted me for the next few nights—squealing piglets escaping my grasp every time.

I gradually settled into my role as the parcel clerk. Hanumantha revealed anecdotes of the parcel booking, and Begum entertained me by singing.

When the CBS took up his post, I returned to the BO. Did I miss the extras? Hmmm. Yes and no. I was relieved that I didn't have to snub my conscience again.

* * *

The one-eyed porter broke my reverie. 'Madam, I hope you know the customs followed for booking parcels.'

'Umm.' Before he could educate me further, my first customer stomped in with a consignment to book.

I carefully prepared the bill based on the details in the consignment form tendered by the customer. Accepting the bill payment, I handed the receipt to the customer and a copy to the porter to keep with the package.

The porter cleared his throat. Once. Twice. And thrice.

'Err, do as the porter tells you,' I mumbled to the customer with a bent head.

Surprisingly, a file of customers waited to book parcels. They kept me busy during the first half of the day. I strolled on the platform post-lunch, when I witnessed a harrowing incident.

I recognized the scrawny woman who had come in earlier to book a parcel of books to her daughter studying engineering in the neighbouring state. I pitied her appearance, more so when the woman took out small change to pay the bill. The others waiting to book parcels groaned. The lady fidgeted and fumbled, which led to her coins scattering all over the room, further delaying the other customers.

I saw Kaatupoochi haggling with the same woman, now sobbing and imploring. Before I could intercede, a colleague called me for coffee.

As the rest of the day moved at a snail's pace, I pondered the episode and was ashamed of my porter's behaviour. The awareness that a share of money thus earned had oiled my wheels in my old station for a brief period distressed and mortified me immensely.

Once, I confided to Sujith (whom I married six months later in a huge elopement drama) about the 'do as the porter says' transaction, and he was appalled. It also petrified him, and he gave me an earful of the risks of my action.

'Promise me that you will never do that.'

'But I no longer work in those places.'

'Promise me even when you are forced, you will refuse.'

Sullenly, I acquiesced, adding, 'But I cannot stop the porters from earning extra money.'

He was infuriated with my careless flippancy. I promised to resist the blatant charm of easy money.

* * *

With an hour to complete my eight hours, I called Kaatupoochi.

He squatted on the floor and handed me some soiled currency.

'Madam, your share.'

'No, Kaatupoochi, I don't want. You can keep it. It is all yours.'

His face blossomed and his eyes sparkled. The glass eye reflected the light in the room.

'You are almost as old as my father. I am embarrassed to talk to you like this. I am no saint. I know how all this works, and I can't stop you from doing it. But can I request that you not demand extra from poor people? That lady with the parcel of books was pleading. I saw it.'

'Madam, sorry. I have three daughters to wed,' he bleated with a lopsided grin.

I sighed and measured my words, but we were interrupted by a customer.

The accounts were tallied, and it annoyed me to tend to a customer at closing time. Mechanically, I drew up the receipt and collected the cash.

'The petrol tank should be dry; the porter will do the required packing.'

In a hurry to catch the train home, I told Kaatupoochi that he should finish packing and lock the office. I intended to remit the day's collection to the BO and board the next train.

Within a few minutes of the porter walking out with the customer, seven men barged inside with Kaatupoochi. His one eye was enormous and red like the signal light. I was perplexed. It looked like a hostage situation in the movies.

A tall man addressed me authoritatively, flashing an identity card, 'Madam, we are vigilance officers. We received complaints about the parcel clerk, and this is a surprise check. We caught your porter red-handed bargaining for extra.'

Ashen-faced, I staggered. I held the desk as the man continued, 'Please cooperate with us. We must check your accounts and tally your "today's earnings". First, please show us how much personal cash you have and bring the "personal cash" register you declared before starting work.'

* * *

My friend Bharathi had sent a letter about her brush with the vigilance officers. When she worked at a manual counter, wagonloads of humans milled the counters.

Even tallying the accounts at the end of the shift was exasperating. People screamed obscenities as they saw the train move without them. The fact was lost to them that accounts had to be tallied before a new person took charge. Many of these transactions couldn't be done at the other counters because her counter was earmarked for special tickets.

An officer from the railway board came for inspection and ordered Bharathi to tally the accounts with the cash on hand. Her limbs shivered as she hurried to count the money. Too many registers and manual refund entries had to be tallied, and the snarling passengers further terrified her. The supervisor also pleaded with the officer that the counter tallying would take a long time and the passengers might get aggressive. He remained stubborn, and my friend tallied every single rupee. She said she wasn't sure if the officer understood the accounts she showed him. Anyway, he left satisfied and let her face the firing squad. A few more minutes of delay would have ensured the breakage of the plexiglass counter windows.

The passengers in the queue often think those inside the counters are chit-chatting and wasting time. But the reality is we have these surprise checks by the Vigilance Inspectors and auditors, for which we have to halt the ticketing. Even during duty change, the passengers create a commotion flustering us.

In another instance, while working the reservations, Bharathi faced a miscreant. The passenger reservation systems all over ceased at 14.00 hrs and reopened at 14.15 hrs. A customer thrust an incomplete reservation form at 13.58; by the time she checked the enquiry about the train availability it was 14.00 and the system shut down. This person, a lawyer, raised his voice, abusing all government staff. He called them servants and told Bharathi to stop using angry words, and to deal with her family issues at home and not at the counter. He said he would show a lawyer's power and asked for the complaint register and registered a complaint.

My friend Bharathi is one of the timidest persons I know, never raises her voice in anger or utters hurtful words. The lawyer's ego had to be mollified with an apology letter. I am not sure how he would have reacted if she had halted the issue of tickets when a Vigilance Inspection happened.

* * *

With these thoughts coiling, I hastily showed the vigilance officers the books. The men checked the registers. This was a well-planned operation. I signed the letter proffered by the vigilance officers, which certified, 'Accounts and personal cash tallied without any discrepancy.'

A young officer was chatty, 'Your signature is shaky. The clerk whose duty you took over must have received a tip-off. That's why he feigned illness, and you were called in as a replacement. Lucky that you are not corrupt.'

I managed a wan smile. My insides were churning, and I excused myself to go to the washroom and retched. I remembered Sujith's words, 'Everything has a domino effect; your casual demands and nonchalance might have dangerous repercussions on everybody around you.' I cringed, imagining being cuffed, taken away and dismissed from service ingloriously.

Later I heard that some of these corrupt staff and the Vigilance Inspectors worked on a symbiotic relationship. One needed a case and the other wanted a peaceful tenure. So, an unsuspecting staff was sacrificed, and life went on for others.

Things did not go well for Kaatupoochi. He was booked on corruption charges and placed under immediate suspension from work. I boarded the last train, head held high. A timely, correct decision saved my career and life.

* * *

I appeared as a witness for the defendant in the trial that unfolded in the vigilance office a few weeks later. Kaatupoochi had only a few months of service left until retirement; my little assistance could save his pension, informed the lawyer appointed by the staff welfare union. The railway unions are strong and work miracles to save their members. One is unassailable if affiliated with the mighty union. Kaatupoochi escaped with a warning and a remark on his service register. He completed the rest of his service and received his pension.

I never received another dime besides my remuneration from the government.

I didn't stay in the parcel office for long or work with the tickets. Cement bags surrounded me for a while. A bandana partly covered my face in feeble protection against the cement dust and the lure of large kickbacks. Steeling myself to 'stay clean,' I furiously calculated wharfage in the goods shed—a frowzier but wealthier place than the parcel office.

PLATFORM NO. 11

AFTER WORKING FOR A FEW months at the station overlooking the water body, I received my transfer orders to a suburban station near my home. It was not an easy feat to finagle this transfer. I met the senior officer, at the divisional office. A brilliant young lady sporting a stylish Indra Gandhi bob and a reputation of being a straightforward terror of our cadre. I requested a transfer to a suburban station. She rejected my application.

The second time did the trick as I claimed that marriage proposals for me weren't materializing because of my posting in a far location. It was a white lie, but it served the purpose, and I received my orders. It's ironical that mine was the last transfer order she signed before receiving her transfer orders to a different division. My guardian angel, perhaps Bholu (mascot of the Indian Railways), continued to look out for me.

My achan wasn't too keen to let me travel alone to my new place of work because of my goof-ups with trains at my earlier station(s), but I convinced him that I would be vigilant this time. What would my new work mates think if I entered my workplace clutching my dad's hand? So, armed with my posting orders, I detrained at the right station and walked up to the ticket window near the foot overbridge. This station had a few leather factories in the vicinity and a talcum powder factory. As the wind rolled, we were assailed by fragrance or tannins.

Just as there were Karnataka Day celebrations when I joined my first station, that day was the festival of Holi. Enthralled by the jubilation of the train commuters and wary of people dunking colours, I reached my station.

The rectangular squat building had a grille door with a large padlock. I rattled it and shouted out a meek, 'Sir . . .!' A thin man waddled towards the door in a folded dhoti revealing his spindly legs. His pencil-line moustache accentuated his cleft lip, which twitched as his eyes sized me up.

'Who are you?' A strange whoosh of air, popped as he spoke.

'Sir, I am the new clerk. Please open the door,' I mumbled, wondering why he was wearing a *veshti*, yellowed and crumpled. I remembered my statistics master. He had long matted hair tied into a loose bun, crooked, stained teeth and was dressed in wrinkled veshti that had never allied with soap.

But this person had oiled and side-partitioned hair and a streak of holy ash on his forehead.

'Ok. Wait for a minute.'

I heard voices, he returned with several keys and opened the door, humming a tune.

These suburban stations had considerable patronage from those waiting for the electric trains, and the safety of the counter clerk and the cash collection had to be safeguarded with large locks. Anyone could walk in and try to run away with an armful of currency.

During my tenure at this station, the neighbouring station reported a burglary attack. The night duty clerk, a man, was alone, and it was a CNC station, i.e., there were no station masters, and the ticketing office staff were in complete charge of the entire railway premises. This clerk alerted the control room from the section phone in the middle of the night and reported the break-in. A few RPF personnel on bikes rushed to the scene. The injured and bruised clerk had blood streaming from a deep cut on the forehead. After administering first aid, the RPF informed GRPF. A thorough investigation progressed; the clerk explained how a masked man broke open the wooden door, attacked him and fled with the station earnings. It was a long weekend with the banks closed for three days; the earnings for three days had accumulated, and it was a whopping amount.

The station was treated as a major crime scene, but they couldn't close the counter as people flocked to the platform from the day's first train until the last train left. It was only at night that it was deserted; sometimes, homeless beggars huddled on the platform.

We discussed the case for a few weeks; the clerk went on sick leave to nurse his wounds. Then we read in a regional newspaper that the booking counter burglary case was solved. The culprit had been apprehended, and the loot was safe in railway custody. It was a staged burglary by the booking clerk. He had gambling debts and had seized an opportunity to swindle the station earnings.

After this incident, the railways sped up the process of arranging a cash van with armed personnel to collect the daily earnings from the station and remit them to a bank. If the banks were closed, the currencies were under safe custody and guarded well at the cash office. Previously, the booking earnings were counted, bundled with a filled cash remittance note and shoved into a leather cash bag. These weathered bags had to be tightly fastened with a cord inserted through the eyelet holes by folding the neck of the bag. This cord should pass through the eyelet holes at least four times and twice around the neck. It had to be drawn firmly and knotted, on which the station seal would be affixed using sealing wax and station insignia. Usually, the seniormost on duty managed the cash remittance, but sometimes I ended up struggling with the cash bag, tape and eyelets, pouring hot wax on my fingers. After obtaining the guard's signature in the cash-deposit register, these bags were dropped into the huge travelling cash chest on the specified trains. The cash chest would be opened at the cash office and the cash was remitted to the bank. Empty cash bags returned through another train. Once my friend Jotheeswaran put his hand in an empty bag to retrieve the cash remittance receipt and pulled out a snake!

* * *

Now at my new suburban posting station, I entered the anteroom of the booking office and said, 'Thank you, sir.' I smiled and he reddened.

I checked out the room, congested with a few Godrej bureaus and a table. Then, doddered to the next room, where there were two counters for issuing tickets and one for season tickets. The walls were in the same paint-peeling stage, once white but having ceased the pretence ages back. The BO in my earlier junction station was in better condition. That station had a stationmaster and a station manager. This was a CNC station. Massive wooden cupboards with racks and racks of card tickets stared at me. I winced at the memory of counting tickets. Luckily, the passenger traffic was voluminous; hence, counting tickets was not pursued.

A square metallic box painted bright green with grooves ejected thin, yellow tickets with a whirring sound and a shudder. This new green contraption intrigued me.

'This is the SPTM—self-printing ticket machine,' said Velu, a dark, muscular colleague, discerning my saucer eyes.

I nodded and looked at the others in the cramped room. A man with a French beard and a punk hairstyle, a fashion from the previous decade, sat on a cluttered corner desk, his long legs dangling at an angle. He was probably the husband of the lady at the season ticket counter. They were discussing something and stopped mid-sentence as I entered. The lady colleague, extremely fair with curly hair, Manimozhi, draped in the blue uniform saree, gawped, and then smiled.

The three ladies in my previous station were friendly, but I couldn't connect with them. Manimozhi had enjoyed the sole ladyship until I barged in. I was jittery and wanted her to like me. She read my transfer letter and sighed. I wondered why.

'The room is already too crowded for all of us,' said a dark rotund man, who hobbled in, pulled up a chair and sat wiping his forehead, complaining about the heat.

Guzzling water, he looked askance at me. The man in the veshti stood near the window and watched all of us.

'I am the new clerk.'

'I am the CBS (Chief Booking Supervisor),' he replied.

'Good morning, sir.' I handed my transfer orders.

He read it, and a short bark of a laugh escaped him, 'Now Anwar Hussain has to go; no more excuses.' He told the others, and I blinked, confused.

A bellowing voice came through the side windows. 'Kathiravan, come on. Let's go.'

'Anwar, Come here. Your replacement has come,' the CBS said.

Anwar rushed inside and peered at me through his thick glasses. A gash ran from his eyebrow to his nose tip on his right cheek. I wondered if someone had slashed him with a knife. He snatched the letter from the supervisor and read it aloud.

'*Malayalee aano*?'

'*Athe.*' I gave him the true Mallu head nod. We skipped the '*Naatil evideya*? (Which place in Kerala)' that followed when one met another Malayalee.

He pushed the supervisor's bag from the table and rested his butt on it. '*Edo*, now that you are here, I must go. My transfer orders have been pending for the last six months. You know I have worked in this station for sixteen years.' He had joined the railways when I was a toddler.

'I am sorry. I didn't mean . . .'

'It's not your fault. Don't be sorry. Ok, sir, give me a week's leave. After that, I will go,' Anwar requested the CBS.

'Oh, Anwar. We will miss you *ahn*,' pouted Manimozhi.

I realized that I was breaking into a close-knit bond when she threw me a hateful look. I wanted to meet that officer who had signed my orders to rethink. My orders to a station within a 2-km radius from home was a dream come true. If my entry was someone's exit . . .

Well, life was like that.

Both the men, Anwar Hussain and Kathiravan, got up from the table and went out. The table swayed, and I noticed one of its legs was shorter and propped on two bricks. Manimozhi followed them, leaving the counter as a passenger poked his head in to glimpse the happenings inside.

* * *

I eased into a routine in the new station. I spent the first two days observing my colleagues and checking the SOB. Wait, I am not referring to my colleagues even though some were SOBs. A standing order book is one in which all the latest rules, or the changes in the route or train timings, etc. were sent to the stations from the head office, duly sealed and signed.

The few months at the non-suburban station had equipped me with knowledge of the stations on the route, but nothing prepared me for the masses in the suburban lines—endless serpentine queues at all three counters with hardly a few minutes of respite. And when a clerk closed the counter for the designated fifteen-minute break for tiffin, the passengers whined.

'These people don't value our time!'

'Look! The counter is closed. I bet they are chit-chatting.'

'Can't you guys eat at home? Why now?'

We stopped explaining that we were humans, not robots and that the timings were designated and painted in front of each counter. Some days, one of us lost our temper, and arguments ripened.

* * *

Everyone addressed the veshti-clad man as Tippy.

'Tippy, go and get tea for all of us.'

'Tippy, pass me that ticket bundle.'

'Tippy, carry this box.'

For many days, I thought he was a class IV employee. A peon. He was mostly seen in the BO when Manimozhi was on duty. Then there was Nalini, a class IV employee who swept the platform and brought us tea in the absence of Tippy. Hers was a compassionate posting on her husband's job. Some eight years ago, her husband went on an errand on a Deepavali morning and never returned home. Nalini and her three children still await his return. She was given a posting three years after his disappearance. And now, seven years later, he has been deemed dead. She was hopeful of his return and said she could have chosen to remarry but decided to wait for her husband, whom she loved dearly. Never once did she deplore him. She crimsoned as she shared details of her romantic married life. (Even now she is still waiting—retired and living with her grandchildren.)

One day, I asked Manimozhi, 'Where is Tippy sir?'

She burst out laughing. 'Tippy sir, ahn?'

'Yes.'

'Don't call him sir more and all, ahn' she guffawed.

'But he looks quite old.'

'Oh, he is old ahn. But he is just a passenger who is always here at the station. He never buys a ticket or goes anywhere. He is soft in the head and stays with his brother and family. They send him off in the morning, ordering him to get home only at mealtime. So, he loiters here ahn. We adopted him, and he does odd jobs for us.'

'But he is so authoritative with me. I thought he worked here.'

'You are young enough to be his daughter; hence, he is bossing you. Don't allow him to do that ahn.' She laughed again.

'What's his name, his real name?'

'Ummm. We don't know. We call him Tippy. I've got no idea how that name came by.'

The CBS joined our conversation. 'He is harmless. However, he likes Manimozhi a lot. He worships her.'

'Sir, nothing like that ahn. I sometimes bring him food, and he . . .' floundered Manimozhi.

'And he likes to watch you. He doesn't come here much when you are on leave or off duty,' parried the CBS.

'Oh, don't pull my leg now. Enough ahn!'

Manimozhi had another admirer, although she said he also watched me when I issued tickets. This man worked in an auditor's firm, and his brother worked in the railways. He always wore white pants and a blue shirt. None of us had seen him in other colours. He waited outside the counters, just gazing at us, and when bored or having memorized every mole, every twitch in our face through the grilled windows, boarded a train and left.

It perturbed us that people simply watched us like zoo animals or lab specimens from outside the glass enclosure. They gather information by observation. Later when I worked in the reservation office, a CRPF customer approached me.

'Madam, your name is Sangeetha?'

'Yes. How did you know?'

'I heard your friend call you.'

I rolled my eyes and kept mum.

'You know, ma'am, Sangeetha is a powerful name. I know two Sangeethas who are devastatingly dangerous.'

I was intrigued. 'Umm, I also know another powerful Sangeetha.'

'My officer is one courageous lady, and the other is a notorious Naxal. One Sangeetha wants us to capture the other one. But the Naxal cleverly escapes.'

The man was travelling to the state where my namesake friend was the District Collector. I blurted this and worried if I had revealed more than necessary.

With every person flaunting a mobile phone nowadays, we are helpless when they click pictures of us. We pretend ignorance and issue tickets.

* * *

I was the youngest and junior-most staff member here and was allotted the season ticket counter most days. It was a split roster: 07.00 hrs to 10.30 hrs and 16.00 hrs to 19.30 hrs. I couldn't make any plans for either morning or evening, and I whizzed in and out of the BO, jumping into the moving trains. On seeing me sprinting out of the counter, some guards waited a few seconds before waving the green flag.

* * *

My batchmate Bharathi, at her first posting station, once had to deal with an aggressive customer and shared her story. Issuing a season ticket took a little longer than the unreserved tickets. We wrote the ID number and the passenger's name after picking the right card from an array of cards displayed like the lottery ticket seller. When Bharathi picked up the card, the customer urged her to issue it quickly because the guard was blowing the whistle. When he left, she noticed that the earlier card was a quarterly ST, whereas the one she issued was a monthly ST. But she had collected the correct monthly fare and returned the balance.

The next day, an older man complained that the counter staff had pocketed the extra money by cheating his son and had issued a monthly ST. (This was in Karnataka; she had yet to master the language to comprehend lengthy sentences.) Her colleagues spoke on her behalf, but the man disregarded everyone and wanted the 'Complaint Register'. After cajoling, he agreed to bring his son, who had purchased the ST. When they came by, the older man whined about the waste of his time. The son refuted that Bharathi had returned the correct balance until much later. The father apologized, smacked his son and pulled him away. The son never again purchased the ST from her station.

* * *

A major chunk of the season ticket traffic in my suburban station were season tickets against concession forms issued by educational institutions. Many schools and colleges neighboured our station, and in the evening season-ticket shift, we had hordes of students swarming the BO. Each concession form had details of six students; we rarely received the form with one name. The counter staff had to tick off specifications before issuing the tickets because these forms were treated as vouchers, and we collected only a meagre amount from the students.

A comprehensive checklist included: no overwriting, valid date, signature and seal of the head of the institution, the round seal of the institution, student name and ID, and the collection of the student's season ticket ID, etc., and then preparing individual season tickets. Sometimes, by oversight, even if one of these criteria was missed, I had to run to the institution to get it rectified. At times, I requested other students who came for season tickets from the same institution to get it altered. Some obliged, some desisted, some took the form and never returned. So, most of the time, I hiked to the institution and collected a new concession form. After a morning shift, I went to the colleges and schools with the invalid concession certificates and waited to get them corrected. Sometimes, I had to go twice to get the forms right.

The railway clerks at other stations, whose jurisdiction the institution was situated in, abstained from issuing STs and asked them to change the issuing station to the next station or one near their homes. The thwarted students got their institution to change the 'from' station to our station because the staff posted here were quicker, kinder and obliged. Manimozhi and I received the maximum concession forms in our shifts. Afterwards we understood the men in our BO were sending them away, asking them to come during our shifts. After issuing the STs, the concession forms with all the details had to be entered into a register. During such days, our work extended beyond the counter timings, and we missed the regular train home.

When Manimozhi or I had to go to an institution to get a form rectified, Tippy accompanied us. Some days, he stood outside our ticket counter and regulated the students' queue. He used an authoritative voice, which he had reserved for me earlier, and the students called him 'sir' and requested if they could be served first. Tippy selected forms from the best-looking girls and brought their ID and cash inside the BO, and we issued them because we knew that Tippy desired to shine and feel valued.

A week later, when Manimozhi rejoined work after a vacation, Tippy came inside wearing a pant, an entire size bigger. He clutched his pants and head bent, glanced at us sideways, a shy smile shadowing his face.

His eyes moistened at our laughter. Then Manimozhi pulled a thread that bundled the tickets and told him to secure his pants with it. He blinked. The CBS took him aside and secured it for him.

Tippy briskly walked like a ramp model and announced, 'From tomorrow, I won't be coming here daily. I have got a job.'

'Where and who gave you a job ahn?'

'Cardboard company that is three stations away. My *anna* (brother) took me today and put me in the job. Now I will get my monthly salary. I will buy you all tea. Sangeetha, I will get you Milk Bikis too.'

Britannia Milk Bikis was my favourite biscuit brand, and I always had a packet next to my counter. When I was a kid, my achan always brought me Milk Bikis and allowed me to dunk it in his cup of tea. The habit stuck; I still view MB as my comfort food.

Tippy took his maiden employment seriously. He waved a cheery hi and a bye every morning, dressed in a borrowed shirt and pants. Velu gave him a belt. Tippy always had holy ash on his forehead in his excessively powdered face in the morning. He held a large empty bag in his hand. He said he had always wished to carry a bag to the office. By evening, when he returned, he looked tired and worn out. An insipid hi and bye wheezed out. If Manimozhi was on evening duty, his face brightened like a full moon. He still bossed over me at times, and I indulged him.

He had a weird talent. Tippy could tell the PIN code of every place in Chennai. It was a game we enjoyed playing. We would name a place, and he was able to immediately give us its PIN code. In addition to that strange talent, he could tell the level crossing gate numbers of every single LC in the suburban line. None of us were aware of the term autism in that period. We joked about his talent.

Some days, he disclosed that his brother's wife did not give him food. She scolded him, telling him to get out and get killed by the train. His nephew had recently taken a job, and they were looking for a bride for him already.

'I will turn fifty next month, but no one in my house is bothered about it.'

Manimozhi and I planned a small celebration for Tippy which never happened. Tippy did not visit our station for the next six months. We worried about him. Since we didn't know his address or even his real name, other than waiting, we could do nothing.

One day, when Manimozhi and I were on duty, Tippy tiptoed inside our office and yelled 'Booo'. He admonished us for not locking the door. We were so happy to see him, our voices cracked. He was overwhelmed by our emotions.

'My anna sent me away to my sister's house in the village. She brought me here because her husband told her she could not stay if I stayed there. So, I will now be able to meet you all daily. My sister-in-law has to feed me; no other go.'

His innocent smile was a burden too heavy for us to bear.

After seven years, I moved out of the station on a promotion to a different cadre. From being a commercial clerk issuing tickets in the suburban section, I would now be working in the Passenger Reservation System issuing computerized reservation tickets. I dropped in at my station whenever possible to meet my friends. They informed me that Tippy had stopped coming. Perhaps he was living with his sister in the village.

We continued to believe that because the alternative was too bleak.

PLATFORM NO. 12

THE STATION WHERE I WORKED, on the suburban line, was 5 km from my home. For the first two, I rode a bike, manoeuvring the morning office rush to the nearest railway station, where I took a train. The 2-km bike ride was like an adventure sport for my twenty-three-year-old self. Bikers, autorickshaws and minibuses vied for their slice of the narrow, potholed road. I shook under my helmet, hyperventilating as I made my way through.

I have always feared roads and traffic. When I appeared for my driving licence test, the RTO (regional transport office) inspector instructed me to do the '8' with my bike.

My friend Gajalakshmi (the one I befriended during kindergarten and who is still my bestie) and I were the first two candidates present for the test. We reached early assuming (and hoping) the inspector would be in a better mood. First, my friend did a flamboyant 8 and parked the bike in style, impressing the inspector.

Although I had practised, plenty of buses and two-wheelers zigzagged on the road, terrifying me. So, we came up with a plan. My friend engaged the inspector in conversation when he signalled me to ride. I drove fast, did a skewed eight, and parked my bike on a side-stand. The inspector snarled: I didn't see your 8. The Lord of the Vehicles answered my prayers. A bus broke down in the middle of the road just then, saving me from doing a 16! I received my licence, but I rarely rode. When I did, I rode pillion. I was the only person in my circle who had a driver for a bike, and everyone teased me about it more times than I care to count. It wasn't as if I hadn't tried. The morning traffic spooked me, so I even attempted to wake up earlier and walk the 2 km to the railway station, but the vehicular fumes and garbage-strewn sidewalks shattered my resolve. And while the teasing continued, I sucked it up and finally put my licence to use.

After three weeks of hard practice and with low confidence, I parked the bike (I never mastered parking my bike on the main stand) and dazzled a beguiling smile to the young man commanding the cycle shed. He tilted his head and gazed at me before offering to straighten my bike.

The bell for the level crossing gate jangled, and as I sneaked across, the heavy metal gate came down, inciting barks from the passers-by.

'What's the hurry?'

'Slow down!'

'Do you have a death wish?'

'Remember, a family is waiting for you.'

My God! People pounced on me, throwing opinions and suggestions. I wasn't dumb; after all, I was a railway employee! I crossed the tracks confirming that the signal was red on all sides. Sheathed in thick skin, I raced toward the platform, ignoring everyone. When the train screeched to a halt on the platform, packs of men, women, and children barged into the already overfull train. Inside the ladies' compartment rubbing shoulders, bellies and whatnot with the jasmine-bedecked women, their pasty talcum powder streaking in sweat rivulets, I travelled the short distance. Like the proverb 'the fragrance of the jasmine is absorbed by the fibre on which it is strung', I sponged the myriad scents encircling me.

This was the first stop after the train left the terminus, the starting point of the EMU on the suburban line. I worked at the next station, so I had to detrain as soon as I wormed in.

As soon as I bustled out, my eyes searched for my favourite beggar. The homeless man under consideration was tall, dark and relatively healthy for a vagrant. With a head full of tousled, thick hair and a luxurious beard, he sat near our ticket counter, brooding. He sometimes angled his head and looked through or beyond me. His intense gaze was scary, yet magnetic. I always thought that in another life, he could have been a model.

He never smiled or talked, nor begged; he just sat in his place, dressed in a chequered lungi and a shirt with a few missing buttons, the rest buttoned wrongly. Passers-by wondered if he was a mendicant or some drunkard before dropping coins. He didn't even have a begging bowl.

Then, one day, a lady with a dented aluminium cup and a cane to swat the stray dogs, joined him. Some days, I watched her comb his hair. While his shirt still missed buttons, the remaining were buttoned right, and the others were secured with safety pins. She cared for him like a mother or an older sibling. And oddly, in time, a smile adorned his otherwise lost features.

When our old corner was razed, we shifted to a brand-new, fancy, hexagonal building suspended on four vertical columns attached to a foot overbridge (FOB). It was a block with three ticket windows and a small storage room for tickets. The significant feature was the attached bathroom. There was a two-shutter window with grills overlooking the busy intersection. Some days, when the passenger traffic was less, I stared through the windows, observing and absorbing the sights. I even made up stories of the people I watched unobtrusively.

After we switched to the newer building, the tramps moved near the stairs to the FOB, inconveniencing the passengers. Many others, the homeless and hawkers, deemed the platform their home and spread their belongings and family over the length and breadth of the four platforms. The vendors vanished without a trace whenever the RPF personnel patrolled. But these two beggars never moved despite repeated warnings for disrupting the commuters from using the stairs, as everyone had to circumvent the young man and the older woman. The neatly buttoned-up man rattled the dented begging bowl. The older woman, clothed in a salwar kameez that I gave her a few months ago, rubbed the bald patch on her head and put on a tobacco-stained smile, mumbling inaudibly, 'Amma, Ayya.'

* * *

I observed the duo daily and almost felt possessive of them. If I couldn't see either of them in their regular spot, I did a 360-degree turn like an owl until I spotted them. The relationship between the two was indecipherable. She wasn't old enough to be his mother, and they didn't behave like lovers.

Oh, there were others on the platform who were most certainly lovers. The visually challenged boarded the trains, singing tunelessly and wringing a harmonium. A few of them had real talent. On the platform, they were entirely oblivious to the moving sea of people. I am not sure why they canoodled in public. Was it because they couldn't see us and thought that we couldn't see them either? Like children. Or was it because they didn't care what others thought?

Often, I've wondered if we should follow their example and stop worrying about what others think about us and our actions. We can learn from everyone. These people bothered no one; they were just blindly in love, thankfully no one bothered them.

Unlike the lovebirds, my beggars seemed to be in a nurturing relationship. The roles reversed often. The woman cared for the man as he lay his head on her lap while she picked lice from his tangles. She bought food parcels from a hotel, and he fed her with his hand before he ate.

I did not watch them all the time; I did have work. But platform assessments did have its virtues.

My junior, Prabhu, who is now in the Indian Army, worked as a TC in a station where the electric traction ended, and diesel locomotives began. During his prowls on the platform to nab ticketless travellers, his keen observation aided in busting a fraud. In his station, every train halted for fifteen to forty-five minutes during which the slip coaches were removed and engines were shunted. At this time, the 'Watch Racketeers' dived into action. These men beguiled the guileless travellers to shell out money to buy the fake luxury watches announced as 'imported from the Gulf'. The railway personnel formed a team and apprehended these con men, facilitating an arrest. Soon after, this action-adventure pushed my friend to take the SSB examination, where his merit in tests that rated him in eighty different aspects and landed him on a post guarding our frontiers.

* * *

I habitually took frequent breaks at work, taking a five to ten-minute pause once every ninety minutes. My officemates condoned it. Who knew I would write about our mutual break indulgences one day and make it a matter of public record.

On my breaks, I sauntered on the platform, bought a magazine, scanned the trains and talked to strangers. During the Polio Eradication Drive, the polio drops booth functioned on the railway platform. I loved to watch the children being immunized. Oh, the kids and their expressions were heart-tugging.

So, I had seen the homeless duo enough, and of course, I tried to converse with them too, but the woman spoke in a strange tongue—not Hindi, perhaps Bhojpuri or Odiya—while the man was mute. I tried a bit of gesturing with the woman, but the man's unblinking stare unnerved me.

Some days later, I was surprised to find a third person with them. He was old, frail and had long limbs (imagine a taller, sapped Amitabh Bachchan) that stretched everywhere, tripping people. Dressed in a khaki shirt, a material that looked like flannel (flannel in the humid Chennai weather), paired with black shorts. He had a buzz cut, more like new hair sprouting on a shaven head. After all these years, I can still picture him; his image is imprinted in my memory.

Nobody knew where this new guest had come from. The woman offered him food and water from her meagre share. And just like that, the three were a family, a complete picture.

Weeks passed. One day, the woman disappeared from the scene, a.k.a. platform. Rumours spread that she was kidnapped. I requested a patrolling RPF to search for her in the other stations, but he dismissed my concerns.

Perhaps beggars did not qualify for attention, passing under the radar of life itself.

The plight of the young man she left behind was terrible. He yowled, running amok, endangering himself, and when we received complaints from the passengers, the RPF removed him from the station. The RPF told me they had him in a holding cell for a few days and then freed him. But he never returned to my station. I never saw him again.

The station fruit vendors took pity on the older man, the one left behind. He survived on the food some of us gave him and moved to the landing on the stairs, closer to us. The emanating stench became unbearable, but no one complained.

* * *

The inevitable happened one night. The CNC stations were desolate once the last suburban train left. At night, the lone clerk was liable for the entire station premises, the tickets, the cash, the beggars, dogs, cats, rats and lizards.

After I tallied the accounts, I arranged a bed sheet on a large table to rest. A safer option as a frightful lot of lizards and rats grazed the floor. I inflated my air pillow and lay on the teakwood table, listening to maestro Ilayaraja's songs on Radio Mirchi FM—my companion on these long, lonely nights. The FM stations had just been launched and were a rage. Youthful, vibrant witty RJs captivated the plenitude of music lovers.

Remember, this was before the era of smartphones. Limited avenues of entertainment besides books, music, daydreams and night-time fancies. All the booking staff pitched in Rs 25 to get a tiny transistor; an assembled set kept alongside the ticket bundles for the night clerk's use. One of my favourites on FM was a programme hosted by R.J. Senthil, 'Neenga Naan and Raja Sir.' The RJ had a velvety voice, and in the silence of the nights, there was no better companion than Ilayaraja—an incomparable pleasure. Kadhal Doctor Siva was another RJ who crept into everyone's hearts with his hilarious answers to love-lorn souls. Daytime was peppy with Deva, Mirchi Suchi and Orampo Sujatha.

Amma began her mornings during my schooldays with Radio Ceylon and Vividh Bharati where she could figure out the accurate time when a particular advertisement played.

A glass-fronted wall over a metal grille shielded the office, and we covered most of the exposed parts with cardboard sheets, leaving only the counter openings and its border. Some nights, I could spot random strangers peering into the darkness. I remained still, fearing the sound of my breath—there was no dearth of drunkards or crazy ones. Like the dead, they were active at night.

That night, someone tapped on the glass enclosure, and a soft voice whispered. 'Madam, madam!'

I didn't respond.

'The old man is dead. No movement. Please come,' the voice said.

My heart clogged, and a piercing ache poked. But there was nothing I could do at that late hour. Once the train services resumed some hours later, I'd report it to the SM at the terminus, who would report to the GRPF.

* * *

By the time I managed to fall asleep in the familiar, uncomfortable surroundings, the wake-up alarm shocked me. The tiny clock was also a joint property purchased by my predecessors in the BO. Some nights the clock would turn truant, the battery petered out and the rattling thuds by passengers on the ticket window catapulted me. I issued tickets, eyes heavy with sleep, hair like Medusa, beseeching my pelvic muscles to cooperate. Once the first train of the day left, I checked on the old man. Ants and flies enshrouded his lips and eyes. I called the SM in the terminus and informed him of the beggar's death.

'Are you sure he is dead?' the SM asked.

'I am not a doctor, sir, but I think he is dead,'

Infuriated by my jibe he slammed the phone saying he would send a team to remove the body.

In thirty minutes, I went to identify the body. The GRPF and two men in lungis waited for me to lock the office.

One of the lungi-clad men kept his finger beneath the beggar's nose.

'What madam! This man is still alive. You wasted our time.'

The GRP bristled. 'Madam, don't you know we pay these men to remove the body? So next time, unless you are sure he is dead, don't call us.'

'But sir, the ants have covered him. Take him away.'

'Not until he is dead. Fully. Call us when he is FULLY dead.'

I took a rag from the floor and swatted the ants from the old man's face. I should have done it earlier. I hoped he would live. I knew hope was futile. When my shift ended, the ants were back.

The old man crawled to death, inch by inch. A few days later, on my evening shift, a passenger reported the beggar's death.

I placed my finger under his nose.

He was FULLY dead.

The same GRP and the same two men came. Satisfied that the beggar was completely dead, the GRP gave me a voucher (actually, I had to write up a voucher on a piece of paper, and the GRP signed and put a seal on it) for 'shroud money'—the cost of a covering shroud to dispose of unclaimed bodies, or death by a train accident. The voucher also included the station details and time of death (reporting time). I filled in my name as the clerk reporting the death. I issued Rs 150 from the station collection against the voucher and made an entry under vouchers in our daily journal.

Along with the official shroud money, I gave another Rs 25 to the GRPF because I was aware of the liquor money spent on the two men for carrying the dead body to the nearest government hospital. These men went to a corner, gulped from a quarter bottle, and performed the thankless task at hand. (Or maybe the dead souls were thankful.) The dead bodies retrieved from the tracks were often mangled and smashed. Sometimes, the men scraped the splattered brains and bones from the tracks. No wonder these men needed courage, or their senses had to be numbed.

One of my friends, John Parangusam, came on a transfer from Mysore and was posted in a station in north Madras. He had never worked in a station when posted in Mysore, but rather held a desk job at the divisional office. His sleep was his primary necessity. To prevent passengers during night shifts who would clang the booking window asking umpteen irrelevant questions or offer him arrack packets, he locked the office and slept on the platform bench. He chose the bench farthest from the office cabins because the equipment inside the SM's cabin made intermittent dings, disturbing him. It is a fact that train sounds do not disrupt a railway person's sleep, the horn or the rumble is melody to our ears.

One night, rankled by arguments interfering with his sleep, he opened his eyes to see an assembly at the platform's end. Two male bodies lay in a disfigured mess on the tracks. Anger giving in to despair, John croaked, 'Call a railway staff immediately.'

The pointsman said, 'Sir, you are the railway clerk. The SM has gone on an emergency break, last night's biryani is creating fireworks in his stomach. So, you please do the identification and report the run-over.'

'But I have never reported such a thing. I have no idea how it's done.'

The RPF clearing the spectators said, 'No worries I will help you out. I have enquired already. The bodies belong to a father and son who have been at loggerheads since last evening. Some property disputes. Looks like they found a solution by jumping on to the tracks. You write a report, I will furnish the age. Come let's find a paper and pen.'

John walked in a trance behind the RPF and followed his orders. He had a few sleepless nights as the mutilated bodies devolved into nightmares. When the summons came for him to be at the mortuary at the General Hospital to identify the bodies, John almost swooned. Rows of freezer boxes were pulled out for him to pick the right ones. Not one but several bodies were stacked up inside one box. John couldn't identify the father–son without the timely help of the RPF again.

During my tenure, I reported a few dead bodies run over by trains, and I still remember every single gruesome detail.

The old beggar's fully dead body was removed. They washed the stairs with phenyl, and the small space my beggars once occupied was empty. One had become two, then two had become three, and now there were none. I missed them. The begging bowl lay face down under the stairs. In time, new tenants occupied the vacant place, but I maintained my distance, wary of attachment and the aftermath.

I don't know what happened to the missing man and woman. They were a strange family of sorts under stranger circumstances. Trains came and went through the station, and life moved on. The beggars became one of the many thousands of people at the station—just passing through. I hope their journeys went on to greener pastures. Whenever I travelled, I continued to check the suburban platforms, hoping to glimpse the young man or the lady.

PLATFORM NO. 12A

EARLIER, WHEN THE BOOKING OFFICE was down on the platform, I took frequent walks, passenger gazing. I perused magazines in the bookstalls, and the shopkeeper allowed me to borrow them. Later, I returned them untarnished. Sometimes my colleagues would ask me to get them Tamil magazines. I read a lot of '*Tell me why*' and cluttered my brain with knowledge that seems to have sieved through now. Oh, I love the book stalls at the railway stations.

Every summer vacation, before boarding the train to Palghat from Madras Central station, I pulled Achan to the Higginbothams stall. I could stare at those books all day, caress them and read the blurbs. Achan bought me the Amar Chitra Katha comics, and when I began earning, I bought fiction paperbacks. I still remember the thrill I felt when I purchased my first expensive paperback, *Gone with the Wind* by Margaret Mitchell.

We had on-the-job training at a few railway stations in Madras during our two-year higher secondary schooling. Once, a cousin filled out a reservation form, and gave me the cash for reserving tickets to Palghat. I had just finished reading *Gone with the Wind*, borrowed from the school library, and was hopelessly in awe of Rhett Butler and Scarlett O'Hara. At the Egmore Station platform, I saw the book displayed at Higginbothams. I couldn't move away without buying the book. From the money my cousin had given to reserve tickets, I spent Rs 160 and purchased my first paperback, which is still displayed in my home library. To see my *Platform Ticket* on these railway stalls would be sensational.

* * *

Like I mentioned earlier, one of the highlights of the new office on the FOB was an attached restroom and tiled floors. Pure luxury, as far as booking office standards go. Earlier the washrooms were located at the other end of the platform—a common washroom the office staff shared with the public. We kept one stall locked exclusively for our use. Each visit to the bathroom meant skipping over dried or fresh faeces and soiled sanitary pads. The filth and odour were unbearable, and I remember deliberately limiting my water consumption, to cut down the washroom breaks during my eight-hour shift. Health complications cropped up off and on.

The BO rarely had attached washrooms. I sensed everyone on the platform staring at me whenever I walked to the restroom. The staring was free of charge for all the ladies, especially during 'that time of the month' when we had to carry sanitary pads in front of ogling eyes. There were no hooks or nails to hang handbags inside the stall, so I carried the pad, hiding it with my dupatta or the sari pallu. The simple act of facilitating a bodily function was like a battle sequence requiring meticulous planning, strategy and technique.

* * *

When I detrained from the EMU train, I weaved my way through the sea of passengers descending the stairs to board the already in-motion train.

Before I could enter the office, my partner Manimozhi completing the night shift was ready with her bag on her shoulders to catch the EMU, inward bound. She hollered instructions about the roster, accounts and related things, as she ran down the stairs. We were trained to grasp the implicit meanings of each other's jabber because I did the same at the end of my shift. The serpentine queue outside the counter audibly growled in disapproval.

So, before I could fling the handbag off my shoulders, I began issuing tickets, sweat clouding my glasses. I exhaled in relief as I cleared the queue within minutes and leaned against the chair.

Once my breathing calmed, I moved to sign the muster roll, declaring the cash on hand in the cash-declaration register. Then I pulled the high chair, a netted wooden chair, and heaved myself on it. I was set for the next few hours. I checked the small pad with papers clipped on it. A few pages down, hidden between blank sheets, was the one

I was looking for. It had a list of staff names with a 'counter shortage' that had yet to be paid. Against each name was an amount between Rs 5 and Rs 100. I also had a pending Rs 25 against my name.

This list was carried forward until the month's end when we received our salaries and this account was adjusted and closed, only to start a new one the next day. Sometimes, we lose money on daily transactions. At the shift's end, while reconciling the accounts, we included this 'shortage list' along with cash on hand, although it was literally only on paper. However, we always carried money equivalent to the shortage-cash list because we had to match the cash and accounts when a vigilance or auditor check happened.

On one of my night shifts, an auditor dropped by for inspection. He was a rotund jovial person whose daughter was named Sangeetha. But, wary of letting a man inside the BO at night, I requested him to come the next morning. He showed his special auditing order and said he was helpless as he was bound by duty. The entire night we stayed awake. He asked for several registers, and schlepping them drained me. Auditing done, we talked about his four daughters. Sangeetha was his youngest. I don't remember his name but a father's pride for his daughters and his dreams for them, oh, how his eyes animated. I hope his daughters are well and taking care of their old man.

So, for the shortage list, each of us carried this amount and kept it separately near the cash collection, and at the end of the shift, we took that cash home. The next clerk did the same. Even though we had money to clear the dues against our names, we let it be carried forward and cleared it only when everyone else had money to spare. It probably sounds strange, but these were our ways, and it worked flawlessly.

My associate at the season ticket (ST) window and I chatted about our spouses, kids, cooking, movies and the change of duties as we continued issuing tickets. We were like robots, entirely mechanical—two women seasoned in multitasking.

Sometimes, the men working at the abutting counters would beg me to shut up as they couldn't concentrate on issuing tickets. How could I tell them I couldn't work without the constant chattering? They blamed their headache on me. I couldn't work in silence, so I chatted with the passengers during the minuscule time they spent at my counter—from the time they thrust the money in the small opening of the ticket counter—and I pulled the right tickets and returned the balance.

The BO worked in three shifts. 06.00–13.00 hrs, 13.00–20.00 hrs and 20.00–06.00 hrs. On some days, if a colleague had an emergency, we had to forgo our rest day and work the counter.

We also had to juggle the season-ticket shifts—a split roster. Amongst the six of us, we managed one 24-hour counter, another that worked only morning and evening shifts, and the ST counter.

It was a hair-splitting job, simply drawing up the weekly roster. We had to adjust our family commitments at home and communicate about it to reflect in the weekly roster, like hospital appointments, kids' school functions, visiting parents and even movie plans. We had to obtain a prior sanction. There was zero space for spontaneity.

Amidst all this juggling of work and life, on the other side of the issuing counter, even a second's delay was greeted with loud protests of indignant fury. Ticketing clerks also have a life. I wanted to tell the nameless and the faceless, but the ocean of hands waiting for their tickets never seemed to care.

Or did they? Some did.

* * *

The death of the old beggar wasn't my first brush with death on the job. The first run-over accident I reported took place right after I joined this station. During an afternoon shift, a passenger informed us of an accident and requested one of us to inspect. The man alongside me in Counter 1, demurred, so I accompanied the passenger.

The remains of a man in a blue-and-red checkered lungi, and a plain blue full shirt lay on the tracks. A completely severed hand rested away from the body. He was lying prone; his legs splayed. Except for the severed hand, there was no other visible damage. When the passenger and I tried to turn his body to check his breath, he remained glued to the tracks. Then, we noticed blood pooling beneath his face. I rushed to alert the SM at the terminus. Before help arrived, a few more EMU trains cruised over the body.

As the booking clerk on duty, it was my responsibility to check the gender and approximate age of the body on the track and alert the GRPF police station to report the accident. These bodies were usually beyond recognition, and deducing the age was agonising.

My RPF friend Jenny—a tall, hefty woman with cropped hair, always smartly dressed in starched khakis—talked about what she saw when accompanying a senior officer to a run-over spot. The body was of a tramp with no identity card, and the person arranged to carry the body briskly flipped it twice and rammed his fist into the mouth of the dead man. Shocked and disgusted, Jenny asked her officer, 'Madam, why is this man harassing a dead body?'

The officer calmly replied with a smile, 'He is not harassing the dead man, Jenny, although it might appear so. They must thoroughly examine the body to locate and record the identification marks. They pry open the mouth of the dead body to identify the approximate age by counting the teeth. I can't be the one to flip the body, so this man does my job.'

'Ahh, ok. No wonder this man reeks of cheap liquor; he needs it to do such tasks.'

Well, I was in my full senses when it required me to jump on the tracks to check the vitals, gauge the age of the deceased and move the crookedly angled hand of a young teenager. I even tried to peel the tattered lungi of a middle-aged man from the track to cover his torso. Once I watched helplessly the twitching henna fingers of a lady gradually coming to a halt. Images that are seared on to my retinas, as fresh, as bloody as they had been then.

* * *

There was a clerk who stayed at the office even after his shift ended, recalled my friend Janaki, who was posted in a suburban station. He was in no hurry to go home because his wife managed a beauty parlour and would be busy at work. He had no one waiting at home, so he helped the other staff, issued tickets allowing them to enjoy breaks.

Some tattled about him and a female employee who worked the second shift while he stayed back. Tongues wagged. A few years later it shocked everyone when the man took his life jumping on the track in front of a train. His colleagues had to identify and report his death and arrange for the removal of his body. It was cruel of him to die this way deserting his wife, and it was no less traumatic for his colleagues, to identify his wreckage. Indeed, we never know what goes on in the human mind. What drove him into a depression to jump on to the tracks will never be answered.

* * *

My friend Inbaraj worked as a railway goods guard, and I asked him how he dealt with the overwhelming presence of death in and around the tracks every single day.

'Dealing with dead bodies is the same as dealing with the goods,' he said without a trace of emotion. 'It's a part of my job description. I stop the train, pull out all the pieces, put them on a stretcher, and hand them over to the nearest level-crossing gate or station. If the train-hit person is still alive, we call the nearest hospital, wait for an ambulance or hand over the injured to the nearest station along with their belongings and proceed further.'

'Do you know what the gate or station does with the body or the . . . remains?'

'The stationmaster hands over the body to GRP and sends it for post-mortem to see whether it is suicide or murder. If nothing is fishy about the death, the body is handed over to relatives.'

His detached voice still haunts me.

In due time, he was promoted as a passenger-train guard and shared one of his haunting experiences.

One day, while working on a passenger train, a man ran up to Inbaraj and said there was a dead body in the coach. Inbaraj headed to the coach and saw a female, roughly forty-years old, lying below the chair-car seat. It appeared as if she had vomited blood; the entire area was blood-soaked. He immediately passed on an 'all concerned message' (a radio message to the stationmaster, GRPF, etc.) The stationmaster arrived on the scene and was afraid to even come near the body. Inbaraj requested him to unload the body, but the scared SM asked him to take it to the next station. My friend insisted, as the sight would disturb other passengers, and waited for the body to be removed so he could signal the train to move. After much deliberation, a cleaning staff was called in to clear the dead body. But just as they were lifting it, the dead body started shouting! It was after midnight, and Inbaraj told me he felt his heart freeze.

Everyone, hysterical, ran in different directions. Soon, Inbaraj guessed it was a case of drug overdose. The 'dead body' came to and wiped her mouth with the back of her hand and walked out of the coach nonchalantly. The 'bloody incident' still tops his scariest moments on the job.

* * *

Another friend, Meenakshi, on a transfer from one of the major stations in Karnataka, was shocked to see her orders to join a station on the elevated line. She went to check her station and applied for sick leave immediately. These station buildings on the MRTS (Mass Rapid Transit System) are huge like a multi-storeyed supermarket, with no shops or person in sight. A mass of waste space. The plan was to have shops that would earn revenue, but the plans remained unexecuted.

Slum dwellers surrounded the cavernous, deserted station building. Hardly any passengers and a single counter. To sit there all alone was harrowing. But even after two months of sick leave, all her requests for a transfer to a different station were denied. She eventually cancelled her sick leave and joined work.

On the first morning, she caught the early 05.20 hrs bus and reached the station. It was October, and the northeast monsoon descended on Chennai with heavy rains. An eerily dark day welcomed her, and the first thing she saw as soon as she reached the office on the first floor was a pair of owls.

She sprinted towards the counter and stumbled over a bundle on the floor. And something rolled away. With a racing pulse, she opened the shutter and entered the office. Shortly after, a group of lungi-garbed men reeking of fish knocked on her counter window.

In local Tamil, in the fisherfolk's slang, a man said. 'I see you are the clerk on duty. We are here to report about the dead body that's bundled and kept outside the counter.'

Her heart lurched. Was that a dead body she had tripped on?

She gingerly closed her office room, and came out to check, worried that the men would assault her. She asked the men what she was supposed to do. Until then, she had worked in a big station with an SM and an entire railway personnel crew; here, she was alone in a new milieu. Although she spoke the local language, these men spoke a chaste local Chennai Tamil, which was difficult to follow.

First, they unwrapped the bundle; Meenakshi swayed as she saw a headless corpse. Then the men opened a cardboard box which had a head matted with blood.

Meenakshi couldn't handle the sight and closed her eyes.

The men told her to inform the RPF, who would be patrolling in one of the adjacent stations, and they would remove the dead body.

My friend dialled the other stations and reported the death. On her first day, Meenakshi stood guard over a stranger's dead body.

Over time, Meenakshi surmised that people left their unwanted old folks from home under the station building to die. Sometimes, from the nearby hospitals, the terminally ill patients with no relatives were discarded near the station building. Some deaths were the result of a gang war. This station was next to a famous fishermen's colony where one of Tamil Nadu's most feared gangsters lived.

This gangster wore thick gold chains around his neck. He led a grand life with the latest cars and security guards. He caught fish using powerboats and sold bootleg liquor. He was the uncrowned king of the volatile fishermen's colonies.

In an extensive sting encounter planned by the police, this gangster was shot dead while sipping juice in a shop near the railway station. All hell broke loose on that day. Riot mobs closed shops and the station. Meenakshi confided that everyone in that area felt safe and secure when he lived. The gangster respected and protected the government personnel.

In her time at this station, she reported several beheaded bodies lying on the track while the heads lay on the platform. The RPF and the local police were involved, and they closed these cases as 'run over by train' to avoid complications.

* * *

The duty of a railway employee isn't just reporting the dead. Sometimes it's to rescue a person. But not everyone thinks fast on their feet and has thought through the consequences of saving a life.

My colleague Anwar Hussain recollected an incident, as a train superintendent (TS) on duty on T No. 12621 TN Express MAS (Madras Central)–NDLS (New Delhi).

The TN Express had a non-stop run once it left MAS at 22.00 hrs until 04.30 hrs when it halted at BZA

(Vijayawada). At about 01.00 hrs, when the train was crossing OGL (Ongole), the pressure began falling, and the train started to slow down. Someone had pulled the alarm chain. Once that happens, the pressure drops by 15 degrees, and then gradually, the train rolls to a stop. Usually, the train travels the length of the train before stopping. Train No. 12621 was approximately 1 km long.

When the train stopped after 1 km, the driver hooted two long and one short signal. Then, the TS and armed RPF personnel carried dragon lamps and detrained. Two RPF men walked to the front, and the TS with two RPF walked to the train's rear to check where exactly the chain was pulled. The hissing sound or the air leak guided them to the right compartment.

In the unreserved compartment, a fourteen-year-old boy sitting with his father on the steps had dozed off and tumbled from the train. The father immediately grabbed the red alarm chain to stop the train. The weeping father informed Anwar of the mishap, and the crew walked a few yards; then, he checked on the walkie-talkie to reach out to any neighbouring station (only up to a radius of 3 km was reachable in that WT). When no railway station responded, Anwar spoke to the driver.

'Can you reverse the train up to 1 km?'

Once the driver hesitantly agreed, the train reversed a few meters, where they found the injured boy on the side of the tracks. It was summer, and the TS had a white towel hanging on his neck to wipe the sweat, which he used as a tourniquet around the boy's bleeding head. They carried him to the brake van, and the TS picked up a few ballast stones.

Anwar Hussain ordered the driver: 'T. No. 12621, proceed at maximum permissible speed.'

He sat with the boy and the father in the brake van. He tore pages from his pocketbook and scribbled notes to alert BZA station about the train needing an ambulance to carry an injured passenger. Wrapping the small stones with these notes, he threw them to the wayside intermediate stations as the train passed through.

Despite the drama of halting and reversing the train midway for some distance, the TN Express reached BZA at the right time, where two ambulances waited, along with the station manager and a high-ranking official. They rushed the injured boy to the hospital. On seeing the official, the TS expected that there would be an inquiry into his actions, and he offered to write a report in quadruplicate at his destination as he didn't wish to cause further delay to the train and its passengers.

The train proceeded; Anwar Hussain filed his report. Surprisingly, he was not reprimanded, nor was an inquiry called for, and no one asked, 'How dare you reverse the train and endanger the lives of other passengers?'

On his next trip after the incident, he checked with the SMR at BZA about the boy. Fortunately, the boy was recuperating in his village. The TS believed that he and his clan had the power to do things to save a passenger's life.

* * *

Jenny, my RPF friend, was posted to a suburban section where a high number of train run-overs were reported. The first day on duty was called learning duty where she was instructed about her duty procedures. Gauge conversion work was happening, and in the broad gauge line, trains shuttled once in thirty minutes. On the second day of her duty she had to walk a portion of the track to reach the spot where a run-over was reported. A youth travelling on the footboard fell from a speeding train as his backpack hooked in an electrical post. He was pulled down the train and immediately succumbed to a head injury. Brain matter had splattered all over, the head was hollow. The rest of the body was twisted grotesquely. The body belonged to an employee of the airport authority, who was to fly to Mumbai the next day to join a higher position.

The first thing an RPF needs to check after confirming that the person is dead is whether the person had a bona fide ticket and was a bona fide railway passenger, to rule out illegal claims. If the person isn't dead but injured, arrangements are made to transport the person to the nearest hospital.

Thankfully, the boy had ID cards and his family was alerted. (In case of a run-over with no ID, the work doubled.) The message that was sent to the family was 'Son injured in a train accident.' It was not revealed that he was dead. Jenny worried about how the deceased person's parents would deal with such a tragedy. Just then she saw a young girl running on the tracks towards the accident site. Jenny called out to her teammate to stop her from coming closer. On enquiry, it was found that the girl was the boy's beloved, and he was on his way to meet her when the accident happened. Jenny said she skipped lunch and dinner that day and kept thinking of the boy.

On one of these spots in 2019, my friend Vasu lost his life. Some say he was under severe financial pressure and ended his life. The last memory I have of him is when he came home, months before the accident. We talked a lot about all our friends and laughed so much. He said, 'Sangee, I have forgotten all my worries while we talked. We should do this more often.'

Perhaps, I should have called him on that day. If only destiny could be changed.

* * *

Now, for a booking clerk, all of this—identifying and reporting a run over, and drawing up the voucher—was 'additional work' on top of their already hectic schedule. For many clerks, the tendency was to push the ball, or the body, to the next shift and the next clerk. Sometimes, the dead bodies on the tracks continued to stay on the tracks as the metaphorical ball was pushed further. Meanwhile, trains came and went, and the bodies got more and more battered. This used to happen mostly at night when the drivers did not want the hassle of reporting the death and increasing their workload. One cannot blame the drivers, because procuring people to carry the bodies at night was daunting. Perhaps, that's why my colleagues couldn't comprehend my alacrity in reporting the deaths as soon as I could.

Well, the most pressing reason was my inability to detach from the dead, unlike my friend Inbaraj. Even as they lay scattered over the tracks or breathing their last on the platforms, I couldn't bring myself to see them as a chore or 'goods' to be dealt with. I saw the dead bodies and wondered if it was an accident or a suicide attempt, and imagined their lives and what could have pushed them under the train. I worried about the families of these lost souls.

I saw it as a part of my duty. My colleagues often teased me, but I let it slide. However, I still have trouble equating the girl who was afraid of driving in traffic with the woman who grew to be unafraid of splattered brains and limbs. But that is how life teaches us and forces us to grow, whether we want to or not.

In all fairness, however, not all booking clerks and railway staff were as immune to the dead on the tracks or unaware of the immense significance of their jobs. There were many for whom their job and passenger/commuter safety were paramount; no matter the extra work, they far outweighed the negligent few.

PLATFORM NO. 13

I WAS WORKING at the season-ticket counter that day when Kathiravan received a call on his new NOKIA 3310. 'Ok. Ok. I will be there. Don't cry.' He turned his blanched face toward us. 'I need to go. Manimozhi has an emergency.'

'Oh, hope it's not . . .'

'Muthu drank rat poison—they're in the hospital.'

Velu said, 'Ok. You go. We will manage.' Although closing the supporting counter and functioning a single counter was a torment.

* * *

The first day I met Manimozhi, I remember that it was Holi. The passengers standing outside the counter came smeared in all sorts of colours, and someone poked his hand through the ticket window with a bit of pink powder. She shrieked as it sprinkled on her blue saree. Instead of getting angry she cheered 'Happy Holi' and waved.

I have a lot of friends; as a single child, I relied on my friends for emotional support. I boast that I make friends for life. Strangely, I have very few female friends. School friends were different, and I wasn't sure if Manimozhi and I could be friends.

Not long after I joined, I figured out my presence was encroaching; a friendship bond had catalysed among these clerks who had entered the railway service within months of each other. They had been together in this station for more than twelve years. Anwar Hussain, Kathiravan and Manimozhi were a trio.

As a rule, all booking clerks had to be transferred every four years, and everyone belonged to one union or another (the railway employee unions were mighty). The posting orders were passed but never carried out. The officer I met to request transfer from the moffusil junction challenged the two strong railway unions, rolled out posting orders and followed it up until everyone joined the station they were transferred to.

Within two days of joining, I took independent shifts. Anwar grudgingly left the station but continued to meet all of us often. The other man, Kathiravan, who was talking to Manimozhi on the first day sitting at the crooked table and whom I mistook for her husband, was actually a colleague. On my first independent duty, he was rostered beside me. He seemed to be hostile, projecting authoritative vibes. He was fastidious about his looks and groomed his French beard like it was studded with diamonds.

Kathiravan managed the roster in our office. A job no one envied. He first filled it with the shifts he wanted. He was into multi-level marketing, and preferred morning or night shifts. Next, he offered Manimozhi her preference. The rest of us got the rejected shifts. After a year of working with them, even when I was initiated into the inner circle and received my choicest shifts, I called out his unfair bias in drawing the roster. He bristled and denied it. When a man and two women form a team, a teeny-weeny extra attention to one woman distressed the other. We treaded on glass striving to maintain a friendly bond.

If Manimozhi got her favourite shifts, work happened without friction. She begrudged me the attention I received at times but never rebuffed me. We had a love–hate relationship. I felt bad about upsetting her kingdom.

When I was newly married, the roster man tried not to give me night shifts. Later, when I had morning sickness during my pregnancy, I was rostered for evening shifts.

Manimozhi and her husband, Muthu, lived with her three children—a son, two daughters, the elder one only a few years younger than I—and her unmarried sister. The sister managed the house while Manimozhi worked shifts. She always believed that with our odd work timings, someone to cook and care for her home was a boon. When the sister visited other relatives, Manimozhi applied for leave. She couldn't manage work and home.

Manimozhi was an excellent cook, and on rare days when she cooked instead of her sister, she often packed lunch for me and even spoon-fed me while I issued tickets. The taste of her drumstick sambar and potato fry still lingers on my tongue. Recently, when we met at Kathiravan's retirement function, I reminded her of it, and she said that day, she had prepared the same combination at home. And if she had known that I still remembered the taste, she could have packed a box for me.

Oh, the two of us were particular about the right food combination. Green banana bhajji (fritters) with coconut chutney (from the Nair tea stall), poori and potato curry (from the hotel across the road), curd rice with mango pickle (when bored to cook anything else), biryani and brinjal salna (from the mobile vendor right below our BO window; the men warned us it would be crow and not chicken that was served, but we relished it) . . . the list goes on.

Our colleague Nalini, who was supposed to sweep the platform, would sit and stare at Kathiravan starry-eyed. The poor woman missed her absconding husband, and although the photo she showed of him did not in any angle resemble Kathiravan, she continued to say, ah, Kathiravan looks like my husband and talks like my lost husband. Kathiravan walks like my dear husband.

Nalini employed a homeless woman, Rani, to sweep the platforms and paid her from her salary. Rani was a short, thin woman with protruding yellow teeth coupled with mouth sores. Manimozhi and I paid Rani to sleep inside the BO during our night shifts. But we ordered her to brush and bathe on those nights, otherwise the unpleasant stink kept us awake. Some nights, she never turned up— her freshly bathed body invited admirers, and she left us kicking our heels while she made quick money.

At least we didn't suffer like my junior Prabhu. I met him recently at the Army Officers Mess. He wrinkled his nose and shuddered remembering his reeking colleague. While working as a TC, Prabhu enjoyed issuing tickets, loading parcels along with the porters and doing all manner of odd jobs in the station whenever he was bored of standing, collecting tickets. He detested his absentee workmate—*Azhukku* (dirty) Thiruvengadam, who bathed once in ten days only. No exaggeration. This Thiruvengadam slept in the running staff restroom and left his colleagues to continue shifts in a row. Prabhu said that the disgusting smell made him gag whenever Azhukku turned up for duty.

At least, our Rani heeded us. We asked Nalini why she would hire someone to sweep and waste her salary. She answered that when her husband was with her, he treated her like a queen, and she hadn't fallen to such lows to sweep platforms. Her dignity was essential. She believed she was on par with us clerks because Kathiravan had trained her to issue tickets, and she cleared the queue while we sipped our tea or relished our bhajjis. Nalini ate with us, but she refrained from sharing food with her 'employed' and treated her with disdain.

Although Manimozhi and I were furious at her double standards, we condoled and included Nalini when we visited the houses of our coworkers during Navaratri Golu, to movie theatres or shopping. But when she tried to boss us, Manimozhi snubbed her. I was young and humoured her. She reminded me of my Zahira Begum.

Sometimes, I think I was a pushover, but I let these people have their little triumphs. I reserved all my temper tantrums for my mother and husband.

Manimozhi was the only colleague who attended my wedding, which took place at a temple. (Manimozhi, too, had a love marriage) She was the oldest among the attendees of my wedding. She was the only colleague who came home during the brief window of my motherhood and saw my firstborn son.

When I rejoined after maternity leave—which coincided with the Twin Tower collapse—where I gained and lost a son, she never treated me with sympathy. When the others gazed at me with cloying commiseration and smothered me, Manimozhi did no such thing. She treated me the usual way, competing for the favourite morning shifts in Counter 2. (Counter 1 was complex, with many tickets and more responsibilities.) We women had seen the worst together, inundated with personal demons we buffed and moved on, although the overshadowing sadness sheathed us like a second skin.

* * *

Once we were on the morning shift, a rare day with less traffic, Manimozhi suddenly jumped from the tall chair and rushed out. I issued tickets, keeping an eye on the happenings outside the counter. A group of college girls were chatting with a stout bald man. Manimozhi smacked the girls and thundered, 'Don't you girls have sense ahn? Your parents are sending you to college with such high hopes, and here you are . . . get lost all of you.' And she raised her hand at the man and shouted, 'If I see you here again, I will report you to the police ahn.'

Manimozhi returned snarling, 'That man is a pimp ahn. I heard from the vendors on the platform that he lures college girls by promising them big pocket money. These girls who dream of luxury fall easy prey to the racket. The girls are pimped to rich men ahn.'

She had read in the regional newspaper that many of the college girls were lured into these easy money-making schemes.

'Shouldn't we report him?' I asked.

'The police demand proof. And he would easily bribe them and get out ahn.'

Anyway, her threats worked; the pimp operated elsewhere, and we never saw him in our station premises again.

A few days later, a regular customer confirmed the activities of the despicable person. This lady frequented our station once or twice a week, attired in bright colours, a truss of jasmine on her thick black mane, a faux leather handbag and a pink flowery umbrella. She waited for the queue to clear, then giggled excessively and chatted before buying her tickets. She addressed us, 'Halloooo friendzzz.' When I told her my name and asked hers, she winked and said, 'Nithya Kalyani.'

Once she left, Manimozhi explained her profession and what she meant by calling herself Nithya Kalyani, roughly translated as 'daily bride.'

* * *

During these years I suffered from a damaged voice box. Yes, too much talking had inflamed my vocal cords, and the railway doctor advised me a week of non-verbal communication. Placed on sick leave and buried in books, my throat and my husband revelled. When the doctor suggested extending the treatment for another week, my husband almost hugged him. Later after my promotion to the Passenger Reservation counter, assailed by severe spondylosis due to bad posture and 'too many neck movements', I worked a few weeks wearing a dog collar. However, Manimozhi who talked a lot never damaged her vocal cords.

* * *

On a day of heavy rush, when the tickets had to be replenished in the tubes once in twenty minutes, Manimozhi and I squeezed into the tiny space between the ticket racks and issued tickets together in a single window. There was no space to open a third counter. After my ST shift, I stayed over to assist others for a little while. A passenger thrust a small coin purse and said it must have fallen off some passenger while buying a ticket. The tiny pouch still held the warmth of the unknown bosom.

We waited for a week, but no one claimed the purse. When we opened the tiny purse, currency notes were crammed into it. Manimozhi and I went to a temple, tucked a little into the hundi, and ordered biryani for everyone in the BO. I had the small purse with me for a long time; I used it as my coin purse until the zipper fell off.

* * *

My friend Bharathi, working in Mysore, shared with me that twenty-eight years ago, someone surrendered a key chain carrying the imprint of Goddess Lakshmi during her morning shift. She informed everyone in the BO to call her if someone came searching for it. The silver key chain still hangs from her bureau locker in her home, reminding her of the unknown stranger.

* * *

There was an influx of youth from northern India selling sugar candy in small plastic packets on trains and platforms. I relished this pink candyfloss until I grasped what goes into its concoction. During my rounds on the platform, I noticed these boys picking up discarded tickets. On further probing, they answered in Tamilish Hindi—the card tickets were one of the main ingredients of the cheap fluffy pink candyfloss. YUCK!

* * *

Manimozhi, Kathiravan and I were besties in our BO, much to the chagrin of the other men working with us. So, the day when Kathiravan attended the call from Manimozhi and deserted his counter, I took up extra work after closing my season-ticket counter. Then I rushed to the hospital to meet Manimozhi. Kathiravan was still there. She lumbered over and hugged me tightly. When the calamity struck, she was in her uniform saree, ready to leave home for the morning shift.

Sometimes I feel guilty that I came in between two friends. When he favoured me over her, allotting me easier shifts, she took it hard.

Kathiravan fell into bad times because of his multi-level marketing business, for which he rented an office with some friends. When things became challenging, his partners scooted, leaving him to face the investors. The situation worsened, and his continuing in the railways became a big question.

Fortunately, saved by the goodwill he enjoyed, Kathiravan was able to rejoin work. Whenever he talks about big money schemes, I warn him to think multiple times and not jeopardize his government salary and secure job.

It was Kathiravan who advised me not to pursue Union activities. There was a time when I managed to draw a considerable population of female employees to attend a railway union meeting, and the higher-ups awarded me a post of some value in our suburban section. I attended a few member meetings along with Kathiravan, who was also someone with clout in the union. But soon, as I gained popularity, he advised me to resign from the post. As expected, I insinuated that he was jealous of my rise. He said, 'You are my good friend. I don't wish you any trouble; you don't know how some people could slander you about your sudden rise in the union. The other women in the Union are older, wiser and can withstand the pressures. You are too outspoken for your own good. You are ill-suited here. Moreover, they will call you for meetings at odd times; I may not always be able to accompany you.'

* * *

At the hospital, Manimozhi crumbled, clinging to me. For some months, Manimozhi was distraught and had fought with Muthu a lot. That day, she had confronted her husband and slurred him. To prove his innocence, the fellow picked up a bottle of rat poison and gulped it. The following day he was discharged with a warning.

After many years, I asked Manimozhi if all was well between her and Muthu. She answered, 'Yes. I need peace. I am unsure if it was all in my head. Maybe Muthu wasn't lying. Anyway, I overlooked it. If my home functions smoothly and I can peacefully do my shifts at the counter, I am ok with it.'

I met many men and women who battled all odds to work the demands of erratic shift duties. Not everyone had someone at home to manage the house. I felt grateful because I had my mother-in-law to cook and deal with other aspects at home. She was my strength, a strong support in times of need. A state government pensioner, she understood the rigours of an office job for a woman.

PLATFORM NO. 14

THE DAY STARTED WITH A bang as I entered the BO
for my morning shift. There was an unusual hustle
and bustle everywhere at the railway station. Summer
holidays had begun, and a few sports meets were
scheduled, so passenger traffic peaked. On top of it was
a local celebration.

A few of us counter staff from the suburban stations
were pulled out of our regular habitat and ordered to work
shifts at the junction station. We manned the counters for
platform tickets and open tickets for express trains.

'Expect some heavy rush,' said the supervisor, adding as he smiled, 'Keep your cool today. Let's avoid any complaints.'

Secretly, I knew his comment was aimed at me and my colleague—my friend and competitor—at the counter. We ensured that we always took our small breaks together. Not just because we were great friends, nope—it was to ensure that the other didn't get undue advantage in our counter collections. We always had the busiest counters.

All trains to the major city were overfilled, and we warned every passenger that we would charge a cancellation fee if they didn't travel. The SPTMs spewed the yellow tickets at supersonic speed, and money was all over our counters. The heated exchanges on change, the odd ones in the lines shouting to make it faster, and the seemingly endless queues added to the tense atmosphere. It was so demanding that we asked the supervisor to lock the door to avoid the many railway staff coming in with requests for tickets for their friends who wished to skip the line outside.

Close to 11.00 hrs, the time for the express to leave, my friend and I galloped to the last lap. We shifted gears, grinning at each other and charged. Frankly, I doubt that we had the time to let out a breath. Imagine plucking the currency from the third person in line while printing the ticket of the one in front of me, and the second person's details already stored in my memory chip. We were clerks with supernatural powers when situations demanded.

And we could be nasty as well. Basically, a customer begets what he throws, err, what he deserves.

* * *

My friend Siluvai who had shared a KitKat with a beggar and me, told me that a passenger had once thrown currency inside the counter on a busy day.

'Hello, why are you throwing the money? Can't you push it inside the counter?' said Siluvai.

'I am in a hurry. Pick it up and issue the ticket. Don't waste my time talking.'

Siluvai picked up the currency and issued the tickets. For the balance of Rs 10 he had to give, he took two five-rupee coins and tossed one in a way that the coin pitched and glided out.

'What are you doing? Tit for tat, eh?'

'No, that was tit, and this is tat.' He tossed the other coin, which rolled down the stairs in front of the counter. The passenger tottered behind his coin.

We believe, 'Give respect, take respect.'

* * *

Once my friend Janaki on a busy shift asked a customer if he had small change to make the transaction easier. The man responded by saying it was the clerk's responsibility to give the balance. She politely asked him to stand aside until she could get the required change by issuing tickets to the other passengers.

Miffed, he lodged a complaint against her. He was a regional transport officer and deemed his time was more important. A supervisor intervened and tried to pacify the egoistic customer. Janaki even apologized and accepted that it was her responsibility to bring small change of Rs 100 to Rs 200 from home to sail through the day.

I never had such an issue of shortage of coins ever at my counter. Because I asked every customer during my shift for small change. Everyone carried coins, they required a nudge to forage. So, when a rowdy customer turned up, I had coins to ward off the devil. At the end of my shift, I accumulated a wealth of coins. My colleagues scorned if

I had been sitting at the counter or with a begging bowl outside the adjoining mosque.

* * *

The last-minute tickets(s) printed out of our counters when the supervisor instructed us to stop as the train might leave at any moment. Vaguely, I felt a presence behind me, or rather at my right side, and not wanting to take my eyes off the counter, I ignored it. A few more moments passed, and I sensed a movement behind me again. Cash was on the floor near my chair, over the SPTM, overflowing in the drawers. Agitated, I shut my cash drawer and turned to the person behind me.

'Just step back. You have no business standing here. If you need anything, meet the supervisor.' Enraged, I called the supervisor and asked why he had allowed anyone near the cash counters. Once again, I pointed to the supervisor's cabin and said, 'Please move from here and go there.'

While the supervisor appeared stunned and speechless, the person said calmly, 'I am very sorry I came near your counter without introducing myself. My name is T and I am from the Railway Board Vigilance.'

I struggled to regain my composure. I apologized for being rude but maintained that he could have stood farther until the counter was closed. Did I just tempt fate? I wondered. But then we (my batchmates and I) were known for our straightforward and bold manner in talking to an officer or anyone. The youthful boiling blood, perhaps.

The Vigilance Inspector said that he understood my reaction. I had to wait and see whether his report would reflect it. He instructed me to close my counter and tally the cash. Rs 6/- was in excess. Fate chuckled looking past my shoulder.

He asked me to explain—my only justification was the abnormal rush.

'Please re-check your collection,' he said.

His expression changed when I replied that I needed to tally only once and that Rs 6/- was certainly excess. Confidence at its zenith. He insisted, and I re-checked it. I was right. He instructed me to remit it and write an explanation, which I did. I made sure to point out that the number of tickets was way higher than the daily average compared to the other counters in the shift, besides mentioning that the excess was a negligible percentage of my transactions. I cannot say if I was afraid or upset. On other days, my collection and ticket count would have demanded a treat from other staff.

I asked, 'What punishment should I expect?'

'I don't know,' the VI said. I looked at his crinkled eyes. 'But it all depends on how you write your report.'

Thud, thud. I heard the loud sound of fate thumping a fist on its head. Too late to scarf my words. I have seen my colleagues writing lengthy explanations for vigilance reports, any amount however small, in excess or shortage, we are accountable. Sometimes this will result in a privilege pass cut and a remark in the service register.

Years later, when I worked the morning shift at the Passenger Reservations System (PRS), a cousin of mine demanded I book a ticket for a train on the opening day of the Advance Reservation Period. When I informed her that inside booking was not possible, especially for the first 30 minutes of the booth opening because rules were strict and the reservation forms of people standing in the queue were numbered, my cousin discredited me, blamed my indifference and since then our relationship has soured.

Many believe it is an easy task for a railway employee to book tickets or release an emergency quota (EQ). But there are many factors involved; in reservation centres, you have these numbered forms and surprise vigilance checks, and in the case of EQ, one never knows when a demand from higher officials might crop up, dwarfing the

EQ application sent by a low-key employee. Moreover, if caught carrying excess cash other than the cash declared in the 'Personal Cash Register' our job would be in peril.

Three months passed, and this incident of Rs 6 in excess ruled my mind; I worried about what punishment awaited me. More than the punishment, the maiden remark that would go into my record bothered me. I never shared it with my family, which I later recognized was a mistake since I could have gotten over it easier and earlier.

* * *

Quite recently, a colleague in the reservation office had a Vigilance Inspection that turned unpleasant. She suffered from a urinary infection and had to use the washroom urgently. An ECRC from a neighbouring station had come by for a chat. She requested him to issue tickets from her counter while she attended the emergency. He was notorious for helping the ticket agents. When she returned, unfortunately, the vigilance officers followed.

Vigilance checks were a regular affair. Several officers would suddenly pop in and ask the clerks to cease ticketing and tally accounts with cash.

When she tallied, she found she had excess cash on hand. Neither she nor the visiting ECRC could utter a word in defence. She was punished with a three-year increment cut.

So, the situation could turn bad anytime. A harmless loo break resulted in a financial drain.

* * *

A vigilance inspector on an enquiry asked my colleague Velu, 'Did you see the Duty Card Pass of this employee when you issued him a ticket?'

As a rule, while booking a ticket on a DCP the PNR must be noted on it. However, when booking, no clerk sees the DCP and fills in the DCP number furnished in the reservation form.

Replying to the VI, Velu said, 'Sir, on record I have seen the DCP. But off the record, I haven't seen it. Why waste papers writing reports and your precious time on a futile enquiry? Tomorrow you will have to wind up the report stating that the clerk has seen the DCP while booking but has no idea if it was an original or duplicate DCP.'

Velu got away with it because he was aware it was only a customary vigilance check.

* * *

One morning, when I received a summons from the main boss's office at the Divisional HQ, I expected the worst. My ordeal of Rs 6 excess would end today.

Eyebrows raised, he asked, 'Do you have any contacts at the Railway Board?'

'I had a contact three months back.' Thankfully, my sarcasm didn't register.

'We received the report of the vigilance check with clear instructions to issue only a strict warning to the employee.'

I was speechless. This warning would not go into my service register.

'Thank you, sir,' I mumbled.

Was it because the VI was such a reasonable man? Or did standing up for myself convince the VI that I didn't belong to the standard breed of railway personnel? Some senior staff accused me of insolence when I expressed my opinion. Was anyone else involved in taking up my case in a personal way to the higher rungs? Or was it pure luck? Fast forward twenty-seven years later, and I still wonder why it ended that way.

PLATFORM NO. 15

THE PHONE TRILLED. I STRETCHED my hand on the side table, checked the caller and cut the call. Why was she calling so early in the morning? The snoring husband and the cosy blanket lulled me back to sleep. The message tone chimed in and I checked the mobile. It was her, again. My colleague and friend Manimozhi. She hadn't contacted me in a long time.

'Ebenezar Johnson passed away.'

Who was this Johnson? I lay awake, trying to remember the dead man. Unable to douse my curiosity, I shifted to the living room and called her mobile. By then, another friend's message flashed on the mobile—the same message accompanied by a picture.

Oh shit! This was Ebe, my old colleague; I dialled Manimozhi. The line was engaged.

Sleep entirely out of my system, I poured water into the kettle and slipped a teabag into a mug. I slid on to the cane chair and watched the inky skies bleeding splotches of pink-orange. I opened my mobile to click a picture, but Ebe's photo popped up and I sat back sipping chai while the sun did its job. The memories unspooled; the tea soothed me.

Ah, Ebe liked his tea with cardamom.

* * *

He joined our station when Sethupathi moved to a place closer home on transfer. Sethu was timid, and all of us took advantage of him. If we were his relievers at work, we turned up late consistently, and if he was our reliever, we demanded that he come early. He complied without ever raising his voice or eyes.

Sethu preferred evening shifts, as in the mornings he had to get his children ready for school every day. His wife was a manager in a company, and she managed him well. He did all housework, was thin as a stick and confided that his wife wasn't interested in cooking. He consumed a lot of tea and biscuits at work.

Oh, how Manimozhi, Kathiravan and I ganged up and ragged him. Poor guy, he was relieved to leave our station. But soon news reached us that we were angels compared to his new colleagues. Sethu suffered his bossy wife at home. At work, he accepted everyone's demands. Manimozhi and I were protective if anyone other than the three of us treated him wrongly. It was our sole right. Such inhumaneness.

But all things come to an end. Ebe was nothing like Sethu.

* * *

Ebe arrived late, exceptionally late, on his first day at our station. A whole ninety minutes late. A raging Manimozhi pushed the chair. She eyed the supervisor to issue a warning to Ebe.

'I brought you biryani. I knew you would be hungry. I am sorry I am late.'

He gave a packet of steaming biryani to Manimozhi and offered one to me (I was at the second counter) and one packet to the CBS. Manimozhi's stomach growled, and she slumped on the chair at the supervisor's table.

'Come, Sangeetha, let's eat ahn.'

I'd had an early lunch, but the aroma enticed me. While the three of us relished our biryani, Ebe, with a practised finesse, issued tickets. It was the first time he had looked at these ticket tubes in our BO, and I wondered how he had adapted so quickly.

But some people are gifted in adapting and adopting new tricks of the trade.

Years later, when I moved to a different station on promotion, there was an influx of recruits from Bihar. The state to which the railway minister belonged. As seniors, we had to train them to issue computerized reservation tickets. Some of my colleagues sniggered, 'They look like duffers; who can train them?' All the recruits were boys aged between 21 and 23. Some seemed scared—new place, new language—reminding me of the day I joined a station in Karnataka. Some looked confident as if they owned the place. A timid, bespectacled boy looked at all of us at the counters and walked toward mine.

'Madam, can I sit beside you? Will you teach me?'

'Sure. Pull up a stool and sit. I will explain the process.'

The remaining boys found their teachers, and we began training them.

Kishore Kumar Jha, my apprentice, displayed such brilliance that within an hour of observing the process and asking questions, he requested, 'Ma'am, can I issue tickets?'

'Really?'

His unwavering confidence stunned me. The teacher moved aside and watched with pride as the student took the reservation form and typed in the keys. After watching Kishore for ten minutes, I took a coffee break. During summer vacation in Palakkad, I watched my amma and *ammamma* sit around a huge mortar grinding rice. While Amma rotated the heavy pestle at regular intervals, ammamma gently nudged the fluffy batter into the grinding pit. Likewise, I gently nudged Kishore whenever he faltered with the language.

Soon, he learned a bit of Tamil needed to function efficiently—*Enge?*(where) *Entha* (which) train? *Illeppa* (no) and *seriya?* (correct)—and took up independent duty at a counter beside me. His mathematical skills amazed me and sometimes I used him as a human calculator. He endeared me with his humbleness and gratitude. I reiterated that it was not my training but his brilliance, yet he continued to treat me as his guru. He left the railways and is now an officer in another government sector. Now, he shares the short stories he pens and works on my input. Something he always said delighted me, 'Madamji, *sar ankhon par.*' (By all means, with great pleasure/your wish is my command.)

* * *

While we relished the biryani, Ebe spoke tenderly, his penetrating gaze bored into each of our eyes. 'My daughter Sofia, my angel, comes home from school at 13.00 hrs. Her school operates in two shifts. Sofia goes to morning school, and my wife is a big shot in a law firm. Every day, I love getting Sofia ready for school, cooking her favourite breakfast, packing her snack box, dropping her at school, and then picking her up and dropping her at my sister's place. So I can only work evening shifts, and I can arrive only at this time. Every day.'

We ate a lot of biryanis during those days.

On days when Sofia's school closed, Ebe did any shift, sometimes even double shifts, and we could go on leave. The biryani never stopped, and when we said we had enough of the biryani, he ordered pizzas and burgers. He was particular about only one holiday—Christmas, because it was Sofia's birthday.

He promised to bring Sofia to our station someday. But before that happened, he was transferred to a station near his home.

Manimozhi called me and gave me the details. Ebe died at home of Covid complications. Sofia was married and stayed in the US. Flight services hadn't resumed yet.

* * *

There was this guy, Chandran, a leave reserve in the section who frequented our station whenever an acute shortfall of workforce arose. A tall, dark baldie with hairy ears, always dressed in a white shirt and black pants. He punched in on time and agreed to work beyond his shift timings if we requested. He was quick and efficient at work. But he helped himself from the station's collections. The person who relieved him would find a shortage ranging from Rs 20 to Rs 500 depending on his necessities on that day. He enjoyed his 'drinks' and wafted a splash of the spirits he had guzzled before taking up duty. And, to top it all, after that day, it would take him months to visit our station; until then, we clerks ran an account on his name against the amount shortage in the earnings.

He shared his birthday with my second-born son. I wished Chandran a happy birthday if he happened to visit us thereabouts his birthday. It made him emotional, and he said, 'No one remembered my birthday.' I am so sorry that your son is no longer alive for you to celebrate his birthday.'

When I heard of his demise due to liver failure, I shed tears. I continue to pray and wish him along with my son on April 10 every year.

* * *

Then there were a few men who treated us women like commodities. Their sly looks and whispers flustered us. One guy complained that my constant chatter with the public gave him headaches. I chatted with every customer while he worked with an evil sneer. Some of the jokes these men spouted were outright nasty and dirty, and Manimozhi and I acted as if we did not get it. Perhaps we never had the guts to confront. I am not sure if they ever got reported.

Looking back, I see that the colleagues at my first station were gentler men. My earlier colleagues were only concerned with my efficiency at work, and I never felt threatened working alongside them. The first clerk who taught me ticketing had a peg or two when he came for the winter night shift. Never once did he forget who I was or where we were. Another clerk made me write all the reservation charts (four coaches of seventy-two passengers each), and that was the way he troubled me rather than giving me sly looks or talking nonsense.

I requested a Commercial Supervisor (CS) of the busiest reservation office in Chennai to sign my relieving order and send me to the smaller reservation office printed on my posting order because I couldn't cope with the multitude of personnel at the large reservation office. My husband worked abroad; I was friendly with everyone. Caste, gender, rich, poor, customer, ticket agent . . . I talked with everyone. When I was promoted to the reservation office, I was sent to work in the main reservation complex to gain experience before being sent to my posting station. This was the norm followed. It was a huge PRS with hundreds of ECRC. And everyone talked behind everyone's backs, there was mud-slinging and name-calling . . . I was horrified.

I met the CS and said, 'Sir, please send me to the smaller PRS. I am terrified to work amongst these people.'

He cocked his head. Earlier, on two occasions, I had met him to request casual leave. The other clerks warned me that he didn't grant leave easily. When he sanctioned my CL, both times, tongues wagged and eyes rolled. I informed my colleagues that I gave the real reason, and he appreciated my honesty. I got my leave sanctioned.

Once: Sir, I have booked tickets for a movie, I need the leave.

Second: Sir, I have a party at home, how can I come the next day?

So, when I asked him to send me to my station, he said, 'Ok. Usually, an ECRC stays here a minimum of a year, some stay on and do not go to their stations. This is the first time someone has been so honest with me. Do not change. All the best.'

Within a day I was sent to my station.

I wasn't aware of dealing with men who thought I was easy prey if I had a cup of tea with them or shared my lunch box. A lady workmate asked me if there was something going on between me and the guy with whom I had tea because he was bragging about it. When the CS released me, the others in our office asked me how I managed that. What did I charm him with?

Perhaps the world was a better place earlier, and it gradually poisoned the inhabitants and turned them dangerous.

Perhaps I was a misfit.

Perhaps . . .

PLATFORM NO. 15A

THEN TWO LADIES JOINED OUR station.

One was a hare-brained older woman, Girija, who was too slow at the counter. Her frizzy hair and constant smile reminded one of an affable aunt. My work doubled if I partnered with her. She was gullible and always had a shortage at the end of her shift. The number of tickets sold and cash on hand never tallied; she spent extra hours in the BO after her shift ended, grappling with the figures on the calculator.

On some days when there was a long queue, Girija would lie flat on the floor announcing that she yearned for a stretch. Like Garfield she did a full body stretch, awakening her muscles. It perplexed me and the passengers. But Girija slackened her taut sinews, purred in satisfaction and recommended ticketing within a minute.

The other, Ranjini, was tall, with her hair in a tightly pulled bun—a single jasmine pinned on it—and a scalding tongue for annoying passengers. All three women, Manimozhi, Girija and Ranjini, were ten or more years older than me. The years I spent with them have changed me. I preferred friendships with wiser women, their experiences forever grounding me. As years passed, my older friends looked up to me for my direct and blunt manner, and valued my opinions. Non-judgemental, they call me (though I disagree), and they prefer sharing the problems and dilemmas of their lives with me. Once I embarked on my writing journey, I asked them if I could write about them, and they readily agreed. Our stories need to be told and heard, is their united opinion.

Now, I am at the age they were when we worked together, and I see many younger women confiding in me their deepest fears, and seeking solace. My husband calls me 'agony aunt,' but I refrain from advising or passing judgement and allow the women to talk through and decide their path. All they need is a listener.

Tell this to my amma and she would scoff: you don't have time to lend me an ear. Oh, that's her relentless complaint.

* * *

It would be an exaggeration to say that Ranjini's creators were pleased to see her born. Her mother pushed her out in an expert technique; after all, she was doing it for the eighth time. The midwife cut the connecting cord with detachment; little did she know she was severing a bond that would never reconnect.

The birth of the eighth child could never be exceptional unless it were in mythology where Lord Krishna was born to greatness. Ranjini's was an average birth destined to no greatness. She heard the proverb in the vernacular language spoken aloud a lot while growing up: the eighth born encountered obstacles wherever it turned. How true, indeed.

Like weeds in the garden, Ranjini grew up unwanted and continued to progress into adolescence. She preferred to stay in the shadows of her elder siblings. The parents did not stop with the eighth release; a few little ones followed after Ranjini. Of all the twelve childbirths her mother underwent, ten went on to live beyond teenage.

Ranjini was a hardworking student and completed her school education, rebelling against her parents, who wanted to lower their burden by marrying her off. A minuscule ray of luck favoured her, and she joined the railways as 'summer staff'. She did odd jobs around the office and trained to issue tickets. When the railways decided to do a lateral absorption of the summer staff into the cadres, Ranjini landed a job designated as 'commercial clerk', a government employee with a pension. The next step in her life was marriage when providence deserted her.

She stayed with her schoolteacher husband for hardly a month before she left his home, broken and bruised. When her parents and siblings advised her to compromise, adjust and return to the teacher, one of her brothers supported her decision to stay back. The teacher waited for her return for a year, then sent the divorce papers to become a new groom again.

Ranjini conformed to divine will. She never had great hopes until she met him, to whom she bequeathed her heart. He was gentle, respected and treated her well— all attributes which would shoot romantic feelings in a vulnerable woman. She discounted the fact that he was her cousin's husband.

When Ranjini and I worked in adjacent counters in our station, she blushed whenever she said her husband would be arriving for the weekend and she needed a leave. A few years into our friendship, she revealed the status of her love life. Neither Manimozhi nor I pronounced any judgements and this further strengthened our bond.

I went through financial tempests combined with the grief of losing not one but two sons in successive years. These friendships and the life lessons of the strong women guided me throughout. This too shall pass—my mantra for life.

I joined the railway union and was conferred a 'post' in our section. I organized a meeting of the Commercial Department lady staff in the section. The ladies had simple demands—provide comfortable (unbroken) working chairs and a restroom inside the BO. The perils and hazards of sharing public toilets, where dangers lurked in the form of infections and rowdy molesters, were plenty.

I paraded into every BO and discussed the duty roster with CBS. In a never-before-seen turnout, the women staff attended the meeting, paving my way into the annals of the railway union. Ah, nothing spectacular happened after that. A few unbroken chairs were brought in from some other stations (and later taken back). The call for tenders and execution was too tedious, so the plans were discarded.

When an opportunity opened, I cleared the department examination, received a promotion, left the CC cadre and became an ECRC—Enquiry cum Reservation Clerk. I joined the new cadre and my new station when India's first female President moved into Rashtrapati Bhavan.

* * *

As an ECRC, I met and worked with more amazing specimens of the fairer sex. Umm, the stronger sex.

Ann Maria was a decade older, and we immediately built an everlasting bond, as are all my bonds. Decked in a neat, pleated saree that never rumpled, her lustrous long hair in a neat plait and a pearl string on her neck. She battled serious health complications but exuded verve. When I befriended female colleagues earlier, I was young and unmarried, and then I went through the phases of a love marriage and my brief stints of motherhood. Those women saw me evolve from a girl to a woman.

Here, I was in my thirties, scarred and blemished, but displaying irrefutable positivity, and my life experiences matched with those of women far beyond my age.

Ann had married young, out of her caste and language, to a man who had weathered the highs and lows of life in quick succession. The couple lived abroad for a while. She availed a long duration of leave and rejoined the railways when they returned to India, losing a chunk of years from her railway service. Ann was placed in the junior category and pushed through years of work to see promotions, while her batchmates superseded her. Her husband tried out new business ventures every other month. Ann supported his idiosyncrasies and her children's education.

We loved working the same shifts in adjoining counters, going on tea breaks together and sharing almost every detail of our lives. There were no secrets between us; we had each other's backs. To have friends who held a position that could turn threatening any day but remained a haven of love always . . . Well, I am blessed.

Ann and I competed, aiming for the maximum number of reservation forms handled at the end of a shift. To have the highest earnings in the sale of tickets was a bonus. There were instances where we issued Rajdhani first AC tickets that escalated our revenues and persuaded cancellation of tickets of extensive amounts to be done at the adjacent counters.

To comprehend our enthusiasm for handling the maximum reservation forms, let me tell you what my diplomat friend divulged the other day. He thumped the table and disclosed, 'Do you know when I worked in a PRS, I issued more or less 180 forms in a shift? I felt such pride. Now, that job satisfaction eludes me.'

Ann and I have always stayed in contact. Ann, afflicted by many losses, recently that of her husband, asked me, 'Will my son get a job if I die before retirement?' It impaled me, but I maintained my composure. 'They don't do that anymore. The rules have changed. So don't bother to think from that angle. Moreover, your son is better suited for other things.'

I met her the day after her husband's funeral. While dressing up to meet her, I hesitated. Should I sport a bindi when her forehead would be empty? Donning a tiny bindi and a pastel kurta, I got there to see her radiant in a bright red saree, a big bindi, and flowers on her head. The tradition demanded her to remain dressed up like a new bride until the third-day ceremony, where they would remove the marks of a married woman and initiate her into widowhood.

We hugged, cried, laughed and spoke of tickets, reservation offices and passengers.

* * *

Girija, my Garfield colleague, celebrated her first Women's Day with me. I believe in Pay it Forward. Do you remember the TTE who bought me tea and biscuits to celebrate my first-ever Women's Day? It seems that until her demise soon after her retirement, Girija always gushed about the one Women's Day we celebrated together. Ranjini met her often, and they always spoke about me and that Women's Day.

I requested the male colleagues in our BO to grant leave to all four women for Women's Day. Ranjini, Manimozhi, Girija and I—dressed in sarees printed in the same design but different colours—met for lunch in a restaurant and watched a movie together. Nalini was on long leave and couldn't join us.

To discern that Girija, who completed almost thirty-five years in the railways, felt that 'one' day was a high point in her life was heartbreaking. Her husband's job paid a trifling. With the education and wedding of her daughters, she had enough troubles compounded by the daily shortage at her counter, but ask anyone if they remember Girija: 'Oh yes, the one who always smiled with her lips and eyes.'

* * *

My batchmate Meenakshi who guarded a headless corpse on her first day, told me of the two women at her station. One was a sweeper, who was like her guardian angel at work. She refers to her as her 'Rail Mother'. This Sandhanamma belonged to the fisherfolk colony and commanded great respect in her community. Her presence by my friend's side assured her a safety net within which she performed her duties surrounded by sordid restrooms and cavernous corridors lurking dangers, where warring factions used the station building to resolve their issues.

Sandhanamma respected Meenakshi to the extent that she involved my friend in a case where two hearts had to be melded.

A young boy from her colony employed as a swimming coach entrusted his heart to the daughter of a Brahmin cook. Meenakshi accompanied the boy and talked to the girl's father on behalf of his family. As expected, the agitated father spewed venom, but my friend calmed him down with objective reasoning. In the wedding invitation, Meenakshi's name was emboldened, and she was the chief guest. The couple are happily married and have named their firstborn Meenakshi.

* * *

As an ECRC, my friend Janaki's first posting was at an MRTS station in Chennai. Janaki was always rostered next to an ECRC, Kanchana, who was extremely loud and wrathful. A tyrant who logged in at 07.59 hrs every day. Her scooter screeched to a halt at 07.58 hrs, and she darted inside the PRS. Immediately, Janaki stuffed cotton in her ears. The poor girl suffered from vertigo since the day she joined this station. The staff could hear Kanchana from the booking counter at the platform's other end. Everyone pitied Janaki. Even the passengers complained to the SM about the unusually loud and foul-mouthed lady clerk. No number of warnings changed her.

Janaki escaped on the pretext of getting coins from the BO or offered to count the station cash, fill up the challan, anything, for a few seconds away from the firing mouth. Kanchana even invaded Janaki's nightmares, and fitful sleep ignited more health issues. The competitive Kanchana never left her seat and wished to issue tickets for her shift's maximum number of forms. Unfortunately, when she registered that Janaki cleared more forms than her, she devised ways to stop the passengers from taking tickets from Janaki.

Kanchana collected one form, and as she checked the availability of a train, she quickly took the form from the next person in the queue. By the time she issued a ticket to the first person, she had snatched the form from the third person. After four years of torture, Janaki was ecstatic to leave on a transfer.

* * *

At her earlier posting, as CC, a young girl joined Janaki's station. She was just nineteen and received a compassionate posting after her father died on the job. The girl's mother met the staff at the station and requested them to take care of her daughter, who exhibited suicidal tendencies.

Janaki took her role seriously and often held the girl's hand, talked and listened to her, and lent her shoulder to cry. The girl suffered from the pangs of a love failure and once even attempted to cut her veins in the BO. Janaki set aside her own family troubles and often spent time cheering this girl. Her dismal chats even distressed Janaki and she keeled into depression with all the negativity and the toll of counselling the girl. Janaki took to yoga, which helped her combat despondency.

When everyone, the staff and the family, sat together and discussed a way to pull this girl out of her morbid urges, marriage was suggested. The mother selected a groom and after a grand wedding, the girl's life turned around. Completely. She was no longer forlorn but transformed into a cheerful person.

Basically, the girl craved attention and well . . .

Janaki felt her situation with her colleagues had been bleak wherever she worked.

* * *

My colleague Ranjini opted for VRS because her cousin's husband promised to leave her as his responsibilities towards his children were complete. He would stay with her if she resigned from her job. Excited as a young bride, Ranjini put up her papers and waited to begin a new chapter of her life.

The husband never came. Ranjini believes he died heartbroken because his family trounced his decision.

Ranjini lives with her widowed, childless sister and her happily married niece—the daughter of the brother who supported her decision to leave the schoolteacher. She enthusiastically talks about her niece's son, loves him like her own, and has made peace with her life.

* * *

PLATFORM NO. 16

I GAZED AT THE BEGUILING backdrop of swiftly passing trees, houses and vehicles in a pleasant, vacant state of mind—a rarity. My brain constantly buzzed with multitudinous thoughts. Startled by the railway station's clamour, I sprung out of the train before the surge of passengers barging in could drag me back to my seat. I then loped, expertly weaving my way, elbowing through the swarm of humans—some idlers, some purposeful. A scabby dog yelped as an urchin landed a kick on his flea-ridden bald patch while another lay sprawled, eyes closed, ears perked.

I was late for work.

I now worked in the railway passenger reservations system (PRS), and my office room was just at the end of the platform. This station was the last stop on the suburban line. A busy place with many business institutions, courts, and famous streets where one could get anything from textiles, paper, iron and industrial spares. In the colonial era, the area around my station was the most vital, flanked by the harbour and important government buildings.

We had to log in by 07.30 hrs, thirty minutes before the commencement of reservations all over India. I travelled by bus from home, then took a train and usually reached by 07.20 hrs. Then I retrieved the keys from the SM, opened the office, switched on the AC, searched for the best chair, wheeled it to my counter and logged into my system, waiting for my colleagues. However, a month earlier, a peculiar incident changed this routine.

When I de-boarded my bus, I had to cross the road and take the train from the penultimate station. Some students (mostly girls) from the bordering dental college and a few like me frequented this station. I was very early that day, and no one was on the stairs. As I reached the top of the bridge, I stopped mid-stride.

It was a day like any other, the regular train, the same platform, yet suddenly nothing was the same. A homeless man on the walkway had his hand underneath the striped cloth covering his lower body. The hand jerked furiously. His eyes met mine; he removed the lungi and flashed. His lusty eyes stripped me. I couldn't move; I couldn't speak.

'Come, honey, come closer. I bet you have seen nothing like this before,' he said, his pale tongue slithering over his dark, cracked lips.

His eyes singed my body, and I lowered mine. That was the moment I inferred that 'violated' had nothing to do with the actual unwanted, unwelcome touch. I was standing at the mouth of the stairs, and he sat some distance away on the bridge. Still, horror and fear stabbed me like someone had reached inside and yanked out a fistful of my gut. My stomach knotted, and my legs turned to slush. I flailed and clasped the railing. A gust of wind wafted the man's fecund reek my way, and bile soared inside me.

When my senses returned, I sprinted down the steps just as the train screeched to stop. The train was usually deserted when it reached this station, so I boarded the general compartment instead of the ladies' compartment. My whole body quivered as I stood near the door, unable to look at anyone or decode what had just happened.

I reached my station and raced to the RPF room where my friend Jenny worked. I stuttered as I recounted everything, and she immediately sent word to the police personnel monitoring the platforms.

It was time for my shift, I gladly embraced the opportunity to do and think about anything other than the thing that stuck to me, like a second disgusting skin. When I cleared the tatkal queue, Jenny showed me a photo from her mobile. It was him. The miscreant had been apprehended and was in custody at the police station across from my counter. After a sound thrashing, a case of nuisance was booked against him.

The relief I felt was palpable. However, I could not muster the courage to board the same bus or train as before. Since that day, I have never come early to work; just in time to sit in my chair and issue tickets.

Recently, I travelled by EMU after many years. When I alighted on the platform and checked the exit stairs, a man dressed in a pink shirt leaning on a long stick, hauling a heavy white sack rambled before me. Just as he was inches away from me, he slightly lifted his elbows and brushed my breast. I recoiled, then seething, slapped his shoulder.

'Do you need to do this at this age?'

'Amma, sorry, I didn't do it purposefully.'

'Don't I know your purpose? Shall I call the RPF?'

'Amma, please forgive me.'

I controlled my impulse to thwack him as the train moved. A boy's merry laughter from the trundling train slunk into my ears.

Perhaps the boy was laughing at something else.

Perhaps I wouldn't have dared if the man was younger and well-built.

Perhaps age has instilled in me a never-care boldness.

* * *

I wasn't the only one who faced a nightmare like this. Meenakshi, posted at a deserted station, also braved a similar incident. Once, a flasher on the train chased her as she dashed to the office. Opening the steel shutter was arduous and an iron door had to be raised too. She opened the inside door without entirely raising the shutter, crawled inside and locked the door, even as the man banged at the locked door. She called the RPF scouting a few stations away while hiding until help arrived.

She worked in an all-ladies office and in another incident, an ardent admirer of the lady clerks dropped love notes inside the counter. The letter was lascivious and quite evidently in poor taste. Fed up with this man's antics, the unsettled women designed a trap. One day, while chitchatting with a regular customer, they saw the perpetrator. Meenakshi quickly apprised the customer of the situation and their plan, and he, most graciously, agreed to help.

Meenakshi yelled at the customer in an angry tone. 'If you do this again, I will call the RPF.'

'Oh, let me see you do it,' said the customer as scripted.

The RPF was called; she directed him to the real culprit, who was apprehended with a love note in his possession.

Whenever I think about that disgusting man on the bridge and all these mighty women, we, the descendants of Jhansi ki Rani, I can't help but marvel at the tenacity of our gender. Eve-teasing, sexual harassment and assaults are a silent world war we have been fighting. Tragically, every ounce of heroism, bravery and courage we show to repel the scum, or to even piece our own lives together, are coated with an unwarranted sheen of shame, guilt and regret, none of which is ours to bear.

* * *

My office was a rectangular room measuring 30 ft in length and 20 ft in width, with fibreglass windows on one side facing a blemished pale grey wall. The reservation clerks sat linearly along the glass casing, issuing tickets. I checked my wristwatch and muttered expletives at no one in particular as I sprinted towards the PRS. Although a one-legged older man leaning on a wall con torted his face in disdain.

The Chief Reservations Supervisor (CRS) frequently warned us against late arrivals. As a workaround, I had a standing adjustment with my friend, Ann Maria. She stayed near and logged in my credentials, VSGEET, so the higher powers wouldn't report me. Some days, I did the same for her if she needed extra time at home.

A few months ago, a fellow ECRC clocked in at 07.59 hrs, settled in quickly and issued her first ticket at 08.00 hrs. Sadly, it was a WL ticket. The agitated passenger screamed, 'You came at the eleventh hour, and by the time you typed, the tickets were sold. I was here at

6:00 a.m. You know I am related to the General Manager of Southern Railways? I am going to file a complaint against you.'

The CRS on duty that day, Cyril Thomas—a rotund, ruddy comrade (Ann and I nicknamed him *Thakkali*, tomato in Tamil)—swooped in to handle the situation. After hearing the passenger, he said, 'There are two options before you. Either you can write a complaint, or I can arrange a confirmed berth for you.'

'How can you do that? Do you see the WL number?'

'Trust me. The mistake is partly yours, too. The clerk logged in before 08.00, but you gave her a credit card. She had to fill in all the numbers, bank details, etc., and precious time was lost. For tatkal tickets, it's preferred that you give cash, that too, exact change, to help the clerk provide quicker service. Tell me, have you taken up my offer to provide you with a confirmed ticket? I can even tell you the coach and berth number, which you can see in the chart tomorrow.'

Pacified, the passenger went without complaining. Cyril Thomas gave him the emergency quota berth number, hoping to send a request to the headquarters immediately. His luck turned, though, as there were already requests for EQ. Thomas contacted a friend who owed him and got him to release a berth in the defence quota. Luckily, the berth was in the same coach promised to the passenger. The CRS was called to a senior officer's cabin to explain how and why the same passenger's EQ letter was in both the HQ and DQ—headquarters and defence quotas. Thomas gabbed his way out without giving away the employee.

* * *

A winding queue waited on shuffling feet to grab the tatkal tickets as soon as the counter opened. I waltzed into the

PRS office with minutes to spare and smiled at my blinking credentials on the screen, unmindful of the steely stare of the CRS. This CRS Rangabashyam, whose eyes twitched incessantly, towered over me thrusting the attendance and personal cash registers towards me. I marked my initials and the standard amount of cash I carried daily to work, then settled in the allotted counter number 4, my favourite.

I checked the date on the calendar on the wall near the railway map of India, a standard issue for all railway offices. The CRS announced the date of advance ticket opening aloud to us inside the counter and those waiting to grab the tickets.

The only air conditioner in the room hung across counter four on the wall, which harboured a dangerously winding crack resembling the 'Great Divide Trail' of Canada and dissipated the muggy air. I glanced at the horde of humans, wondering where these people found the money *and* leave to travel?!

I curled my toes, sat upright and puckered my forehead. The person who turned up last for work ended up with the worst chair in the office. I groaned, thinking about sitting for six hours in the creaky chair that slanted to the side whenever I shifted my frame.

'Sir, when are they replacing our chairs?' No ergonomic chairs for us.

Rangabashyam shrugged, stood next to his protégé's counter (everyone had favourites) peering outside the glass windows with his twitching eyes, every twitch counting the passengers.

I perused the form rendered; the CRS had numbered the reservation forms of the first thirty passengers waiting in the queue to avoid touts bargaining their way into booking additional tickets. Another 60 seconds remained for the clock to strike 08.00.

I peered at the first man in the queue—gaunt with grey bristles.

'Since when are you waiting?'

'Good morning, Madam. I had my man here at 2.00 a.m. last night; I relieved him at 5 this morning. Please, get me confirmed tickets.'

'I hope you have the exact amount . . .'

'Yes, Madam. We calculated the fare, I have it down to the rupee.' He pushed the currency inside.

'Hey! Keep it with you for now; give it to me once I issue the ticket.'

The man grinned at me. I knew he was an agent and would make a commission of a few hundred on a confirmed ticket. It was easy to pick these men out of the line-up. They were positioned at the front, never fumbled for exact change or passenger details and projected a swagger of self-confidence. Regular passengers wishing to reserve a tatkal ticket usually sported worried frowns of uncertainty until after they held their tickets.

My colleague on Counter 5 begrudged these agents and invariably slowed her typing, delivering the wait-listed tickets to them. I had once argued with her about the insincerity of her actions, contesting that the person proffering the first form after spending a sleepless night waiting in the queue must be rewarded with a confirmed ticket, if possible, be it an agent or an ordinary passenger. She attacked me with the rule book, which said that for *tatkal* tickets, only the person who travels should come with their relevant ID or if sending a representative, a letter explaining the details should be given. Although she was technically correct, I could never approve her lopsided righteousness. What stopped these agents from framing a letter signed by the ones who employed them?

Unlike her, I worked my best during the *tatkal* time. Like a trained monkey, I performed the monotonous repetitive action of pulling a form, punching the details, yanking the cash, tearing the ticket—all in a circuit.

The tatkal tickets for the train furnished on the form in front of me were limited. For the six allotted berths for 2AC for the entire train, hundreds would attempt to procure the same six berths all over India's reservation centres. Not to account for the many thousands typing on their systems at home through the IRCTC website. And my target for tatkal was to issue four tickets. A tall order, if any.

I memorized the names, ages and genders of the four passengers on the form. The smart agents filled the forms with short names, unlike the normal public who wrote their first, middle and last names. The form in my hand had N Sharma F 42, C Sharma M 45, N Sharma F 13, B Sharma M 10.

Imagine the ticking seconds if I had to type Narayana Venkatapathy Iyer, Ramakant Pyarelal Rathod or such lengthy names.

At the stroke of eight, distraction would be disastrous.

Precisely twenty seconds past 08.00 hrs, I had my first ticket printed, with three berths confirmed and one on the waiting list, aided and abetted by the passengers, who usually tendered the exact change for quick disposal.

This worked even though I typed using one finger and used one for the space bar. I was a complete computer noob, like most of us back in the day.

Some days, after typing in all the particulars, the ticket printer would not cooperate, or the system might hang: no buttons would work. Oh, the tension we'd undergo, the ones inside and those standing in the queue, was immense. By then a WL ticket would pop up.

A typical twenty-five minutes past 08.00 hrs in a PRS office functioned like this: I took the form, eyed the details as my fingers went clackety-clack on the keyboard, pressed 'Enter' with a flourish as I informed the ticket's position, confirmed or WL. Quickly counting the cash and dropping it into the drawer (time couldn't be wasted in arranging the notes; they were in heaps in the drawer), I tore the ticket from the printer. At the same time, my left hand handed over the ticket and took the next reservation form; my right hand scribbled on the rear side of the earlier form the details of the berth issued, the cash received and the change tendered.

All this happened in under a minute. And then, hit repeat! For these twenty-five minutes, our office was a cacophony of keys tapping, printing static, grumbling passengers and creaking chairs as we issued tickets non-stop.

Sometimes, the number of berths for luxury classes was limited in tatkal, or even on the opening day of advance reservation. In a frenzy to issue confirmed tickets from my counter, in a moment of pride (yes, I was vain), I would mug up the reservation forms (my matriculation rote learning served), type on the keyboard and an ECRC assigned to the general shift would come early to help and tear the tickets from the printer. At the same time, the CRS would collect the cash. On these days, we printed three tickets in under 60 seconds.

'Let's get all the confirmed berths!' Our CRS Cyril Thomas whooped his motto like a sports team coach, motivating us to do our best during tatkal.

The workmate at Counter 6 used to marvel at my flash-like speed. 'VS, didn't I see you arrive just minutes before 08.00 hrs? How did you log in and issue all those tickets so quickly?'

'Shush! Don't remind the supervisor now. I cleared the queue, that's what counts.'

'However late you come, you don't forget to spray your heady perfume.' The lady at counter 9 quipped with a teasing lilt.

'Don't you ladies have anything else to gossip about?' I blushed. 'Always joking about my Dubai perfume. Next time, I will ask my husband to get one for you.'

My husband had joined a construction firm in Dubai, and I visited him a few months ago. I brought chocolates for all, and perfumes for my clique.

I overheard a customer at the next counter earnestly advising my colleague on the right method of washing rice. The colleague had apparently told the customer that he'd been on leave because of stomach pain caused by kidney stones.

'You bachelors don't take care of yourselves,' the customer said, shaking his head and wagging a finger. 'I know you are cooking for yourself. While washing rice, take care, sift the stones out, don't boil the stones and eat. Kidney stones happen when you don't wash the rice properly.'

Whoever said you never get anything 'free' must never have passed through our remarkably generous nation. Advice has always been freely dispensed here and will continue to be done so in the future.

Tickets issued, I called Ann Maria at counter 8 for a coffee break after a quick cash tally. Rangabashyam peered at me, wiping his glasses clean.

'I am tired of warning you to come early. Don't you know you must log in to the system at 07.30 hrs?'

I smiled and didn't retort about the counter being logged in with or without me. 'Sir, I know, but what to do? On some days, the bus driver's watch runs five minutes slow. I should register a complaint at the bus depot.'

'You are a genius in giving excuses.'

'*And* tickets, no?' I winked and went outside. 'A sugarless coffee coming up for you, sir!'

'Don't forget, the shift is not over yet. Don't take the train home. Come back soon.'

The other day, an ECRC went out for tea outside the station, his usual tea shop. While sipping his tea, he saw his neighbour crossing the road. He called out to him and offered him tea. Both smoked a cigarette. Then suddenly, the men saw the bus to their home route slowing down at the bus stop. Quickly, they stubbed the ciggies and jumped on the bus. After ten minutes, the CRS covering for him—sitting at his counter and issuing tickets—lost his cool. He sent a customer in the queue to the tea shop. The customer returned and said the clerk wasn't at the teashop. They learned later that he had boarded a bus home. An incensed supervisor called his home and asked the wife to send her husband back to the station as soon as he reached home.

Ann and I laughed thinking of that incident and walked to the hotel outlet at the station. A famous chain of hotels had opened outlets in many of the stations on the suburban line. We never waited in line to receive special coffee at a concessional rate. Being popular had its merits, as did being the fastest ticketing clerk.

Ah, looking back, I sometimes miss those moments. The adrenaline rush carried me through the strenuous tatkal timings. I would clear the winding queue and stretch out my arms like Christ on the cross, smiling smugly. I was one of the quickest reservation clerks. The moniker 'The Express Lady' followed me from my first station, and the passengers waiting for tatkal believed I had magical fingers. The agents coaxed my co-worker on previous evenings to reveal the counter number allotted to me and saw to it they stayed in the line corresponding to my counter.

Honestly, it's a pity I never ventured into *Kaun Banega Crorepati*; I would be the *Fastest Fingers First* every single time!

PLATFORM NO. 16A

BY THE TIME I RETURNED from my coffee break, I had a visitor waiting.

'VS, this man says you issued him the wrong ticket, and the TTE fined him.' Rangabashyam pushed a receipt towards me.

There were supervisors, and there were SUPERvisors. Some nurtured vengeance, drawing pleasure when their disfavoured clerks were distressed. Another kind, with their presence of mind, rescued their clerks from peril.

Once, at a Current Booking Counter in the Chennai central railway station, the ticket clerk was accused of bribery. He dialled his supervisor for help.

'Sir, can you pacify a passenger and clear the commotion?'

'What is the issue?'

'The passenger is accusing me of asking Rs 50 extra for a ticket.'

'Did you?'

'Umm, Sirrr . . .'

'Ok, I will handle it.'

CRS Cyril Thomas called the angry passenger, a hulk of a man, inside and offered him a chair. When he agitatedly explained what had conspired, CRS addressed the clerk.

'Don't you know how to deal with a passenger? They are most important to us.'

Thomas typed on the keyboard and turned the monitor towards the passenger. The screen displayed: tatkal charges Rs 50.

'See this? The clerk wasn't demanding extra from you; he was offering you a tatkal ticket, which has a good chance of confirmation, although it is showing a waiting list now. Poor guy, he didn't convey it properly. I can do you a favour.'

The passenger relaxed his flexed fists and a smile slunk on to his face.

Then Thomas addressed the clerk. 'You do one thing. Issue him a normal waiting list ticket. Let's help him save the tatkal charges. I will allot a confirmed berth to him while preparing the chart. After all, he is our esteemed customer. And the two of you also share a mother tongue.'

The clerk and the passenger shared cordial words in their common language. The CRS had checked all the details of the vacant quota (ladies, defence, headquarters, etc.) on the train the angry passenger was to travel to, before mediation. Equipped with the information, he arranged a berth. All was well—a happy customer and a thankful clerk.

* * *

I wished that Cyril Thomas was on duty instead of this smirking buffoon.

'The TTE harassed me.' The visitor jutted in.

'Wrong ticket? I don't think that's possible. What's wrong? The date?' I asked, my nose up in the air.

'No. Wrong gender. It's marked F instead of M.'

'What was the name in the form? Maybe you filled up the wrong details in the form.'

'I bought the ticket for myself. You can check the forms. I filled it up correctly.'

I puffed a sigh. 'Ok. Wait here. Let's get the forms and check.'

I quickly disposed the passengers in the queue, bearing in that mind the top brass demanded an explanation if the system idled.

If the clerks vacated their seats at any time other than the timings painted on each counter (the fifteen-minute break for food), whether for coffee/tea or even to use the washroom, the customers created a furore. We had to specify, 'I need a loo break, or I have a splitting headache, or let me get a tea.'

Some customers acquiesced, while others went on a tirade about the value of (their) time and how we were public servants stationed there to serve the public. To our collective annoyance, some even pointed to the poster on the railway premises where the Mahatma said, 'The customer is always right.'

While I ticketed, the supervisor found out the issuing window, time and booking date from the ticket given by the complainant and procured the forms bundle from the storage. The reservation forms were stored in the reservation offices for six months and then sent to the central repository. After checking the musty records, Rangabashyam concluded I was at fault. The triumphant visitor sneered.

'Kamakshi M 60? But Kamakshi is a female name,' I grumped.

'Agree. But my parents named me Kamakshi after the goddess who granted them a boon of parenthood.'

'Hmmm. Looking at the name, I must have automatically typed F. But you should have also checked the ticket before leaving the counter. You purchased this ticket seventy days back!'

'Yes. I should have checked instead of trusting you to do your job right. But what is the answer for the fine and the harassment meted out, huh? I want to lodge an official complaint.'

Rangabashyam intervened, shook his head at my bristling visage and adopted his wheedling voice.

'We will take action on the TTE. The clerk will pay you the amount mentioned in the fine receipt. In future, you check the tickets and inform the counter clerk about the name and gender. It's a human error. What will a complaint solve?'

I grudgingly parted with the money and pocketed the TTE's receipt. Then, I drooped into my crooked chair and resumed the counter duties sans the usual exuberance. This was a rare occurrence, and I took the mistake hard; I am a Virgo, a perfectionist.

* * *

Later in my ECRC years, I issued tickets to Santosh F 24, Rajkumari M 45 and Gauri M 56, all as per the reservation form tendered. People had weird names. There was a 'Firstborn' in a reservation form. Such ingenuity. I asked the passenger if his sibling was named Second-born. He sheepishly raked his hair.

There were instances when a passenger asked, 'Madam, I studied till class 7; shall I fill that out here?'

Making them understand that 'class' in the reservation form meant class of travel and not the educational level completed in school was challenging—to keep a poker face and not burst out laughing. The lower berth was spelt lower birth, lower breath. The train number column was filled in with a lucky number, mostly the date of birth.

Initially, when I joined the PRS, the trains never filled up on Tuesdays. Superstitious people avoided travel on Tuesdays, but later, I saw a change in the trend. The trains were filled to the brim every day of the week.

Oh, we saw all sorts at the ticket counter.

* * *

The day dragged on. There were periods of lull and activity. Ann and I went on another coffee break. After coffee, I bought gum and chewed it vigorously. Usually after coffee, I would peruse the pirated CDs displayed in tiny shops adjoining the station. A grainy copy was available in these shops on the day any movie was released anywhere in the world. A dull ache lingered between my eyes, and I massaged my temples. Purchasing a Saridon from the local pharmacy, we entered the reservation office, and I excused myself to the toilet—a tiny cubicle outside the PRS.

Since joining railways, I have always used the toilet shared by male and female colleagues. Once, a cousin working in a private firm hung out at my office, and she was appalled to know there were no separate toilets for men and women. And there I was, never even knowing that separate toilets existed at workplaces.

The toilet was outside the BO in the station, where my friend Meenakshi worked: a dingy, dark place with an erratic supply of water and electricity. Once, a vile man took advantage of the darkness and isolation and assaulted a colleague of hers. Luckily, the lady escaped his clutches, ran and locked herself in her cabin.

After this incident, all the ladies protested, demanding an attached toilet. They highlighted this incident and others where the counter clerks had to rush to a stationary express train and 'do it' within the few minutes the train halted at a station. Imagine the train moving from the station with the clerk locked in the toilet.

The ladies were reluctant to work shifts until the authorities satisfied their demands. That's how some of the railway booking offices acquired toilets. I was grateful that a toilet existed at all at my station, unisexual or not.

* * *

When I returned after my break, I found the door of the reservation office locked. A surprise vigilance check was in progress. I persuaded the officers to open the door and let me in. They were not happy about my explanation of the unauthorized restroom break. Angry, I resumed work, while the vigilance personnel closed the counters one after the other and ordered us to tally the cash.

When it was my turn to tally the cash with the number indicated on the computer, there was a shortage of Rs 500. Sweat streaked down my face. I pulled the drawer on my table, lifted the PC and fluttered the forms, but I could not find the missing 500. My headache aggravated, and in a foul mood, I signed the register, acknowledging the shortage of funds.

My shift ended soon, and after handing over the earnings of the morning shift to the cashier in charge, I relinquished my seat.

On his way out, the clerk from counter 1 murmured in a subdued voice, 'Biju, who is on leave, checked some availability when you went out for coffee. He used your system. Do you think he might have slipped a 500-rupee note into his pocket?'

I glared at my colleague and did not dignify his remark with a reply. I ordered tea and MilkBikis for myself and moved to the cashier's table. It was an enclosed space within the metal locker bureau, where each of us had a tiny locker to keep our belongings. This was the only place away from the prying eyes of the customers who rubbernecked to see where we were, if not at the counter.

Sipping my tea, I checked all the reservation forms for the shift. I recalculated the details of the currency tendered, and the balance returned. Painstakingly I analysed all the 210 reservation forms and found nothing faulty. The doubt on Biju threatened to sprout. My stomach rumbled, and I belched. Drowning the doubts with water, I tarried to the ATM and remitted the shortage to the cashier. Exhausted and hungry, I boarded the train.

* * *

A few months ago, a colleague had a cash shortage of Rs 7000 at the end of his shift. It was a festival holiday, so there was hardly any queue for reservations. The PRS worked only the morning shift during important days like Gandhi Jayanthi, Republic Day, Christmas, etc. Seniors or anyone newly married or with young children were given a preference, granted a holiday and allowed to celebrate at home with family. Some luckless souls left all the delicacies and the special programmes on TV and trudged to work. Even buses and trains operated holiday services.

The only change in our schedule was that we took turns coming early and opening all the counters. We knew most of the IDs and passwords. Only a handful of the staff guarded their login info, the rest giving in to convenience over confidentiality. We hopped around engaging all the counters and issued tickets in intervals so that no counter would show long periods of non-activity and get flagged. The latecomers would bring sweets and a special breakfast for the rest of us. Ann was an excellent cook, and she cooked me yummy food. Sometimes, they joked that I was like Lord Ganapathy, to whom everyone offers food first. I would honestly review the food I tasted, and luckily, everyone tolerated my outspokenness.

So, when a shortage of such a considerable amount was discovered at the end of the shift, especially with a meagre turnout and fewer forms, and when all of us issued tickets in that window, the onus fell on everyone to trace the lost money.

The festivities abandoned, we fervently checked the reservation forms, called random customers from the phone number on the forms, retraced the events since the opening of the counters, pulled out chairs and drawers, and swept under the raised platform on which we sat with the systems and the printers. But to no avail; the cash was nowhere to be found.

Ultimately, we all pitched in, tallied the cash at the end of the shift, and locked up the office. We moped the rest of the day, wondering what went wrong.

Despite all the everyday drama of ticketing, the only thing that kept us going was the satisfaction of a job well done—issuing confirmed tickets to tatkal passengers or when happy customers leave the counter on the opening day of the Advance Reservation Period with their tickets in hand. The aberration in the funds, of course, gave us sleepless nights.

The next day, a lady came to my colleague's counter and asked if he had any issues tallying his cash yesterday.

The lady said, 'I had withdrawn cash from the bank and ran some errands yesterday. When I reached home, I checked my cash and found a surplus. I retraced all the places I went to yesterday, but no one had any cash shortage. This is the last place.'

My colleague was jubilant. 'Yes! I had a shortage in my counter yesterday.'

'What was the amount?'

'Rs 7000.'

'Exactly the surplus I have.'

So, this is what happened. While booking the tickets, this lady had to give the clerk a small change of Rs 5, so she went to a shop to get the coins after booking her tickets. My colleague kept the cash the customer paid, along with the ticket. On collecting the Rs 5 coin, the ticket clerk pushed the ticket out of the counter, forgetting to take the amount he had collected earlier, and handed over the Rs 400 change that had to be returned to her upon receipt of Rs 5. We all thanked the lady, and my colleague treated us to special tea and samosas that day.

If only something similar could happen with my Rs 500. My mood curdled. The splitting headache made sure I quarrelled with my husband.

Another time, such a counter shortage happened and an ECRC used brute force to recover her money. This lady traced the customer in question from the details we wrote overleaf the reservation forms, some clerks even wrote the denominations of cash received and given. She called the phone number on the form, and a shopkeeper said his office boy had booked the ticket and returned the exact change to him. The boy was unavailable, and he would check with him and call back.

Later, when he called and reiterated that the cash was correct, my colleague, who was sure the office boy was the culprit, went to the shop with her boxer husband. When the boy said he had received the correct balance, her husband landed a solid punch to his gut.

Immediately, the office boy returned the excess amount and said he had spent Rs 100.

I wondered if I should call my husband from Dubai to punch a customer to retrieve my lost cash.

* * *

The next day, as soon as I entered my office, I was informed that an older man had come to the office in my absence and approached the supervisor.

'Sir, I sent my driver in the morning to book tickets. The clerk has given an extra 500 rupees along with the tickets. Take this money. I am a retired government employee. I know how everyone works hard to make ends meet.'

Rangabashyam had informed the vigilance inspection officials that it was just an oversight by the counter clerk, and no memo was issued to me. But he had conveniently forgotten to inform me of the return of Rs 500.

Unaware of the events at the office, I had an uneasy evening and night at home. And to compound my misery, my maid bunked. The brimming kitchen sink and a thousand different chores warranted my attention, but my mind focused on the missing 500 rupees. I relinquished my 16.00 hrs nap. (Even now after all these years, every day just about 16.00, I feel drowsy wherever I happen to be—theatre, flight, family function . . . I have to get my forty winks.)

When my supervisor apprised me the next day of the money being returned, I felt relief and gratitude for the older man. I sent a prayer of thanks to him and others of his ilk—honest, hard-working people. I had prayed for a miracle, which had come my way. What a happy, happy happenstance.

PLATFORM NO. 17

AT AGES NINETEEN OR TWENTY, when my batch of forty joined the Southern Railways (forty each year for seven years, 1991 to 1997, in every zone in the Indian Railways), we brought in a youthful vibrancy and new thinking into this archaic department where the clerks always grumbled, dissatisfied. The seniors bogged down by family issues, struggled to muddle through and carried the spite to work. Frequent skirmishes with the public and slow working styles created permanent friction. In contrast, we bubbled with excitement at the novelty of dealing with customers.

Our cheerful inquisitiveness helped us forge endearing relationships with the customers.

Experiences with a few fussy people who yelled at us and cursed our families pushed us into depression but helped strengthen us in facing challenges anywhere. We had 'special' customers and had a list of the ones to be cautious about.

A mother worried about her child's wayward ways found a listening ear in us. We calmed her. When her child cleared the board examinations, she distributed chocolates through the counter opening and celebrated. We received a grandfather's blessings as we secured lower berth tickets for his pilgrimage, and he returned with sacred gifts from the temples. One passenger sought my friend Janaki to bless the bangle for his sister's *valagaapu* (baby shower).

When people said, our journey is safe when you issue tickets, we glowed.

We received wedding invitations from couples whose honeymoon we helped plan. We provided them side berths in 2AC or allotted a coupe.

Being customer-friendly was infused in us. Not all staff from the older generation were grumblers, I have worked with some of the best counter staff and seen the worst too.

Sometimes, the computer system would issue two tickets furnished in a reservation form in different compartments or provide lower berths in different bays. Ann and I worked to help these passengers. I would block a LB in a different bay by filling out proxy details, and she would fill in the particulars from the reservation form, and voila, the berths in opposite lower berths could be issued. Of course, this was possible only if several berths were available for the train and in the class requested.

We advised them to ask for help on the train if nothing worked. But the passengers returned saying no one swapped berths on the train. A young man occupying a lower berth had screamed, 'Don't disturb me. I will not move from this berth.'

The older man had to be appeased, 'Sir, we cannot refuse lower berths to people who come early for booking. When customers, even young, healthy ones, demand an LB, we must oblige if they are available. Some people also demand their favourite or lucky number. I cannot travel in berth no 13, says one. Another says, I must sleep on a berth facing the train's direction. The system allocates the berths. Still, we aim for customer satisfaction.' We managed to send them away mollified. Such lectures were absorbed by others standing in the queue, allowing us to perform without disputes. Sometimes customers who booked tickets through IRCTC too came to us yearning for a human interface.

* * *

There are instances when a beautiful friendship blossoms between the clerk and the passenger who travelled kilometres, leaving their work midway, to return the money that wasn't theirs. Ann Maria called a lady from the phone number on the reservation form and asked her if she had received extra cash when she had her tickets cancelled. The lady immediately switched off the stove while frying fish for her husband and travelled 10 km by bus back to the station.

Soaked in sweat, she said, 'Madam, I don't know if you gave me extra; I didn't even open the cancelled tickets and the cash you gave. I was frying fish when you called. Please check.' She pushed the crumpled tickets with cash inside the counter. Ann recovered the excess amount wrongly given to her. Since then, the lady called Ann (whose mobile displayed: The fish lady) and ascertaining her duty particulars, turned up to book her tickets, chit-chatted and left. She even attended Ann's daughter's wedding.

We served them all, from funny to cranky, from polite, honest customers to rules-spouting angry customers.

* * *

You wouldn't believe me if I said that once, by issuing a ticket, we were arrayed as a witness in a case, a sexual abuse case.

Once, the daughter of a high-ranking government official and her young child travelled in a 2AC coach. A politician occupied the opposite berth. Around midnight, the politician, in an inebriated state, misbehaved with the lady. She raised an alarm, called the TTE and complained to him. The TTE was caught between the victim, the daughter of a senior government official, and a politician with clout. He tried to diffuse the situation by allotting the lady and the child to another bay. But she wasn't assuaged. When the train stopped at the next station, she rushed to the station master's office and entered a complaint in the Complaints Register. Incidentally, the politician detrained at that station.

When the case proceedings commenced, the wily politician alleged that his assistant who travelled with him was the culprit. He said he had many assistants, but wasn't sure who travelled with him on that date in question. They checked the ticket to ascertain the issuing station and the ID of the ticketing clerk. They summoned Ann to testify which assistant had come to the reservation office for the ticket.

Ann, the ECRC, was paid a travel allowance and issued a ticket marked 'On Duty' to travel to the station where the case proceeded. She went thrice over three years. The case dragged on for six years. When, at last, she was called to testify, tired of being a part of the proceedings, Ann stated the fact, 'It's been so many years, I do not remember the face.'

I'm not sure if the case ever saw justice served.

* * *

During a busy shift, I spotted a regular customer in the queue. A jobless person, he lingered in the reservation office to reserve tickets for his neighbours and friends. His notoriety for irritating the counter clerks with inane queries remained unmatched. Somedays, he would enquire about trains and destinations he fancied. We knew he enjoyed seeing us fumble, searching for the station he wrote in a reservation form. When we'd dig into our resources, call up the main PRS in the section and collect details, he would say, 'My uncle called; his trip is cancelled, so I don't want a ticket. Sorry.' The standing joke amongst us was, 'Who would be his next prey?'

My colleague sitting beside snickered, 'Your day couldn't get any worse.'

Already, I was fuming sitting at the counter farthest from the only air-conditioner in the office, continuously dabbing my neck with a handkerchief. Moreover, my chair was aslant and groaned every time I shifted my body. Lunchtime neared. My stomach acids roiled as the scent of the tempered curry leaves wafted from the Saravana Bhavan kitchen across our office. And the troublesome passenger chose the queue at my counter.

The oily fingerprints smeared on the glass window screamed at me when I peered through, trying to catch a better view of the pretty young one extending a cancellation ticket.

'Why are you cancelling the ticket?'

'Oh, my examination dates have changed. I will buy a new one later,' the pretty customer answered.

'You can change the date on this one without cancelling it.'

'Yeah, but I might drive over. Not sure, cancel it.'

'You are losing a lot of money.'

She nodded, uninterested in my advice as she was busy texting.

I saw a lot of students and IT professionals buying tickets to and fro for every weekend of a month in advance. The retired fathers stood in the queue again and again. Sometimes I felt sorry for them and kept them waiting beside the counter as I issued their forms one by one after every third form. It was not advisable to issue reservation forms with the same address in bulk because it was an offence in our rule book.

I contemplated closing my counter for a coffee break to avoid the scraggly bearded troubleshooter who closed in every minute. But having taken a break twenty minutes ago, I persevered. It was his turn after a senior citizen and a defence guy with a warrant.

Slouching, he tendered the form, scratching his beard as white flecks fell on the grey granite counter. His reticence surprised me. The handwriting on the reservation form was illegible, and the letters appeared double in places.

'What have you written? What station is this?' I asked.

'Madam, I have the map here. It is in Karnataka.' He pushed a wrinkled map of India through the gap.

Although familiar with the station and railway code, I pushed the reservation form outside the counter.

'Do you expect me to search the map and find a train? Can't you see the queue? Go to the enquiry counter.'

'I am disabled. Please check the system. There's a lengthy queue at the inquiry counter. I need to join at that station soon. I have got a job in a rural bank.' He grinned, baring his crooked teeth.

I rolled my eyes, 'Don't fool me. You are a healthy man and our regular customer for the last two years. And lucky you! To have landed a bank job.'

He winced as he lifted his right hand, fitted with an artificial limb, and dropped it on the counter. The office room swirled, and sweat trickled down my nose, 'What happ… happened?'

Aware of the people behind him, who would soon lose patience and remark at my sluggishness, I quickly entered the station name to check the details in the system. At the same time, he answered in a subdued voice, 'A few months ago, on the way back from my village, my bus collided with another bus and fell into a river. It was in the news, too. Many died. I survived but lost my arm. I am working on writing with my left hand.'

Instinctively, I splayed my fingers on my heart, 'I am sorry. And this job?'

'The government granted me a job in the disability quota. A blessing in disguise.'

I requested the next person in the queue to fill the form for him legibly and sighed with relief when a confirmed ticket popped up on the screen.

He thanked me and added, 'I will not irritate you guys for some time. Though, the person in that station should be pitied.'

Mumbling a short prayer for his well-being, I smiled at my next customer, a short-statured, stout man.

'Madam, please get me a lower berth. I cannot climb up.'

That train displayed waiting list 201, and he appeared to be an obstinate man—tough luck. I needed a dose of caffeine to sail through the rest of the shift.

* * *

During the trying Covid times, my friend Bharathi faced a prickly customer. All stations operated a single counter and received instructions with a list detailing people allowed to travel by train. Tickets were to be issued only to those who satisfied the criteria. Railway staff on duty and persons working in essential services, like nurses, doctors, sanitary workers, etc., had to show their work ID to travel. People visiting hospitals for dialysis or other regular, systematic treatments had to produce a doctor's certificate.

A passenger approached the booking counter and said he had to visit a patient in the government hospital and wanted a ticket. Bharathi said she couldn't issue tickets for him because he did not fit the criteria of persons allowed to travel. Secondly, it was advisable to curtail hospital visits to curb the spread of Covid.

The livid passenger began abusing in a raised voice and cursed that her spouse would be killed in an accident, her children would rot in jail and she would meet death like the chief minister of Tamil Nadu, who had died alone without her family.

This shook my sensitive friend, and she began to cry. For days, Bharathi was depressed and worried for her family. It took many months for her to get out of the gloom.

* * *

Whereas at a wayside station, in a famous tourist area, Sunil Warrier had a different experience.

He was on a busy evening shift and a surprise visit from a railway zone officer drained him.

The officer and his entourage were visiting a tourist spot and decided to do a surprise check on the lonesome ticket clerk. The officer's assistant warned Sunil that the officer always penalized the clerks during any inspection.

The officer checked the station earnings, 'The collection is too little.'

'Yes, sir, traffic is low.'

'So, if a passenger comes for cancellation of a ticket with a large fare, how do you handle the situation? How do you manage if you get cancellations far above the booking cash?'

'Sir, that's a big problem. We cannot tell the passenger with a confirmed ticket to wait until the revenue matches the cancellation amount because as days or hours pass the cancellation charges go up. Most customers are rich plantation owners, so I convince one of them to book a 2AC ticket to a farther place on a date that shows a waiting list. And against the cash received, I refund the amount on cancellation. Once I get enough collection, I call them to cancel the WL tickets. They lose only Rs 10 on a WL ticket. Passengers are happy that they immediately get money. We have a relationship like that.'

'But this is not legal.'

'I know. But I don't have a way out. Moreover, I convince the passengers, and they don't have an issue. If they had, they would have complained.'

The officer, a bit stunned, could not say whether he approved of it or not.

'Sir, people cooperate with the railways. Tickets build relationships, too.'

This convinced the inspector in the officer's posse that Sunil was crazy and would be penalized heftily. Little did he know that the officer would reward the clerk with a certificate of recognition and a cash award for his expertise in handling the situation instead of inviting complaints from customers.

* * *

Booking counters not only build relationships with the passengers but build strong bonds of friendship and love within the four walls, too.

Mangaiyarkarasi sashayed in her green cotton sari, the pleats starched to stand like knives, was ready to draw blood if anyone dared to warm her face with their breath. Yes, like in all offices, some men breathed down the necks of unwitting women, peeking at their cleavages. Mangaiyarkarasi was famed for her acidic tongue-lashing to such men, a protector of the ladies who worked the shift beside her.

Once, she happened to overhear a conversation between a young girl, fresh from college, the new breed with newfangled ideas, and a senior clerk, a fair tall man, shirt tucked in, shoes and all. Dropping compliments on her salwar, he asked her to join him for tea. The girl, happy at being noticed, agreed immediately, and they walked to the tea shop outside the office for a cuppa. Mangaiyarkarasi waited for the girl to return and took her aside.

'Next time he or any male staff asks you out for tea, coffee or buttermilk, do not go.'

'Oh, what's your problem? It was just outside the counter, inside the station premises. Are you jealous?'

'Not at all. I tell you this because "I have been there, done that". These guys are not as harmless as they seem; they would tell everybody you had accompanied them to a hotel. The roadside tea shop would become a lodge, and a cup of tea would become a theatre until his rotten imagination peters out. Think twice unless you want to see the creepy smiles on all their faces.'

That was how Mangaiyarkarasi was, always looking out for her lot.

Mangaiyarkarasi, her thinning, curly, coloured hair perfectly clamped into a ponytail by a green floral hair clip, fanned herself with the end of her sari. She exhibited her manicured nails, polished green, and rested her shapely back on the rickety chair. There was a running bet amongst the staff on the colour in which she would be seen the next day. It was a wonder how she colour-coded her accessories down to the hair clip, slippers and even a flower pinned on the side above her left ear, the side visible to the public when she sat on the ticket counter.

'Oh, It's too hot. Crank up the AC. And can someone get me a better chair? How can one work six hours sitting on this?' Mangaiyarkarasi cooed in her nasal twang.

The AC on the far wall hummed in a low tone, the air blowing not-so-cool but hot, humid air. During the rainy season, dank air circulated. This was the lone AC in the office that was in working condition. The other AC was taken down for repair a couple of weeks ago.

Chennai sizzled. Certified torture, working in the decrepit reservation office where eight counters were cooped up in a straight line with hardly any moving space within the confines of the computer, the keyboard, the printer and the cash drawer. One must jiggle and wriggle to relieve the aching back and neck without upsetting the adjacent counter's printer. If a person printed a ticket, the one at the next counter felt the tremors, a chain reaction. If only the chairs were comfortable, it would be an enjoyable free massage.

It was an ordeal if the ticket roll had to be changed. One had to stand with body parts touching the individual beside us while adjusting the ancient printers, coaxing them into issuing a ticket. If one was heavyset, then sometimes the neighbouring counter clerk excused themselves and closed their counter until you fought or pleaded with your printer to comply. By then, the masses outside the counters would riot: this guy just came to work and is taking a break; they don't value our time; railway servants they are but behave like they rule us. So on and so forth, while the clerk inside jostled with the printer.

But Mangaiyarkarasi never faced any of these issues. There was someone who answered her beck and call and sometimes even waited for her mouth to utter a word or her mind to think of something that would be handed to her before she finished the sentence. He was not the peon; the reservation office never had peons—if you needed something, you fetched it yourself unless you were Mangaiyarkarasi the charmer. The charmed was none other than the reservation supervisor, the short and fair boss. He had a puffy pompadour slick with Brylcreem and comb marks, his voice boomed in the station, but when he spoke to her, no one heard other than the intended.

The romance that played out in the confines of the cracked reservation walls and the scuffed plexiglass counters would put Laila Majnu to shame. Both the hero and the heroine were in their fifties with spouses and grown children at home, but what to do? They spent a solid seven hours together every day. They had their weekly off together. Rain or shine, they turned up to look into each other's eyes.

I usually worked the morning shifts. I preferred returning home by 15.30 hrs instead of reaching home late after 21.30. However, a colleague working the evening shift wanted an adjustment for a month because his wife worked the evening shift at her office. Someone had to be at home when the kids returned from school. I traded places because I had no children, and my husband was in the Middle East.

I was like the Queen's Lady in Waiting for one month of the evening shift. Yep, Mangaiyarkarasi, as her name suggested, 'queen of women', was the reigning queen of the evening shift, and at first, she did not warm up to me. She accepted my bouquet of friendship only after she knew I wasn't a threat to her kingdom nor had any designs on her aged, wrinkled man. All the others working in the evening shift were men. Why do some women perceive another woman as a threat instead of seeing a friend? It must be in the DNA.

The men paid no heed to whatever conspired between the couple. I faked nonchalance but couldn't help observing. Their compatibility was endearing. But I wondered, if one of them got transferred, what would happen to Cupid's game?

Many such couples felt comfortable sharing their deepest fears and happiness with the 'office spouse' rather than the ones at home. But, every day after the office closed everyone returned home to their family.

* * *

Recently, I heard from Ann that many of our friends met at a wedding last month. Our colleagues, a woman and a man who worked the same shifts, took their office romance to the next level. They had a daughter together and while the man continued staying with his wife, the woman divorced her husband. Last month, Ann attended their daughter's wedding.

There was this ticket agent who waited only at my counter during the tatkal booking—a young fellow who worshipped me for the only reason that I guaranteed confirmed tickets for the first few passengers standing at my counter. Rules were laid to curb booking by touts. But even if I wanted a tatkal for a relative I had to stand in the queue or get the relative to wait in the line. People felt that a railway counter clerk could book as many tickets as they wanted for themselves. This is not the case—we had checks that allowed that firstly, only numbered forms of those standing outside the counter were to be issued the tickets. So, when my relative wanted a ticket, I requested the ticket agent to stand in the queue and render the form.

As with every equation in this world, you help others, so they owe it to you. This agent showed his joy in getting a confirmed ticket by getting me my morning tea which led to my colleagues' whispers.

As if a man and woman can only have one thing between them. Malicious whispers actually led to a young colleague hanging herself—a young widow, she couldn't handle the rumours spread by those who smiled but stabbed her in the back.

My supervisor Cyril Thomas, Ann Maria and I shared a beautiful friendship. The three of us took coffee breaks together, shared jokes and laughed a lot. We created a joyful atmosphere at work. After I went on long leave, the other two never met for coffee. When I asked, he said, 'It was difficult to handle the gossip, beti.'

It takes all sorts to make up our society.

* * *

My friend Inbaraj worked in a tiny station with few passing trains before becoming a guard. Once, after a surprisingly busy day, while tallying the day's earnings, a man approached the counter with two children, a boy and a girl, of approximately seven and ten.

'Sir, when is the train to Bangalore?'

'Tomorrow morning.'

'Oh. Sir, when is the train to Hubli?'

'The last train to Hubli left an hour ago. Next only tomorrow at 7 a.m.'

'Ohho.'

Then he went away with the nagging children.

Returning after a while, he asked, 'Sir, when is the train to Mysore?'

A slightly irritated Inbaraj, unhappy at being disturbed, said, 'Not before tomorrow morning. No more passenger trains for the day.'

'Is there a train going anywhere?'

'No trains.'

He continued reconciling his books.

After ten minutes, the man peeped into the counter again.

'Sir . . . sir.'

Inbaraj feigned indifference.

'SIR . . . SIR'

'Now, what do you want?'

'Sir, are there any goods trains? Going somewhere? Anywhere?'

He lost his cool.

'Are you crazy? Where do you want to go? You cannot board a goods train.'

'Sir, I know, Sir. I don't want to go anywhere. These children were troubling us at home. My wife sent us out saying, Daddy will show you the train. Now, these brats are unwilling to return home without seeing a train. I don't know how to make them understand. What do I do?'

We loved our passengers without whom we wouldn't exist.

PLATFORM NO. 18

BEFORE WRITING THIS BOOK, I felt that my tenure in the railways had been unique and filled with memorable incidents. I lived such an enriching life that I had to pen them down. But I was humbled when I began collecting anecdotes from my railway fraternity. Each one had faced such challenges and soared high.

And my memoir could never be complete without their anecdotes.

* * *

It was a December morning, and Chennai languidly stirred from the celebratory dinner of Christmas. Meenakshi (the one who encountered a headless corpse on her first day) wrapped a shawl tightly and traipsed to the BO at the MRTS station. The premises were desolate and barren.

It was the end-of-the year holidays, so there were hardly any passengers. Moreover, the maintenance of MRTS stations and tracks was in progress: the trains plied only from 07.00 hrs to 11.00 hrs, halted between 11.00 hrs and 15.00 hrs and recommenced.

At 08.00 hrs., the sweeper woman, Sandhanamma, began cleaning the station premises. After some time, bored of swatting flies, Meenakshi opened her tiffin box to eat.

That's when Sandhanamma came sprinting, as much as her creaky knees allowed. She gushed, panting, 'Amma! The sea is swelling. Huge waves. Come and see.'

Meenakshi hiccupped as she swallowed the morsel of idly and, without wasting time to clean up, snatched the keys from the nail, yanked the door close and locked it. The women bounded the steps to the highest floor.

Meenakshi witnessed the tremendous second wave of the tsunami on 26 December 2004. Her jaws grazed the unswept floor.

'Amma, what is this? The sea goddess is angry. I must rush home to my fisherman colony to warn my folks,' screeched Sandhamma and hurtled down the stairs.

Meenakshi watched in horror as cars floated, the seesaw and swings uprooted, trees dashing to pieces.

For a Chennaite, the tallest building was the LIC building in Anna Salai. Although now tall skyscrapers dot the skyline, we still swear by the LIC building. Meenakshi dialled the railway phone and informed the commercial controller that a wave as high as the LIC building had crashed across from her station. Then she called her mother on the BSNL line amidst crackling sounds and urged her to switch on the Sun TV news.

She confirmed her worst fears, and soon Meenakshi received instructions from the controller's office to lock up the station and go home safely.

Outside, the scene was chaotic. People rallied to watch the waves, their curiosity heightened instead of the need for safety. Even the regular waves looked alarming. There were no buses on the road, so Meenakshi pleaded with an auto driver who agreed to take her to the next bus stop. She walked a few kilometres and found another autorickshaw to take her home because she found no buses there.

The word 'tsunami', hitherto hidden in textbooks was on everyone's lips. For the next few days, she did nothing but watch the rerun of the tsunami waves and the devastation caused on all the news channels, and answer phone calls from top railway officials because she was the only railway employee who had witnessed the spectacle. The humongous MRTS station buildings saw their full utilization during this period. Home-wrecked people accumulated in these station premises, to whom the government distributed food packets, and they stayed there until rehabilitation measures were planned.

Meenakshi has been nicknamed 'Tsunami Paartha Sundari' since then. The beauty who saw Tsunami.

* * *

According to Jenny, there was a gap of about fifteen to twenty years without any ladies in the RPF, Southern Railways zone. My friend Jenny was among the forty-eight candidates who joined a few years ago. Jenny had always dreamt of a job in uniform, and when her dad read out the advertisement for recruitment of women in the RPF, she grabbed the opportunity. She was in the first year of an undergraduate course when she applied for the job. There was no further news or information about the examination until she joined her post-graduation course.

When the call letter for a physical examination came during her study holidays, Jenny and her mother took a bus from Neyveli to Chennai. To join the RPF, one had to pass the physicals first, then a written examination followed by an interview. The main criteria to ace the physicals were the requisite height, speed and stamina to run a 400 m race and leap a long jump of 8 ft. Jenny sprinted and jumped her way to victory. Immediately, in the afternoon, she sat a written test. The results were out by the following day, and an interview session quickly ensued.

The result and a letter for training came after three months. She discontinued her post-graduation studies. The training was at zonal training school at TPJ for eight months—a mix of physical exercises, theory classes, and arms and ammunition training. Then, she travelled to the Trivandrum division for a month of on-the-job training.

Her first posting was at the suburban station of Madras Moore Market (MMC) complex. Two months into her job, Jenny became the star of the Railway Protection Force.

An EMU from Arakkonam Jn (AJJ) rolled in as she patrolled the platform. From the first coach, a passenger shouted that a woman in the rear coach was experiencing labour pains. Jenny saw that the mother in labour was in the vendor's compartment, and thankfully, a few older women accompanied her.

'Police Amma, come soon; the baby is half out. We need to deliver the baby now.'

An unmarried Jenny almost swooned at the sight of blood and the screaming woman. But she quickly closed the compartment doors and controlled those who had gathered to watch the episode. Jenny wielded her lathi and blew her whistle to clear the onlookers. From the VLR stall, she grabbed a few scraps of clothes and gave them to the women inside. The young woman squalled in pain.

'Police Amma, quickly get me something sharp to cut the umbilical cord.'

Jenny screeched at the VLR guy, 'Anna, get me a blade.'

They cut the umbilical cord with the knife used to chop onions and tomatoes in VLR. Meanwhile, Jenny had sent a message to the control room through her walkie-talkie to arrange for an ambulance from the Government Hospital

The new mother and her daughter were rushed to the hospital. Jenny checked the next day and was happy that the mother–daughter duo was healthy.

The Chief Security Commissioner congratulated Jenny on her timely action; all the season's awards went to her. Newspapers ran the news with her name. She became a star. Jenny hailed as the Delivery Queen, admits she was scared to witness the labour pain, and wondered how she would birth children. Even today, her batchmates call her Delivery Queen.

* * *

On Sundays, the reservation offices work only one shift, 08.00 hrs to 14.00 hrs. One such Sunday, the busiest and the most pivotal train in Chennai Central, the Coromandel Express, departed at 08.45 hrs with two empty reserved coaches. The incoming Trivandrum Mail, which was to arrive at 07.00 hrs., arrived late, and 144 passengers who had made onward bookings by Coromandel Express were left stranded at MAS.

Soaked in communism, the people from Kerala travelling to West Bengal created havoc, demanding their rights at the Chennai Central Station.

The Dy SMR and the Reservation Supervisor Cyril Thomas devised a plan to calm the riotous passengers. They would attach one extra coach to the night Howrah mail. But 144 passengers couldn't be accommodated into a 72-berth coach, and the agitated passengers refused to calm down. The RS requested one more coach, but it couldn't be arranged.

Thomas persuaded the passengers to come by 21.00 hrs and that he would arrange something.

He re-did the charts of the HWH mail. On Sundays, the charts of the evening trains are prepared in advance. For some of the RAC passengers booked in one PNR, the RS confirmed only one or two on a PNR. If a PNR had six passengers, he confirmed three tickets and was sure the other three would somehow manage in the three confirmed berths (this was before the days of SMS alert). So basically, he managed to accommodate 144 passengers in a 72-berth coach. The railways and the passengers had a win-win deal. His prudent thinking avoided a major catastrophe. However, the TTE's managing the reserved coaches would have had a nightmarish run that day.

* * *

On the morning of 6 December, at 07.30 hrs, the Chennai–Alleppey Express rumbled into Trichur station when my batchmate Karthik entered for work. He was back after a prolonged leave on loss of pay courtesy jaundice and the nightmares that resulted from the suicide of a local on the tracks near the counter.

A loud explosion ripped the air. For a few seconds, all Karthik could hear was the ringing sound. The same day, blasts occurred in Pandian and Cheran Express, too. He rushed to the platform. A gaping hole on the roof of the platform warned them of the sights in the general compartment where an IED bomb had blown the compartment, instantly killing a few and grievously injuring some. Passengers pierced with iron and wooden pieces wailing in agony—the horrendous sight is still imprinted in Karthik's memory. The junior clerk swung into action, helping the other rail workers in gathering the dead bodies, transporting the injured to the nearest government hospital, and securing the tracks.

When the higher officials reached the scene, they ordered the twenty-one-year-old Karthik to carry Rs 5 lakh from the station earnings and accompany the officer. At the hospital, unaccustomed to handling such a colossal amount, Karthik quailed as he distributed ex gratia of Rs 50,000 to the family of the dead and Rs 20,000 to the attendant of the grievously injured. Other passengers needing first aid and attention, received Rs 2000.

He recalls how the next day, life was normal. There were no signs of a calamity.

* * *

Shortly, Karthik cleared the guard exams and became a running staff. He worked as a guard for three years but felt it gave him thirty years of experience. The guards followed a 'continuous roster'. Karthik was in position at 07.00 hrs, but the goods train enroute from another railway zone trailed, giving way to express trains, so by the time he climbed the brake van on duty by 17.00 hrs after a few non-productive hours, he was already fatigued. A guard was eligible for eight hours of rest only at the end of his run. They lived with a confused circadian rhythm.

A goods guard must carry food and water for drinking and washing up. The closet was a raised manhole with no water/flush. In a train formation, the lightest was the brake van (BV), which sometimes oscillated if the train exceeded a speed of 40 km. Karthik said some SM in the section ordered the loco pilot to run the train at 60 km to inconvenience the guard. One of the main occupational hazards arose due to the condition of the wheel suspension in a goods train (GT). It juddered the BV, damaging the knees and spine of the guard. So when you observe a long-time goods guard, you can notice that they walk funnily.

Once on a run, he encountered a fire in the engine. The driver halted the train, and Karthik discussed the course of action before transmitting a control message to the train controllers. This was the period before the walkie-talkie (WT), and the guard had to find a point near the tracks to plug in his portable telephone to send messages to all concerned. (The WT was first issued to the passenger guards and later to the goods guards.) The first thing to do was to safeguard the train and tracks. Karthik walked 1000 yards from the BV, fixed a detonator and then another one after 1500 yards. The driver walked to the front of the train and did the same. So, in case another train rolled on to the track, the detonation would inform the driver that an obstacle was on the way and slow down the train. Karthik waited with the driver in the eerie darkness surrounded by barking foxes, until assistance came into view.

The theft and pilferage of goods the BVs carried were other issues. In some sections, when the goods train waited in the loop line to let another train pass, the locals climbed the open wagons and carried whatever they found. With a customary shout at them, Karthik shut himself inside the BV, worried for his life. It was when lightweight and small Australian coal blocks were imported and carried by GTs; the locals on the route conceived an ingenious way to steal the coal. They tied a thorny stem on a long bamboo pole and held it over the open wagons. When the train moved, the thorny stem pushed the coal blocks to the side of the tracks, later carried by the people and sold.

Did you know the length of a goods train (GT) equals the shortest loop line in the section/route? The wagons areraked keeping in mind the loop line length to enable parking the train on the loop line to let other trains pass by.

When Karthik parked the train in a loop near a station, he observed a man sitting on the platform edge. For three hours, the man sat there; a passenger train crossed the station, and the man still waited. When the GT was cleared to move, the man jumped on to the tracks, and the wagons wheeled unhurriedly. The slow-moving train bit by bit crushed the body. When an express train or a fast-moving train hits a body, it gets thrown away, and instant death occurs, whereas if a slow train hits a body, the body is tumbled and crushed beyond recognition. Perhaps the victim was aware of this; hence, he let the earlier train cross. Fortunately for Karthik, it was within the station premises, so the dead body was taken care of by the SM. Some days, cattle got hit, and the cattle guard in front of the engine pushed the carcass. Cattle bone is sturdy and dangerous; it can derail a train quickly.

Numerous dangers filled a goods guard's life. A buddy of Karthik's succumbed to a massive heart attack while on duty—imagine lying dead alone as the train lolled away. On wintry days and nights, the open BV was cold as a mortuary. If it rained, the guard stood shivering in a raincoat. All that the others saw was the hefty pay cheque a guard carried home. The running allowance was a sizable amount; indeed, it helped these men provide a better life for their families but in the bargain they lost their health.

Karthik left railways for a better job in the private sector and is happy to spend nights peacefully at home.

* * *

I chatted with a friend about the Covid days.

PRS counters were closed from the day the lockdown was announced and reopened sometime in June–July. Circulars and advertisements announced that people should visit the PRS only for cancellations. A few major locations worked two shifts while others worked general shifts. Full refunds were granted for all cancelled trains after 22 March 2020 up to 180 days from the journey date. We posted timetables with journey commencing dates and dates of refund—specific periods for cancellation of tickets held for certain dates. Still, these measures sometimes didn't work as everyone cited various reasons for an urgent requirement of the cancelled fare, and thronged the counters.

When it was the peak of Corona, mid-May 2020, I was asked to work in the main PRS for two days. There were no buses, autos or cars, only the Workmen's Special train shuttled. My husband dropped and picked me up. The roads were deserted. Policemen, at regular intervals, checked IDs. I was terrified to get out of the house because I had aging parents at home. What if I passed on the infection to them? Yet, I felt proud that not only doctors but I, too, provided an essential service. There were water-can suppliers who fought for rail tickets, claiming they were also essential services. The corporation workers were commendable, cleaning and sanitizing every nook.

In any case, I can't say I was unlucky to have to handle those counters. I had no idea Chennai had so many migrants, and to see the masked rows of heads seated inside a chalked circle, maintaining social distancing, waiting to board the 'Shramik Specials' to their states . . . Have you seen the thousands of water pots in temples for bathing the idols on special days? These people reminded me of the pots. Just waiting . . . This continued for many days. State governments, NGOs and normal households, all provided packed food. The booking office printed tickets in bulk; I had to cross-check the details of the number of people allowed to travel from the comprehensive lists received from the Chennai Corporation and hand them over to the policemen. There were so many who had come for treatment and were stuck, pathetic.

We were provided with sanitizers and masks at the station, but we carried our own and worked with double masks and gloves. We sanitized our hands every minute. Counting cash with gloves and speaking with masks on was torture. Then they gave us microphones.

We handled Rs 30 to 50 lakh worth of cancellations per day. The commercial inspectors brought cash from RBI and disbursed it to each station. Change was the biggest issue. My mom shared this 'change' problem with a neighbour, he was a temple treasurer. He gave me the hundi collection, and I carried it to work.

Not just COVID-19, we coped with the floods in 2015, the Varada hurricane and demonetization. The public gave Rs 500 for a Rs 5 ticket. They booked bulk tickets for higher classes and cancelled them the next day, they used railway counters to exchange the demonetized currencies. Railways instructed us to accept all denominations.

* * *

When I filled the application and signed my name for the RRB examinations, I was sixteen years old. My parents reiterated the importance of landing a government job with a pension. With no lofty ambitions of becoming a doctor, scientist or an astronaut, I knew I would be writing competitive examinations like RRB, SSB, etc. after graduation. So why not try it now? That was my sole reasoning when I pored over the GK book. After the written examination, interview, medical tests, schooling, and then training at the railway institute, I joined my posting station.

I coped in a new environment surrounded by a new language, new food and new people, learning and mastering new ways of life. When my work journey took me to platforms in the home turf, I recognized the language and food, but the people I met were new, further embellishing my experiences. From some, I learned time management and planning; from a few, I absorbed humility. I trained to let go, to compromise, to demand, to trust, to smile, to bury the grief deep inside. After all, people who meet me and don't know me well never know that I still grieve my two sons.

The scar never fades. My unending personal grief is one of the main reasons I took a life-altering decision to quit my stable government job and fly to the Middle East to be with my husband.

Life has been a learning experience. Wherever I worked, each person taught me something. I made lifelong relationships.

The biggest take from my tenure at the ticket counter is that I can start a conversation with ANYONE.

I joined the Indian Railways to cater to my family's financial needs. Although I always said I never wanted to work but read books, I metamorphosed into a different person when I sat in the chair and faced the public. I relished every moment spent at the ticket counter.

When a relative saw me working he said, 'Sangeetha, for a person who says I don't want to work but stay at home with books, you seem to have a flair for dealing with customers. Will you not miss this?'

'Oh no. I love this when I am here. But I will surround myself at home with books, friends and conversations.'

Little did I know that it would be my tagline for life.

When my husband took a job in the Middle East, I visited him for three months. After my return, within a few months, I decided to go on a prolonged Ex-India leave. India had just won her second Cricket World Cup. A year later, I extended my leave. I had a lot of time to read. Every year, I read seventy to hundred books. I experimented with cooking during this period. Until then, I had my ammas cook for me.

The railways treated my absence from work as unauthorized, and I attended the Railway Enquiry held at the Divisional Office in Chennai. The Commercial Inspector and the clerk in charge of my case were kind people who listened and empathized.

Writing was something I stumbled upon after my achan's demise. Amma and I were on a train to Palakkad for the sixteenth-day ceremony. Emotionally wrought about travelling without Achan to his ancestral home, lying on the upper berth, I let my tears blind me as I typed on my mobile 'The journey home without Achan.'

A therapeutic relief, if one may give it a name; I haven't stopped typing since then.

Soon, I recognized almost all my writings had a shadow of my railway life. Even now I think of station names in railway code. In fact, since I contemplated quitting my government job, much against my amma's wishes, I had this recurring dream of missing a train. Yes, frequently, I woke up drenched in sweat and distressed to see the brake van displaying a huge X. I have never missed a train in my life; I wondered if it was an ominous warning for the future or if it was telling me to rethink about quitting. I ruminated for days. If my children were alive, I would want to work, earn, save, provide them the best of everything, but now I needn't slog at counters, separated from my husband. He is all that I have. The weight of shared grief decided the course.

I boarded a few wrong trains as a railway employee and had indelible adventures; likewise, opting for the untravelled path certainly unravelled incredible treasures.

The missing-train dream resurfaced every time my life showed me two paths—when my husband decided to move back to India, then again, we moved back to the Middle East, then to a different country in the Middle East. Sometimes, I caught the train at a different station; sometimes, the guard waved a red flag and let me board. But every time, there was a fork in the road, the anxiety of missing a train revisited.

Since I began writing this book, reliving the past through the point of view of my present cognizance, the train has never left the platform without me on it.

Now, I own the train—the platforms, the engine and the compartments.

Epilogue: *Last Van X*

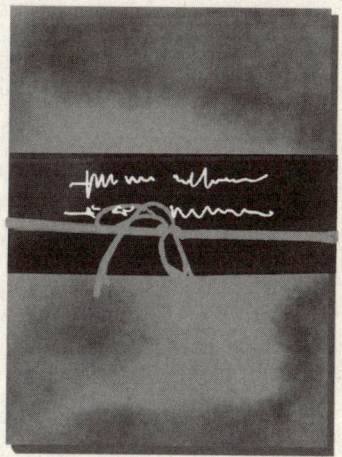

Office Memorandum of even number dated ****

The inquiry officer nominated to inquire into the charges framed against you has submitted his findings after the preliminary and the regular hearing.

On careful examination of the evidence on record and evidence produced by Ms Sangeetha in her defence, the following are considered.

Ms Sangeetha attended all the inquiries and, in a clear state of mind without any compulsion, accepted that the period of unauthorized absence was unintentional, and circumstances prevailed then.

The employee has presented the required documents to substantiate her claim of unemployment.

As requested by the employee, we allow her to relinquish her responsibilities as a railway employee.

Ms Sangeetha has been cleared of all the charges.

Acknowledgements

EVENTS AS I REMEMBER would not have reached their destination without these compartments and passengers enriching the journey.

I am indebted to each one of you:

- ◆ Amma and Achan, for instilling a love for reading and providing me with an endearing childhood.
- ◆ Amma, thank you for your unwavering support and understanding; you are the best mother-in-law.
- ◆ Natasha Sharma, you germinated the seed of *Platform Ticket* and guided it to fruition.
- ◆ Reshma Manoj, for the delightful illustrations.
- ◆ Jyothi Ramakrishnan, for the catchy title.
- ◆ Deepthi Talwar, my editor at Penguin Random House India, for your impeccable taste in literature and trust in *PT*.
- ◆ Latakumari, Vishwanathan Sir, Mercy, Kanthi, Sridevi, Col Prabhu and Roneo, my fellow rail workers, for all the valuable anecdotes.
- ◆ Sunny, Skanthagiri, Ramnath, Vijay, Dinesh, Kannan, Vidhyadhar, Santhosh, Bala, Satish, Malathi, Ranjana, Usha, Subashini, Jayashree and Lakshmi—the glorious batch of SR VCRC 92–94. We share a bond like no other. *PT* is our memoir.

- Monica, Aparna and Khushboo, the writing sisterhood whose intervention shaped this book.
- Sarves, my honest critic, whose approval I constantly seek.
- Ambili and Prakash, for believing in me from the first write-up I sent from the train.
- Sandra Miss, my kindergarten teacher.
- Anu, Sudha, Sanchari, Priyan and Kruti— my knights.
- Karun Uncle, Sashi Aunty and Sam Ammai for all the books I read in my early years.
- My other friends and colleagues.
- ArtoonsInn and Penmancy and their members for nurturing aspiring writers.
- The Bangalore Literature Festival: LitMart—for an excellent platform and exposure to writers.
- Saba Nehal, my copy editor; Rachna, Himanshi, the legal team at PRHI; and Milee Ashwarya, publisher of PRHI.
- My Vallat and Vavullipathy clan.
- Sujith, my best half—without you nothing is possible.
- Finally, to everyone who picks up this book and becomes a part of my journey.

You all are the reason behind my beautiful yesterdays, todays and tomorrows.

Scan QR code to access the
Penguin Random House India website